Pro Eclipse JST

Plug-ins for J2EE Development

Christopher M. Judd
and Hakeem Shittu

Apress®

Pro Eclipse JST: Plug-ins for J2EE Development

Copyright © 2005 by Christopher M. Judd and Hakeem Shittu

ISBN (pbk): 1-59059-493-2

Lead Editor: Steve Anglin
Technical Reviewer: Ben Houston
Editorial Board: Steve Anglin, Dan Appleman, Ewan Buckingham, Gary Cornell, Tony Davis, Jason Gilmore, Jonathan Hassell, Chris Mills, Dominic Shakeshaft, Jim Sumser
Associate Publisher: Grace Wong
Project Manager: Kylie Johnston
Copy Edit Manager: Nicole LeClerc
Copy Editor: Ami Knox
Assistant Production Director: Kari Brooks-Copony
Production Editor: Kelly Winquist
Compositor: Kinetic Publishing Services, LLC
Proofreader: April Eddy
Indexer: Michael Brinkman
Artist: Kinetic Publishing Services, LLC
Cover Designer: Kurt Krames
Manufacturing Manager: Tom Debolski

Distributed to the book trade worldwide by Springer-Verlag New York, Inc., 233 Spring Street, 6th Floor, New York, NY 10013. Phone 1-800-SPRINGER, fax 201-348-4505, e-mail orders-ny@springer-sbm.com, or visit http://www.springeronline.com.

For information on translations, please contact Apress directly at 2560 Ninth Street, Suite 219, Berkeley, CA 94710. Phone 510-549-5930, fax 510-549-5939, e-mail info@apress.com, or visit http://www.apress.com.

The source code for this book is available to readers at http://www.apress.com in the Downloads section.

To my supportive wife and best friend, Sue; my son, Blake; to all the individuals and organizations who have contributed their time, talents, and treasures to Open Source; and to my Heavenly Father for all the blessings He has bestowed upon me.
—Chris

To my loving family, and to Callie for immeasurable support.
—Hakeem

Contents at a Glance

Contents

About the Authors

CHRISTOPHER M. JUDD is the president and primary consultant for Judd Solutions, LLC. (`www.juddsolutions.com`), international speaker, open source evangelist, Central Ohio Java Users Group (`www.cojug.org`) coordinator, and coauthor of *Enterprise Java Development on a Budget*, as well as author of the children's book *Bearable Moments*. He has spent ten years developing software in the insurance, retail, government, manufacturing, service, and transportation industries. His current focus is consulting, mentoring, and training with Java, J2EE, J2ME, Web Services, and related technologies.

HAKEEM SHITTU is currently a senior enterprise programmer for Compuware (`http://www.compuware.com`) where he designs and develops software using J2EE technologies. He also manages Gen!x (`http:/www.genixcorp.com`), a software consulting and technology training outfit. Hakeem has seven years of software development experience in such industries as defense, transportation, biogenetics, and telecommunication.

About the Technical Reviewer

BEN HOUSTON is a senior software engineer for CollegeNET, Inc., of Portland, OR. He uses Eclipse daily in the continuing development of Applyweb, CollegeNET's answer to the forms processing, contact management, and e-commerce needs of over 1,000 educational and nonprofit organizations. Applyweb's J2EE architecture serves millions of requests per day and helps process over a million forms a year. Ben holds a degree in physics and astronomy from Whitman College in Walla Walla, WA.

He would like to thank Jeni, his beautiful wife, for being patient with his late-night editing streaks, and the pets, Bailey and Nikita, for providing plenty of needed breaks.

Acknowledgments

The authors would like to thank all of those who were involved in putting this book together, giving us support and encouragement and influencing us throughout our professional careers.

To our editor, Steve Anglin, who gave us the opportunity and idea to write this book.

To our project manager, Kylie Johnston; copy editor, Ami Knox; production editor, Kelly Winquist; technical reviewer, Ben Houston; and the rest of the dedicated Apress staff who worked so hard to complete this book and keep us on schedule.

To our friend, Geoffrey Goetz, for connecting "the author without a book with the book needing another author."

To our early reviewers, Matt Arnett and Floyd Carver, for reading our chicken scratch and incomplete thoughts.

To our friends and mentors, Dr. Mike Drushal, Brian Sam-Bodden, Mike Rozlog, Steve Swing, Floyd Carver, Kevin Smith, David Bailey, Jim Shingler, Dave Lucas, Ken Faw, Geoff Goetz, Jay Zimmerman, Ted Neward, Neal Ford, Dave Thomas, Erik Hatcher, Stuart Halloway, and Bruce Tate, for helping to shape the way we think about developing software.

To the dedicated contributors of time and money who have made Eclipse and Web Tools a great product.

Chris would also like to thank his wife, Sue, and son, Blake, for their endless patience and inspiration.

Introduction

Developing enterprise Java applications using Java 2 Enterprise Edition (J2EE) is difficult enough. Developers need to use good integrated development environments (IDEs) and tools to simplify the complexity and increase developer productivity. The Eclipse Web Tools Platform (WTP) project is one such collection of tools. WTP is the first open source comprehensive collection of tools for building J2EE applications on top of the Eclipse Platform.

WTP is an Eclipse project found at http://www.eclipse.org/webtools/. It contains two subprojects. The first is the Web Standard Tools (WST) project, which is primarily focused on supporting web development with tools for HTML and XML, and managing servers. The second is the primary focus of this book, the J2EE Standard Tools (JST) project, which contains tools for developing J2EE components like EJB, JavaServer Pages, servlets, and Web Services.

This book is intended to teach developers how to become productive J2EE developers using a combination of JST and Eclipse.

Who This Book Is For

This book is for Java and J2EE developers wanting to learn how to develop enterprise Java applications using the Eclipse Web Tools Platform and specifically the J2EE Standard Tools subproject.

This book is also intended for architects and managers evaluating Java and J2EE development tools.

How This Book Is Structured

The following is a rundown of what is covered in each of the chapters in this book:

- **Chapter 1, "J2EE Specification"**: This chapter provides a basic J2EE primer, a refresher of the terms and technologies defined in the J2EE Specification. The subsequent chapters assume the reader has an understanding of the information contained within this chapter. However, if you are knowledgeable and experienced with J2EE, feel free to skip it.

- **Chapter 2, "Eclipse Plug-in Paradigm"**: This chapter explains the Eclipse platform and how plug-ins like Web Tools are used to extend Eclipse.

- **Chapter 3, "Eclipse Web Tools Platform Project"**: This chapter provides a brief history of WTP as well as an understanding of the scopes of WST and JST.

- **Chapter 4, "Introduction to JST"**: This chapter provides a basic overview of the wizards, views, editors, and perspectives included in the JST for creating EJBs, servlets, JSP pages, and Web Services.

- **Chapter 5, "Introduction to WST"**: This chapter provides a basic overview of the wizards, views, and editors included in WST for managing servers, editing XML, and creating Web Services.

- **Chapter 6, "Eclipse Web Tools Installation"**: This chapter explains how to install Eclipse Web Tools and its dependencies.

- **Chapter 7, "J2EE Standard Tools Projects"**: This chapter explains how to organize, create, and manage a J2EE project. It also explains how to set up a J2EE server configuration to manage application servers from within Eclipse.

- **Chapter 8, "Session Beans"**: This chapter explains how to create session beans using the Enterprise Bean wizard and XDoclet.

- **Chapter 9, "Entity Beans"**: This chapter explains how to create entity beans using the Enterprise Bean wizard and XDoclet.

- **Chapter 10, "Message-Driven Beans"**: This chapter explains how to create message-driven beans using the Enterprise Bean wizard and XDoclet.

- **Chapter 11, "EJB Packaging and Deployment"**: This chapter explains how to package EJBs in EJB JARs and EARs. It also explains how to deploy the packages to a managed J2EE server for testing.

- **Chapter 12, "JavaServer Pages"**: This chapter explains how to use the wizards and editors to create JSP pages. It also explains how to configure and use Struts in JST.

- **Chapter 13, "Servlets"**: This chapter explains how to use the wizards and XDoclet to create servlets.

- **Chapter 14, "Web Packaging and Deployment"**: This chapter explains how to package web artifacts such as JSP pages and servlets in WARs and EARs. It also shows how to deploy the packages using JST or Apache Ant.

- **Chapter 15, "Web Services"**: This chapter explains how to produce and consume Web Services.

- **Chapter 16, "Relational Databases"**: This chapter explains how to connect and interact with a relational database during development.

- **Appendix A, "Apache Derby"**: This appendix explains how to install and configure the Apache Derby database.

- **Appendix B, "JBoss Application Server"**: This appendix explains how to install and configure the JBoss Application Server.

Downloading the Code

You can download the source code accompanying this book from either the Apress website, http://www.apress.com, or the companion website, http://www.projst.com.

Contacting the Authors

Feel free to send us feedback or ask us questions. Our e-mail addresses are cjudd@juddsolutions.com (Chris) and hshittu@genixcorp.com (Hakeem).

Also, make sure you visit the companion website at http://www.projst.com for additional tips and tricks.

J2EE Specification

Building upon the success of its Java programming language, Sun Microsystems decided to extend the benefits of the Java platform to the enterprise application space. The goal was to create a reliable, high-performance, secure, transactional, distributed architecture that would support concurrent user access. The architecture was also to allow the creation of applications that would seamlessly integrate with existing (presumably non-Java-based) systems while supporting future modifications and scaling to match demand with relative ease.

In response to this challenging problem, Sun Microsystems developed a component-based architecture for the development and management of multitier, server-centric applications known as the *Java 2 Platform, Enterprise Edition* (J2EE). This technology extended the existing Java 2 Platform, Standard Edition (J2SE) to provide platform-independent portability to enterprise applications in addition to other features like modularity and reusability. Initially released in 1999, the specification has been revised several times, with the most recent release being the J2EE 1.4 specification. Revision to the J2EE Specification is coordinated and managed by members of the Java Community Process (http://www.jcp.org), ensuring that input from the active community of Java stakeholders is absorbed into future releases.

This chapter will provide an overview of the J2EE Specification as well as supply an in-depth discussion on the components that make up the J2EE Platform. The technologies available within this platform will also be discussed, including how developers use them to create enterprise applications.

Enterprise Application Architecture

Enterprise applications are large-scale business applications that are complex, data-centric, and mission critical. Their complexity is often based on their encapsulation of the intricate business processes, rules, and standards of the application domain for which they are created. Stated simply, these are applications that companies rely on for the smooth functioning of their business.

Figure 1-1 shows the typical architecture of an enterprise application. The application can basically be broken down into three general layers: a presentation layer through which users interact with the application, a business logic layer that encapsulates the functionality and feature set of the application, and a persistence layer in which data created or modified by the application is stored.

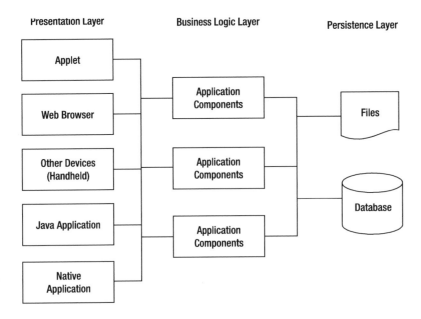

Figure 1-1. *Enterprise application architecture*

As the figure shows, enterprise applications often provide support for one or more different types of clients. In recent years, due to the ubiquity of the Web, HTML has been increasingly used as the preferred presentation format. This is expected to continue as many new connected computing devices include support for web browsers. The business logic layer contains one or more applications that function cohesively to provide a concrete business function. Data needed to complete the requested function is often retrieved from the persistence layer, and on conclusion of the task, the resulting data product is often stored within the persistence layer.

Among other needs, a robust enterprise application design seeks to create an application that is

- **Highly available**, by replicating the business logic layer across multiple server instances

- **Scalable**, by dynamically managing resources to support demand without the need for code modification

- **Modular**, by having components that can be individually modified without impacting the entire application

- **Reusable**, by creating components that manage specific tasks and can be reused in several applications without having to be modified

J2EE Architecture

The J2EE architecture is a distributed, component-based architecture that supports the creation of enterprise applications using the Java programming language. It builds upon the application program interfaces (APIs) and services that are available in the J2SE Specification to achieve this.

A four-tier approach is used that comprises a Client Tier, Web Tier, Business Tier, and Enterprise Information Tier. This is shown in Figure 1-2.

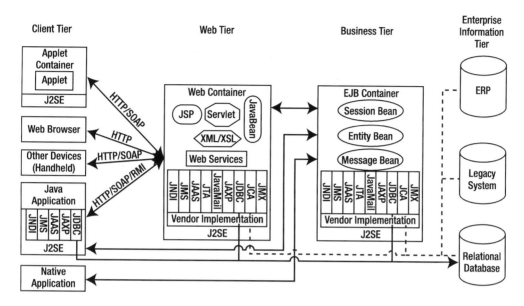

Figure 1-2. *J2EE architecture*

The *Client Tier* provides support for a large number of client types and also allows flexible access from the front end of the application to many of the server-based tiers. The *Web Tier* and the *Business Tier*, also known as the *Middle Tier*, collectively provide a set of services that aid in the rapid development of enterprise applications. At design time, they allow a developer to concentrate on the task of modeling the logic of an application by handling all the low-level details necessary to create an application. Additionally, at runtime, they ensure the existence of services that could be used to manage, monitor, and interact with other parts of the enterprise system. The Enterprise Information Tier comprises Enterprise Resource Planning (ERP) applications, legacy systems such as CICS, relational databases, and file systems.

The J2EE architecture is described at length in the J2EE Specification, which is available from Sun at http://java.sun.com/j2ee.

Overview of the Specification

The J2EE Specification is a standard for the development, deployment, and management of multitiered, server-based Java applications. It defines a collection of components that are available within each tier of an enterprise application, how these components are hosted within a runtime environment, and the services that are available to these components to allow them to interact between each other and with other external applications.

The architecture, contents, and constraints of the J2EE Platform are described by the specification. This J2EE Platform hosts Java-based enterprise applications and allows them to be properly accessed. The minimal set of services that must be supported by a J2EE Platform implementation are described and the contents and services that a developer can expect the platform to provide are also described. It is crucial to understand that the J2EE Specification is just a specification and not a concrete implementation. The services it describes are the minimal set that must be supported by any concrete implementation of the specification.

Commercial vendors and open source projects have then created their implementations of this specification in programs known as *application servers*. These application servers can, and often do, include functionalities and value-added services beyond those laid out in the specification as long as they don't violate any of the requirements. Every application server is subjected to a grueling battery of tests known as the *J2EE Compatibility Test Suite* before it can gain certification as being J2EE compliant. The difference in the implementation, among other factors, guides end users in choosing which vendors' containers would be most suitable for their needs.

J2EE Platform

As we stated previously, the J2EE Specification describes the architecture, services, and resources that must be supported at runtime by an implementation of the J2EE Platform. In addition to this, it dictates what facilities the platform must make available to developers at runtime. These available services are accessible to the developer through the use of APIs.

Figure 1-2 displays the architecture of the J2EE Platform and shows the required relationships between the elements of the platform. The figure also shows the usage of containers to host application components. Many low-level services are supported by each of these containers and are made available to the application component through J2EE APIs.

In addition to the features of a high-quality enterprise application design mentioned earlier such as high availability, scalability, and reusability, implementations using J2EE provide the following additional benefits:

- **Portability**: The platform independence of the Java programming language allows for code that can be deployed on a variety of hardware infrastructures.

- **Vendor independence**: By using the standard J2EE interfaces, applications can be moved easily between application servers from different vendors.

- **Integration**: This benefit is enabled by utilizing interoperability services based on standard protocols and required by the specification to connect to other non-J2EE applications.

J2EE APIs

J2EE APIs are essentially a contract interface between the J2EE Platform implementation and the developer-created application components. The specification defines the entire collection of APIs that must be supported by an application server. Furthermore, it specifies what platform services developers can access, how they can access it, and what information must be provided before the access is allowed.

It should be noted that not all services, and therefore APIs, are available to all application component types. We have, however, provided a description of the entire standard set of J2EE 1.4 APIs:

- **Enterprise Java Beans (EJB) 2.1**: Provides an infrastructure for creating, hosting, and accessing server-based, distributed business components.

- **Servlet 2.4**: Provides a concise mechanism for creating and accessing web-based applications that are server and platform independent.

- **JavaServer Pages (JSP) 2.0**: Represents an extension of the servlet framework to support the rapid, template-based development of web-based applications.

- **Java Message Service (JMS) 1.1**: Provides support for reliable synchronous and asynchronous point-to-point and publish-subscribe messaging models.

- **Java Transaction API (JTA) 1.0**: Handles transaction management within a distributed system.

- **JavaMail 1.3**: Provides complete support for the access, creation, and sending of e-mail messages using common protocols like IMAP, POP, and SMTP.

- **JavaBeans Activation Framework 1.0**: Integrates support for dynamic MIME data type access and utilization.

- **Java API for XML Processing (JAXP) 1.2**: Facilitates the parsing and transformation of XML documents.

- **J2EE Connector Architecture 1.5**: Provides support for the integration of legacy systems with J2EE applications.

- **Web Services for J2EE 1.1**: Specifies the support an application server must provide to support any web service deployed within it.

- **Java API for XML-based RPC (JAX-RPC) 1.1**: Describes how to access web services using XML-based remote procedure calls.

- **SOAP with Attachments API for Java (SAAJ) 1.2**: Provides a simplified mechanism for manipulating SOAP messages.

- **Java API for XML Registries (JAXR) 1.0**: Supports client access to a variety of XML-based registries such as the ebXML and UDDI registries.

- **J2EE Management API 1.0**: Specifies the API for tools that would enable the runtime querying and management of a J2EE application server.

- **Java Management Extensions (JMX) 1.2**: Represents an extension of the J2EE Management API. It introduces the usage of Managed Beans (MBeans) to provide the support required in the J2EE Management API.

- **J2EE Deployment API 1.1**: Defines the interaction between the runtime deployment environment within an application server and application components being deployed.

- **Java Authorization Service Provider Contract for Containers (JACC) 1.0**: Defines a contract between a J2EE application server and authorization policy providers.

J2SE APIs are also available to J2EE applications with such APIs as JDBC, JNDI, and JAAS being among those that are frequently used. We have described some of these additional APIs in the "Services" section found later in this chapter.

Application Components

The J2EE Specification describes four types of components that can be created by a developer. Each component is a modular software unit that is deployed within the application server and interacts with its host environment and other components through the J2EE APIs that are available to it. The APIs available to the components determine the facilities that the components have access to.

In Figure 1-2, we have shown you these four application component types, and here we provide a further description of them:

- **Applet component**: These are client-side GUI components that are hosted by an applet container, which is typically a web browser. They have the ability to provide a feature-rich user interface to an enterprise application.

- **Application client component**: These are Java-based programs that can execute within a supported JVM. They offer a user interface similar to what exists on the native client while accessing J2EE Business Tier facilities.

- **Web component**: These are components that have the ability to respond to HTTP requests. They comprise servlets, JSP pages, filters, and web event listeners:

  - **Servlets**: These extend a web server's functionality to support the dynamic processing of application logic. Servlets can be used in any request/response programming models but are most often used with HTTP. In this method, they utilize data embedded within HTTP requests for input and provide resulting output using the HTTP response, making the processing facilities of the J2EE Platform available to the information input on the source web page.

  - **JavaServer Pages**: Similar to servlets, JSP pages provide dynamic web application capability to the J2EE Platform. JSP pages achieve this goal through the introduction of templating functionality. A JSP page begins with HTML elements that remain static throughout the lifetime of the page; this forms the base template. Dynamic elements are then added through the embedding of Java code and/or special tags within the page. It should be noted that JSP pages are indeed converted to servlets before execution, but the intricacies of this process are managed by the web container.

  - **Filters**: These components provide the ability to intercept requests by clients for resources on a server and also responses provided to these requests by the web container with the goal of transforming the content of either the request or response communication. Filters provide a reusable mechanism to handle recurring tasks such as authentication, logging, etc., that are applicable to items within the web container.

  - **Web event listeners**: These are components that are created to perform a particular function when a specific event occurs within the web container. These components provide developers with the flexibility to respond in a certain way when different types of web application–related events such as the creation or invalidation of a session occurs.

- **Enterprise JavaBeans components**: These are server-side components that singularly or collectively encapsulate the application logic of an enterprise application. EJB technology enables rapid and simplified development of distributed, transactional, secure, and portable applications based on Java technology. There are three types of EJBs defined by the specification:

  - **Session beans**: A session bean is a server-side extension of a client that exists to service requests made by the client. As the name implies, it simulates an interactive session between a client and the server-based component. Session beans exist in two forms. There are *stateful* session beans, which are said to maintain a "conversational state" with a client by virtue of retaining instance variable data on multiple method invocations. Because of this, they are wedded to a unique client throughout the instance existence. *Stateless* session beans, on the other hand, exist to service requests from multiple clients. They perform transient services for their clients, fulfilling whatever request is made of them and returning to their original initialized states.

  - **Entity beans**: Entity beans are an encapsulated representation of business objects made available with a persistence mechanism. They represent an object to relational mapping of the data stored within these persistence layers, thereby facilitating the modification of the underlying business objects while preserving referential and data integrity constraints demanded by the specific business process.

  - **Message-driven beans**: These are stateless, server-side components invoked by the EJB container on the receipt of a message in an associated JMS Queue or Topic. This component allows the EJB container to provide support for asynchronous message processing.

Containers

Although we mentioned containers earlier in this chapter without describing them, from our use of the term *container* in preceding sections, it should be easy to infer that containers are structures within which application components exist. Formally, containers are described as the runtime environment within which application components are deployed.

Containers manage the life cycles of these components and provide many low-level services such as resource pooling, transaction management, and access to resources like database connections for the application components that run within them. These services are provided without the application developer having to dabble in low-level system programming. The benefit from this architecture is that it allows for the creation of abstracted, highly portable software units that are not welded to the functionality of a specific platform. The developer is free to concentrate on modeling the application logic of the enterprise application, thereby shortening the development cycle.

As required by the specification, the container additionally provides several useful services to the application component that the component can access through the use of J2EE APIs. Four types of containers are described in the J2EE spec:

1. **Applet container**: For hosting applets

2. **Application client container**: For hosting standard Java applications

3. **Web component container**: For hosting Java servlets and JSP pages

4. **Enterprise JavaBean container**: For hosting Enterprise JavaBean components

Most commercial application servers typically provide support for more than one container, thereby providing the developer with the greatest possible set of design choices. However, with J2EE being a pluggable architecture, vendors could implement a limited set of services and then plug in available components to complement their offering. An example of this is the popular JBoss open source application server, which provides its own EJB container but uses other open source web containers.

Note The examples we provide in this book use version 4.01 of the JBoss application server. We have provided instruction in Appendix B on how to install the program.

TheServerSide.com (`http://www.theserverside.com`), an online community of enterprise Java developers, maintains an exhaustive matrix of available application servers including the platforms they run on, their J2EE certification status, and the JDK versions they support.

Services

There are several standard services made available by the container. Each of these services has a specific purpose and benefit to the constituent application component. However, not all services are required to be available to all types of components. The following list contains a selection of some of the standard services available:

- **JDBC**: Provides the ability to connect to a database

- **JMS**: Provides a unified mechanism to create, send, and receive messages between application components in both a synchronous and an asynchronous form

- **JTA**: Provides a mechanism for making and reversing a group of changes to a datasource

- **JNDI**: Provides support for looking up distributed resources, services, and application components

- **JavaMail**: Provides J2EE applications with the ability to create, send, and read mail messages

Deployment

The specification details how J2EE application components are to be prepared for deployment. A *deployed application* is an application in an active state, ready to respond to client invocations.

Deployment typically occurs in archive files, and the structure of these files is described by the specification. XML, a flexible document format for describing data, is used to create deployment descriptors for each deployment module. *Deployment descriptors* are self-describing documents about the application components, how they should be deployed, and what additional information should be made available to services within the container.

A *deployment module* is typically an archive file containing one or more application components and any supporting files that they may need. The deployment descriptor is located within the archive file in either the WEB-INF or META-INF folder depending on the module type being packaged. The three available module types are

- **Web module**: This is used to package web application components for deployment. They are packaged into a web archive file known as a *WAR file* and contain a deployment descriptor that must be named web.xml within a WEB-INF folder.

- **EJB module**: This contains application components created for deployment within an EJB container. The archive file used to package this is known as a *JAR file*. The deployment descriptor required for an EJB module is the ejb-jar.xml file, which is located in a META-INF folder.

- **Java module**: This consists of a collection of application client component classes packaged together in a JAR file. Java modules contain a deployment descriptor named application-client.xml within a META-INF folder.

As shown in Figure 1-3, J2EE also supports the composition of a collection of these modules into a package that represents an application. This lends itself to the creation of small task-specific modules such that an assembly of these can be reused in many different applications.

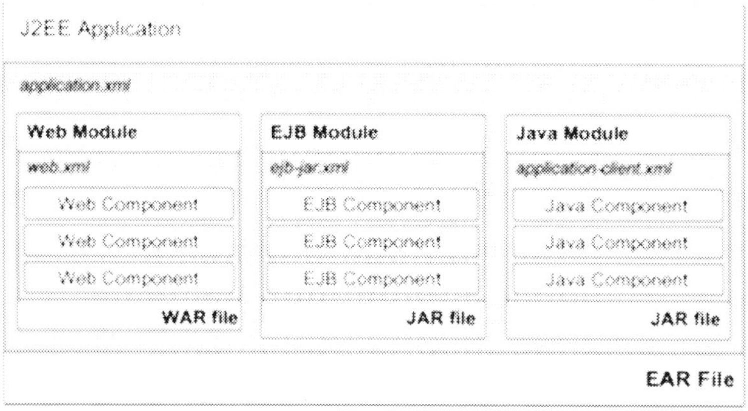

Figure 1-3. *J2EE application deployment*

This figure shows a deployment unit representing an enterprise application. The modules that make up this application are packaged into an enterprise archive file known as an EAR file. This file contains a deployment descriptor called application.xml. It should be noted that many applications and modules can be hosted within a single application server.

It should be noted that most application servers provide support for hosting applications in an unarchived state. In such a situation, the directory structure that would have existed within the archive remains intact, and the deployment descriptor must also be included in the META-INF or WEB-INF subfolder of the deployed module.

Summary

In this chapter, you learned about enterprise applications and how the J2EE architecture was designed to provide benefits such as modularity, reusability, and scalability to such applications. You also learned about the J2EE Platform being the runtime infrastructure within which enterprise applications are deployed. The platform contains four containers, or runtime environments, each of which in turn contains application components. You also saw that some of the services that J2EE demands must be available to these components and that the components access the services using the J2EE API.

Eclipse Plug-in Paradigm

In the late 1990s and early 2000s, IBM endeavored to replace their VisualAge product line, which included integrated development environments (IDEs) for developing C++, COBOL, PL/I, Smalltalk, and Java, with a single seamless development tool. Rather than develop a single application, the standard practice at that time, IBM created a language and vendor-independent tools platform that enabled plug-ins from various vendors to be seamlessly integrated. The platform enabled a developer to live in a single tool for the entire development life cycle. Plug-ins enabled developers to model their applications using UML, connect to a database, develop and debug source code, deploy applications, and connect to version control. Initially the platform was used to form the foundation of IBM's WebSphere Studio products, which primarily focused on developing Java and J2EE applications.

Fortunately, vendors did not flock to the platform because they felt it was still a proprietary IBM product. So, in order to realize the vision of a seamless integrated tool, IBM separated the platform from their enterprise Java tools, renamed the platform Eclipse, and released it as open source.

Today the Eclipse Platform is a model of an active open source community and an open extensible architecture. This chapter will explain the basic Eclipse Platform architecture, Eclipse hosted plug-ins, and the open source and commercial plug-in market.

Eclipse Architecture

A pluggable architecture is a powerful means for assembling individual components to achieve a complete and integrated product. In the 1980s, IBM did this with hardware, by assembling off-the-shelf computer components with well-defined interfaces to produce personal computers. This new architecture revolutionized the computer market by allowing individuals to assemble the right components for their memory, input, and space needs.

Eclipse is providing this same flexibility in the development software arena by enabling developers to assemble different plug-ins to meet their specific development needs. The Eclipse documentation describes a plug-in as a structured bundle of code and/or data that contributes functionality to a system. The well-defined interfaces that enable plug-ins to integrate with Eclipse are referred to as *extension points*.

Platform Layers

The Eclipse Platform consists of four basic layers and three primary components, or extension points, as shown in Figure 2-1.

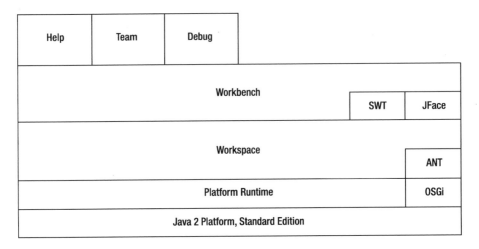

Figure 2-1. *Eclipse Platform architecture*

Java 2 Platform Layer

The Eclipse Platform is built with the popular Java 2 Platform. While Eclipse itself is written in Java, it is not restricted to Java development. In fact, Eclipse has plug-ins for C/C++, C#, COBOL, XML, and HTML. Building Eclipse with the Java 2 Platform enables Eclipse to run on many platforms including Microsoft Windows, Linux, Solaris, AIX, HP-UX, and Mac OSX. Eclipse is also able to take advantage of Java's dynamic loading capabilities, delaying the initialization of plug-ins until they are needed.

Platform Runtime Layer

On top of the Java 2 Platform sits a very thin layer referred to as the *Eclipse Platform Runtime*. This is the only part of Eclipse that is not a plug-in. That is right: Eclipse itself is a collection of plug-ins. The Runtime layer is a microkernel responsible for bootstrapping the plug-ins. At startup, it iterates through the subdirectories of the plugins directory loading the manifest file (plugin.xml). The manifest file is basically a deployment descriptor for Eclipse plug-ins. It describes how to register a plug-in with its respective extension points. The Runtime layer is also responsible for loading the plug-in the first time it is needed and not a moment sooner, reducing resource consumption and improving startup time. For example, menu attributes like label, icon, and tooltip are described within the manifest file along with the name of the associated action class. The action class is not loaded until the first time a user actually selects the menu item.

As of Eclipse 3.0, the Eclipse team began replacing the proprietary plug-in framework with the OSGi standard (http://www.osgi.org). The OSGi specification is focused on defining a service platform for component-based network services. It explains the execution environment, modules, life cycle, and registration of components called *bundles*. Development tools share the same metaphor as network services, enabling Eclipse to appropriately apply the OSGi standards. It is foreseeable that Eclipse will replace the term *plug-ins* with *bundles*. Some of the developer plug-in documentation has already started this process.

Workspace Layer

The Workspace layer acts as an abstraction of the underlying file system. It is used to mount a discreet location on the file system and manage all the resources contained within. The resources are projects, folders, and files. A workspace can and often does manage multiple projects at a time. A project is a location on the file system that maps directly to directories and files. The file system abstraction adds change tracking, resource metadata, and plug-in state.

Contained within the Workspace layer is the Ant component. Apache Ant is an extremely popular open source Java-based build tool used for automating the building of Java applications and performing unit testing. It takes the place of other build tools such as make and nmake. Ant scripting is XML based and is stored commonly in a `build.xml` file. Common tasks supported by Ant include java, javac, zip, copy, delete, and jar. Ant can be downloaded from `http://ant.apache.org` and used separately. However, you will find Eclipse provides great support for building and executing Ant scripts.

Note Ant stands for Another Neat Tool.

Workbench Layer

Eclipse would be hard to use without a user interface (UI), so the Workbench layer is a graphical user interface (GUI) used to interact with the workspace and the resources it manages. The Workbench layer is organized into perspectives, views, and editors. A *perspective* is a named collection of views and editors as well as the available menu items and commands. It manages the views' and editors' visibility and layout. An example is the Java perspective shown later in this chapter in Figure 2-3, which contains the Java Package Explorer View, Basic Outline View, Basic Problems View, and several other helpful views along with the Java source editor. Views and editors are visual components. They differ in that editors are primarily used to edit documents or are input-centric with an emphasis on the open/save/close life cycle; whereas views are used to manage properties of objects and update things immediately, so they do not have to go through the open/save/close life cycle. The best example of an editor is the Java source code editor, which enables Java files to be opened and edited with special features such as syntax highlighting, code assist, code formatting, and refactoring. The Basic Outline View is a good example of a view. The Basic Outline View displays a tree representation of the active item in the editor. If the active item in the editor is a Java file (as shown later in this chapter in Figure 2-3), the Outline View will display the methods and fields of the class. The Basic Outline View also eases navigation. As elements such as methods are selected in the Basic Outline View, the editor repositions itself to show the element. Context-sensitive menus such as Source, Refactoring, and Declarations are also available in the Basic Outline View. If the editor contains an XML document, the Basic Outline View displays a document object model (DOM) tree.

Contained within the Workbench are two UI frameworks for developing desktop applications: Standard Widget Toolkit (SWT) and JFace. The Eclipse developers did not feel the Swing and Abstract Window Toolkit (AWT) included with the Java 2 Standard Edition would meet the needs of the Eclipse Platform, so they developed their own. SWT is a set of widgets that provide the best of Swing and AWT. SWT uses the native operating system components, when available, to get the best look and feel and performance. However, on operating systems where a native component does not exist, SWT provides a Java implementation similar to Swing. For developers wanting to use SWT in their own applications as a replacement for Swing and AWT, SWT is available as the SWT Binary and Source download on the Eclipse downloads page (`http://www.eclipse.org/downloads/`).

The JFace framework is an abstraction that sits on top of SWT. It provides a higher-level API that wraps but does not hide SWT to provide windows, views, dialog boxes, actions, and wizards. While the JFace framework is also available to be used by developers outside of Eclipse, as of this writing there is no separate download. Instead, you have to collect the appropriate JAR files from the Eclipse installation if you want to include JFace in your own applications.

Platform Components

The Eclipse Platform includes the Help, Team, and Debug components, which extend the platform layers. The Help component enables an easy way to incorporate indexed and searchable HTML help. It internally uses the Apache Tomcat (`http://jakarta.apache.org/tomcat/`) web container to serve up the HTML pages and Apache Lucene (`http://jakarta.apache.org/lucene/`) for searching. The Team component provides integration with source configuration management (SCM) tools. Eclipse provides a CVS client implementation. The Debug component provides for language-independent debugger integration.

Obtaining the Eclipse Platform

While uncommon, it is possible to download just the Eclipse Platform. On the Eclipse downloads page, the platform is available as the Platform Runtime Binary, or the Platform Software Development Kit (SDK). The Platform Runtime Binary includes a runable Eclipse Workbench with user documentation. The Platform SDK includes the Platform Runtime Binary, source code, and programmer documentation.

This flavor of Eclipse could be used to assemble plug-ins for a non-Java-related IDE. For example, if you wanted to build a C/C++ IDE, you could start with the Platform Runtime Binary and add the C/C++ Development Tools (CDT) found at `http://www.eclipse.org/cdt/`.

Eclipse Software Development Kit

The Eclipse SDK builds on top of the Eclipse Platform by providing basic Java support through the Java Development Tools (JDT) and the ability to extend Eclipse through the Plug-in Development Environment (PDE). Figure 2-2 shows how JDT and PDE build on top of the Eclipse Platform.

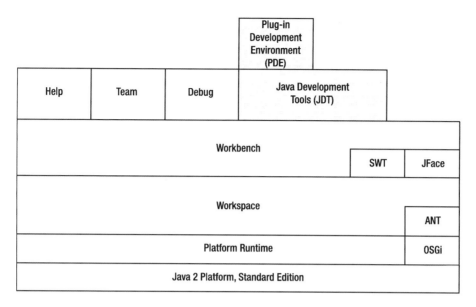

Figure 2-2. *Eclipse SDK architecture*

Java Development Tools

JDT provides many tools for developing simple Java applications. The tools include wizards for creating projects, classes, interfaces, and packages. It also provides the Java perspective shown in Figure 2-3, which includes views for Class outlines, Package Explorer, Javadoc, and Declarations. Additional views are Members, Types, Hierarchy, and Call Hierarchy.

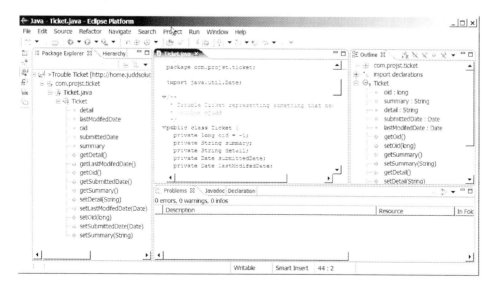

Figure 2-3. *JDT Java perspective*

Unit testing is a vital part of the development and quality assurance process of many Java applications today. So JDT includes wizards for generating JUnit test cases and suites. Eclipse also provides a custom JUnit runner that integrates with Eclipse as a view.

JDT also provides a powerful Java debugger implementation that includes watches, breakpoints, thread monitors, and remote debugging.

Plug-in Development Environment

For those who feel Eclipse does not meet their specific development needs, Eclipse can be extended by using the Plug-in Development Environment (PDE), which extends JDT, since Eclipse plug-ins are written in Java. PDE provides a couple of wizards for developing plug-ins, features, and fragments. It also includes a Plug-in Development perspective, which looks similar to the Java perspective, except it adds a Plug-ins Explorer View, which provides a tree of installed plug-ins, and an Error Log View to display the contents of Eclipse's error log file.

Because plug-ins must be hosted by Eclipse, the runner and debugger in the PDE are configured to start up a new instance of Eclipse, which is referred to as the *runtime instance* for testing and debugging. The version performing the debugging is referred to as the *host instance*.

Note If you are interested in learning to write plug-ins, I suggest you start with the "PDE Does Plug-ins" article found at http://www.eclipse.org/articles/Article-PDE-does-plugins/PDE-intro.html.

Obtaining the Eclipse SDK

The Eclipse SDK is the most common way to get started with Eclipse. It can be downloaded from the Eclipse downloads page (http://www.eclipse.org/downloads/). It includes the Eclipse Platform, JDT, PDE, source code, and both user and programmer documentation. It includes everything necessary to begin developing a simple Java application or developing Eclipse plug-ins.

Extension Points

Eclipse's open plug-in architecture provides many points to which applications can be integrated. Figure 2-4 shows some of the common points in which applications can be added.

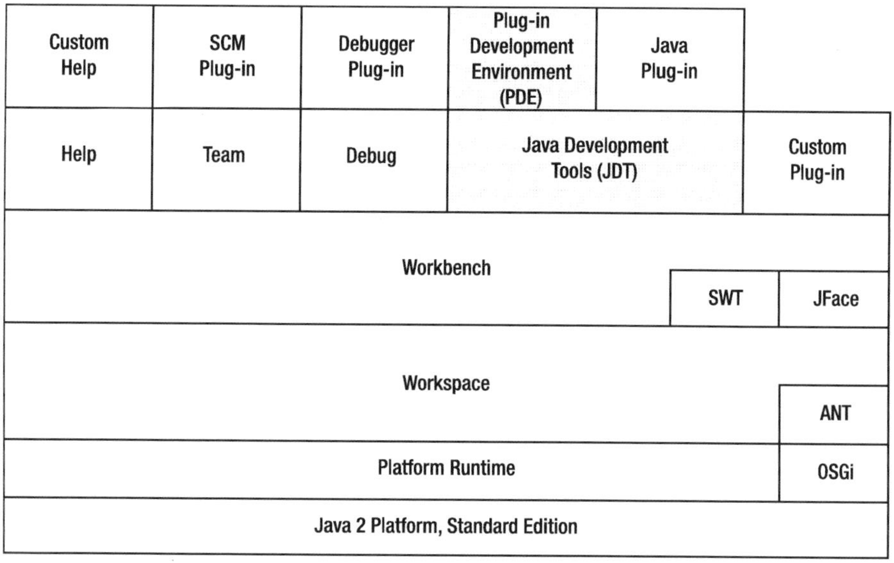

Custom Help	SCM Plug-in	Debugger Plug-in	Plug-in Development Environment (PDE)	Java Plug-in	
Help	Team	Debug	Java Development Tools (JDT)		Custom Plug-in
Workbench					
				SWT	JFace
Workspace					
					ANT
Platform Runtime					OSGi
Java 2 Platform, Standard Edition					

Figure 2-4. *Eclipse extension points*

Most plug-ins extend the workbench directly. These types of plug-ins often include perspectives, views, menus, editors, and wizards. Examples would include other language plug-ins like the CDT mentioned earlier. Language plug-ins are also likely to require extensions to the Debug component.

Plug-ins related to new or evolving Java application programming interfaces (APIs) are likely to extend an already existing JDT plug-in. The J2EE Standard Tools (JST) is an example of such an extension.

There are also plug-ins for the common source code management tools like Microsoft's Visual Source Safe, IBM/Rational's ClearCase, and Subversion, all of which extend the Team component.

The Help component enables plug-ins to include integrated documentation.

Independent Plug-ins

Eclipse boasts of having hundreds of commercial and open source plug-ins available. These plug-ins include additional language support such as C#, new Java APIs like JavaServer Faces (JSF), database integration, modeling, web services, and just about any other imaginable area of development. The Eclipse foundation hosts some of the projects themselves at http://www.eclipse.org/projects/. Other plug-ins can be found at the Eclipse community projects and plug-ins page (http://www.eclipse.org/community/plugins.html) and/or Eclipse-Plugins.info's searchable catalog (http://www.eclipse-plugins.info/).

Summary

In this chapter, you learned Eclipse's plug-in architecture makes it an extremely flexible and customizable platform for developing many kinds of applications. You also learned Eclipse's architecture is built on the Java 2 Platform and includes the Runtime, Workspace, and Workbench layers. The platform also includes the Help, Team, and Debug components as well as the Java Development Tools and Plug-in Development Environment plug-ins. The chapter concludes by identifying areas Eclipse can be extended and where to find additional plug-ins.

CHAPTER 3

Eclipse Web Tools Platform Project

Since the initial release of Eclipse, many critical features have been missing for advanced J2EE application development. Neither the Eclipse platform nor the Java Development Tools (JDT) contain an XML or JSP editor, wizards for creating EJBs, or a mechanism for managing an application server. Up until now this gap has been filled by commercial and open source plug-ins. However, many developers and organizations have been unsatisfied because there is no standard open source set of Eclipse plug-ins for developing web and J2EE applications. They complain the commercial plug-ins are too expensive, and collecting the right open source plug-ins takes too much time and effort to locate and install. The Eclipse Web Tools Platform (WTP) project—http://www.eclipse.org/webtools/—was created to alleviate these complaints. This chapter explains the history, goals, and organization of WTP.

WTP History

WTP was proposed almost immediately after the release of the Eclipse Platform. At the time, current industry focus was on developing web and J2EE applications. Eclipse did not provide any such tools. While many people were excited about the announcement of WTP, there was almost no support or volunteers. The project sat dormant for several years. In the meantime, many open source plug-ins began springing up to meet these needs. For example, Sysdeo (http://www.sysdeo.com/eclipse/tomcatPlugin.html) provided a Tomcat Launcher for starting and stopping the open source Apache Tomcat web container from within Eclipse.

Unfortunately, many of the open source plug-ins did not cover the breadth or depth of the development community needs. In addition, many of the open source plug-ins did not have the quality Eclipse users had come to expect from native Eclipse projects. This enabled commercial vendors to provide higher-quality plug-ins for a price. For example, Eteration (http://www.eteration.com) released Lomboz, which provided support for JSP, EJBs, and most of the J2EE stack. Shortly after the first Eclipse conference in 2004, Eteration made Lomboz open source (http://www.objectlearn.com) and donated it to the ObjectWeb consortium (http://www.objectweb.org). Another noteworthy commercial plug-in is MyEclipse (http://www.myeclipseide.com) by Genuitec, LLC, which took the unique approach of assembling the best of the open source plug-ins, providing some additional value-added features, and selling the whole by subscription. In the meantime, IBM continued to extend Eclipse with its WebSphere Studio tools.

WTP came back to life in the summer of 2004 when ObjectWeb announced it would kick-start WTP by donating its Lomboz code base. The contribution was contingent on WTP being separated into two subprojects, the first subproject being the Web Standard Tools (WST) aimed at providing the development tools necessary for web-enabled applications, and the second being the J2EE Standard Tools (JST), which provides development tools for J2EE-based development.

IBM did not want to be outdone, so it subsequently offered to provide a code donation from its WebSphere Studio Application Developer (WSAD). The IBM contributions contained lots of editor support for XML, JSP, JavaScript, etc., as well as connectivity to relational databases. The strength of the Lomboz donation was the concept of flexible project layouts using modules along with the ability to support many open source and commercial application servers.

Over the year since, many people and organizations donated their time and resources in order to merge and extend the two donations to provide the first release of WTP.

WTP Goals

The primary goals of WTP are quite simple: to provide quality, open source, vendor-neutral, standards-based development tools for web and J2EE applications.

WTP wants to provide the quality users of the Eclipse Platform and JDT have come to expect. Therefore, WTP provides many perspectives, views, editors, and wizards. Many of the editors in WTP are very complex since they have to support a hybrid of formats. For example, a JSP editor must support formatting and code assist for HTML, Java, and JavaScript.

WTP is made available under the open source Eclipse Public License (EPL) version 1.0, an approved license of the Open Source Initiative, or OSI (http://www.opensource.org). You may read the license for yourself at http://www.eclipse.org/legal/epl-v10.html, but a brief summary follows. The EPL is a very flexible license, with few restrictions. It gives you and anybody else the rights to use, distribute, and extend WTP as source code, libraries, or a complete application, all royalty free. The license even includes provisions to distribute WTP as is or in a commercial product. This is all great news; however, there are a couple of downsides. First, if you distribute EPL software, you must provide access to the original source code and any extensions you offer under the EPL. Second, the EPL does not provide any indemnity. This means you are not protected if somebody claims the EPL infringes on their patents or intellectual property rights. If that person wins such a lawsuit and you continue to use or distribute the software, you may be expected to pay a royalty or discontinue such activities.

Warning The authors of this book are not attorneys. Legal questions and concerns about use and distribution of EPL-licensed software should be directed to appropriate legal counsel.

WTP provides development tools rather than a runtime environment. This means nothing from WTP will be required during the execution of an application developed with WTP. Therefore, WTP must integrate with existing web servers and applications servers. WTP is committed to remaining vendor neutral. This is very important in the J2EE space, since there are many application server vendors. TheServerSide.com's Application Server Matrix (http://www.theserverside.com/reviews/matrix.tss) identifies 34 vendors of application servers, and it does not even include Apache's new Geronimo server (http://geronimo.apache.org). In order to support vendor neutrality, WTP includes a service provider interface (SPI) enabling vendors to plug their implementations into WTP.

WTP's primary focus is on providing development tools for standards-based technologies. Figure 3-1 shows the standards-based technologies within the WST and JST scopes. Since WST and JST focus on different types of standards, the next two sections detail the standards in each subproject.

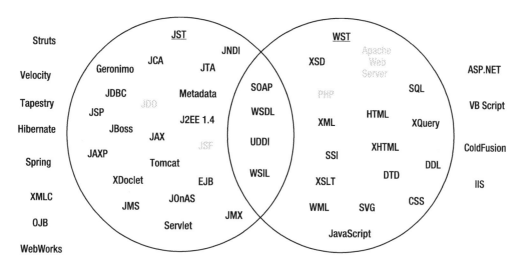

Figure 3-1. *WTP scope and standards*

WST Scope

WST focuses on web-centric application development based on standards defined by the following standards bodies:

- *World Wide Web Consortium (W3C)*—http://www.w3.org: Defines the standards for many web technologies including HTTP, HTML, XHTML, CSS, SVG, XML, XSLT, XML Schema, XML Query, and many more.

- *European Computer Manufacturers Association (ECMA)*—http://www.ecma-international.org: Defines scripting and programming languages such as JavaScript (ECMAScript) and C#.

- *Internet Engineering Task Force (IETF)*—http://www.ietf.org: Defines standards related to the Internet architecture such as the Transmission Control Protocol and Internet Protocol, which make up the TCP/IP standards.

- *American National Standards Institute (ANSI)*—http://www.ansi.org: Defines a wide variety of technology standards in order to improve competitiveness of companies, including the ASCII character sets, Structured Query Language (SQL), and the C/C++ programming languages.

- *Organization for the Advancement of Structured Information Standards (OASIS)*—http://www.oasis-open.org: Defines e-business standards for web services.

- *Web Services Interoperability Organization (WS-I)*—http://www.ws-i.org: Defines generic protocols for the interoperable exchange of messages between web services.

As illustrated in Figure 3-1, WST includes the common web technologies you would expect such as HTML, Cascading Style Sheets (CSS), and JavaScript. It also includes the suite of eXtensible Markup Language (XML) related technologies including XHTML, Wireless Markup Language (WML), XML Schema (XSD), Document Type Definition (DTD), eXtensible Stylesheet Language (XSL), XSL Transformations (XSLT), XSL Formatting Objects (XSL-FO), XML Query (XQuery), and Scalable Vector Graphics (SVG). Of course, WST also includes support for web service technologies such as Simple Object Access Protocol (SOAP), Web Service Description Language (WSDL), Universal Description Discovery and Integration (UDDI), and Web Service Inspection Language (WSIL). Notice in Figure 3-1 that the web services technologies overlap between WST and JST. WST is responsible for supporting the generic web services functionality, while JST is responsible for providing a Java-specific implementation using the Apache Axis framework (http://ws.apache.org/axis/). At first glance, SQL and Database Definition Language may seem out of place in WST since they are not traditionally considered web technologies; however, SQL is defined by the ANSI committee, which brings it into the WST scope. In the future, WST may also grow to encompass open source Internet languages such as PHP and Perl. WST will also consider including support for starting and stopping open source web servers. The most obvious, Apache Web Server, will likely be included at some point.

Outside the scope of WST are proprietary Internet languages such as Microsoft's ASP.NET and VBScript, as well as Macromedia's ColdFusion. Commercial web servers such as Microsoft's Internet Information Server (IIS) will also not be supported. Microsoft or another group would be responsible for extending WTP through the SPI to support IIS.

JST Scope

JST focuses on providing the tools to develop enterprise Java applications based on Java Specification Requests (JSRs) defined by the Java Community Process (JCP), found at http://www.jcp.org. JST's primary focus is on JSR 151, Java 2 Platform Enterprise Edition (J2EE) 1.4 (http://java.sun.com/j2ee/), which includes the following technologies discussed in Chapter 2:

- Enterprise JavaBeans (EJB) 2.1—JSR 153

- Servlets 2.4—JSR 154

- JavaServer Pages (JSP) 2.0—JSR 152

- Java Message Service (JMS) 1.1—JSR 914

- Java Transaction API (JTA) 1.0

- JavaMail 1.3—JSR 919

- Java Naming and Directory Interface (JNDI)

- JDBC API 3.0—JSR 54

- Java Authentication and Authorization Service (JAAS)

- Java API for XML Parsing (JAXP) 1.2—JSR 5

- J2EE Connector Architecture (JCA) 1.5—JSR 112

- Web Services 1.1—JSR 921

- Java API for XML-based RPC (JAX-RPC) 1.1—JSR 101

- SOAP with Attachments API for Java (SAAJ) 1.2

- Java API for XML Registries (JAXR) 1.0—JSR 93

- J2EE Management API 1.0—JSR 77

- Java Management Extensions (JMX) 1.2—JSR 3

- J2EE Deployment API 1.1—JSR 88

- Java Authorization Service Provider Contract for Containers (JACC) 1.0—JSR 115

In addition to these J2EE 1.4 technologies, JST will include JSR 45—Debugging Support. Ultimately, JST will include JSR 175—Metadata, and JSR 181—Metadata for Web Services, based on the metadata support added to J2SE 5.0. Until the metadata frameworks can be implemented, the open source attribute-oriented programming framework XDoclet (`http://xdoclet.sourceforge.net`) will provide an alternative.

JST also plans on including integration with the most popular open source applications servers including Tomcat, Jetty, JBoss, Geronimo, and JOnAS. Commercial application servers such as WebLogic and WebSphere will rely on the vendors providing integration.

What's missing from the JST scope may be just as important as what is included. Initially, JST does not plan on providing support for JavaServer Faces (JSF) or Java Data Objects (JDO) because they are not required by the J2EE 1.4 specification. However, because they are finalized JSRs, it is likely they will be added at some point in the future. The other area that is out of scope is the plethora of open source projects that have really enhanced the Java platform. There are many common open source MVC frameworks that are not included such as Struts, Tapestry, Velocity, and WebWorks. JST also does not provide support for the open source object relational mapping frameworks like Hibernate and OJB. You can also forget about support for the light-weight or inversion of control containers like Spring.

Contributing

Because WTP is open source, you should consider contributing back to the WTP community. Many individuals and organizations have donated their time and money in order to provide a quality tool set. A contribution could consist of source code or simply your comments on the project or the reporting of bugs.

To contribute your ideas or suggestions, you can subscribe to the WTP newsgroup. The newsgroup is frequented by WTP committers to get ideas and answer questions. Because WTP is so young and there are many ways to develop J2EE and web applications, the WTP community needs to hear from you. The newsgroup, `eclipse.webtools`, is available from the `news.eclipse.org` news server.

Equally important is letting the committers know when you have found a bug so they can continue providing a quality product. WTP and Eclipse use a Bugzilla database to maintain defects. Bugs can be submitted by going to `http://bugs.eclipse.org/bugs/`.

The easiest way to contribute source code is to submit it as a patch on a bug report. In order to do this, you must first get the code from the CVS repository. Eclipse has great CVS integration and makes the retrieval, modification, and patch generation really easy. If you want to contribute to WTP, read the "Developing the WTP with Eclipse" tutorial at `http://www.eclipse.org/webtools/testtutorials/developingwtp/DevelopingWTP.html`.

Note WTP CVSROOT is `:pserver:anonymous@dev.eclipse.org:/home/webtools`.

Summary

In this chapter, you learned about how the Lomboz project and IBM jump-started the fledgling WTP project by making code donations. You also learned how WST scope is centered around common Internet standard consortiums, and JST is driven by the J2EE 1.4 specification and the Java Community Process. We concluded by explaining how you might contribute to the future of WTP by sharing your ideas, bugs, or source code.

CHAPTER 4

Introduction to JST

The J2EE Standard Tools (JST) project is an effort by the Eclipse development team to provide users of the Eclipse Platform a standardized framework for the creation of tools for the development of enterprise applications based on the J2EE Specification. The JST project together with the Web Standard Tools (WST) project, discussed in the next chapter, make up the Web Tools Platform (WTP) and jointly provide developers an arsenal of tools produced from the frameworks created by the respective projects. These tools are useful for the development, testing, and management of Java-based enterprise applications. The JST and WST projects are closely related because Java-based enterprise applications often rely heavily on non-Java technologies for core functionalities. The editing of XML-based deployment descriptors, which play an important part in the deployment of J2EE components, is one such example of this close relationship.

The development tools supplied by the project provide users of the ubiquitous Eclipse Platform with a cohesive set of plug-ins integrated into the Eclipse development environment to allow developers to create, debug, test, and deploy multitiered J2EE applications. Some of the tools are provided for use in the creation and maintenance of J2EE source artifacts such as JavaServer Pages (JSP), servlets, EJBs, and other deployable assets. Other tools are meant for activities that provide support to the development process such as the packaging of artifacts into deployable modules, the exploring of available Web Services, and also the management of application servers.

JST limits its scope to providing support for J2EE technologies even though, as we have earlier indicated, many non-Java technologies are often found within an enterprise application. Support for many of these non-Java technologies falls within the scope of the WST project. Expectedly, not all enterprise Java technologies are supported by JST. Support is provided for the standards that comprise the J2EE 1.4 Specification as well as a few other JCP-approved standards. XDoclet, a popular technology for annotating source artifacts, is also supported, even though it is not a JCP standard. Other popular enterprise Java technologies such as Hibernate and Velocity, which are not based on JCP standards, are, however, unsupported.

It is important to bear in mind that JST goes significantly beyond the provision of tools for enterprise development and additionally provides a framework from which further tools of usefulness to Java enterprise development can be created. A brief example of this is that Struts, the popular web development framework which is not supported by JST, could have support provided for it by tool extenders using the framework provided by JST. This way, the new plug-in seamlessly coexists with those provided by JST.

We begin this chapter by describing the scope of the JST project; we will also explore the benefits provided by this project. Discussion of the foundation provided by JST for the creation of J2EE-focused tools will follow, and we will conclude the chapter with an extensive overview of the tools provided by JST. We will be demonstrating the use of these tools more comprehensively throughout the entire book.

JST Scope

JST provides Eclipse with a comprehensive suite of tools for the development of Java-based enterprise applications conforming to the J2EE 1.4 Specification. Due to J2EE support being its core purpose, JST limits its scope to Java-based technologies. Many of the supported technologies, however, such as JavaServer Pages, have a dependence on open standards such as HTML and CSS. In these cases, the open standards fall within the scope of the WST project.

JCP standards, which lie at the core of the J2EE Specification, feature heavily in the list of supported technologies, though some newer JCP standards that are not a part of the J2EE 1.4 Specification are not supported. Notable items in this list include JDO (JSR 243—Java Data Objects 2.0), which defines Java object persistence, and JSF (JSR 252—JavaServer Faces), which provides standard APIs and tag libraries for web interface development.

Additionally, many non-JCP technologies are beyond the scope of JST, including such popular frameworks as Struts, Velocity, and XMLC. XDoclet, as we noted earlier, is supported, however, largely due to the absence of a JCP standard for J2EE annotation.

We present in Table 4-1 a list of supported technologies in JST and the JSR that defines each technology where applicable. You can view any of these specifications by visiting the Java Community Process website at http://www.jcp.org.

Table 4-1. *JST-supported Technologies by JCP Standards*

JCP Standard	Title
JSR 3	Java Management Extensions (JMX) 1.2
JSR 5	Java API for XML Parsing (JAXP) 1.2
JSR 45	Debugging Support
JSR 54	JDBC API 3.0
JSR 67	SOAP with Attachments API for Java (SAAJ) 1.2
JSR 77	J2EE Management API 1.0
JSR 88	Deployment API 1.1
JSR 93	Java API for XML Registries (JAXR) 1.0
JSR 101	Java API for XML-based RPC (JAX-RPC) 1.1
JSR 109	Web Services
JSR 112	J2EE Connector Architecture (JCA) 1.5
JSR 115	Java Authorization Contract for Containers (JACC)
JSR 152	JavaServer Pages (JSP) 2.0
JSR 153	Enterprise JavaBeans (EJB) 2.1
JSR 154	Servlets 2.4
JSR 907	Java Transaction API (JTA) 1.0
JSR 914	Java Message Service (JMS) 1.1
JSR 919	JavaMail 1.3

In addition to these JCP standards, the following non-JCP standards and technologies are also within the scope of JST:

- Java Authentication and Authorization Service (JAAS)

- Java Naming and Directory Interface (JNDI)

- XDoclet

Note XDoclet is supported by JST as a vehicle for J2EE annotation pending the creation of a JSR for this important purpose. An expanded discussion of the role, configuration, and usage of XDoclet in JST is provided in Chapter 8.

JST Goals

A major goal of JST is to extend the Eclipse Platform into the enterprise software development space in the hopes of expanding usage of the platform. Similar to how the Java Development Tools (JDT) provided Eclipse with the necessary tools for the creation and management of standard Java components, and was thus rewarded with a major influx of users who adopted the platform, so does JST expect to generate an influx of new users to adopt the platform.

Although third-party plug-ins exist that provide Eclipse with support for the creation of J2EE applications, there remains some associated difficulty with the process of finding and using these plug-ins for a project. Chief among these difficulties is the need for developers to individually seek and assemble the right collection of commercial and open source plug-ins that suit the needs of their project. A developer could eventually find a suitable assembly of plug-ins to use for a specific project, but the lack of a standard set of tools remained a significant source of complaint due to the time—and sometimes cost—intensive nature of the searching for and assembling of components. Sites like Eclipse Plugin Central (http://www.eclipseplugincentral.com/) try to make the process of assembly easier by providing users with a repository of different plug-ins as well as information about these plug-ins and tutorials on how to use them. This service is, however, only available to paid subscribers.

It is reasonable to expect that users of Eclipse would want a readily available set of tools immediately accessible to them for their development needs. This is especially prevalent among users new to Eclipse and probably more familiar with IDEs that provide readily available development tools. In fact, this requirement of assembling plug-ins for developing J2EE applications is seen as a deterrent to the adoption of the platform for many new users. The JST project intends to remove this barrier by providing the necessary development tools that can be used for J2EE development.

It should be noted that support for third-party plug-ins remains a fundamental part of the Eclipse architecture, and the Web Tools Project was created to enhance rather than diminish this purpose. In fact, beyond providing a standardized set of development tools, the JST project importantly provides a framework for the development of additional tools for the enterprise Java community. This framework, known as the *J2EE Core Model* (JCM), is provided to allow the development of tools that would seamlessly integrate with existing JST tools and the Eclipse Platform. It is hoped that this would encourage vendors to extend support for their proprietary tools to the Eclipse Platform and also for other companies and groups to develop plug-ins for Eclipse to support whatever technology or standard the platform might not currently be providing support for.

The aggregate goal of the JST project is a continued expansion of the user base of the platform, and this is a welcome proposition as it helps to strengthen the platform as an invaluable tool in the software development process. The JST project hopes the release of its toolkit will bring about an inflow of new users to the platform and also swell the ranks of J2EE developers. This growth is expected to in turn encourage vendors to continue to provide the platform with support for their commercial tools, and also encourage open source developers to provide plug-ins that support newer technologies that developers might become interested in.

J2EE Core Model

We have mentioned earlier that JST provides a foundation for the development of J2EE-focused tools. This foundation is known as the J2EE Core Model (JCM), and it comprises frameworks and object models that abstract out core functionalities of J2EE artifacts and components. It additionally provides APIs for accessing and manipulating these functionalities. The JCM is made available to third-party developers to extend the number of tools available for the Eclipse Platform and importantly provide support for additional technologies not currently supported.

It should be understood that the JCM is not provided for use in the creation of J2EE applications, but instead as a base infrastructure for creating J2EE development tools. The commitment of Eclipse to the extension of the platform is thus apparent. The tools provided by the JST project are actually themselves an extension of the JCM. We will discuss these tools at length later in the chapter, but we must first examine the models that are provided by the JCM, which are listed here:

- **J2EE Project Model**: This provides the Eclipse Platform with the framework for managing a J2EE project. The project model supports a flexible structure whereby a project contains a collection of artifacts that constitute either a complete J2EE application or deployment modules that represent a portion of such an application. It also provides a mechanism for the management of build activities and deployment of created artifacts.

- **J2EE Editor Model**: This model extends the standard Eclipse editor to provide support for the creation and editing of J2EE source artifacts such as JSPs, servlets, EJBs, etc. It provides a base for the creation of various text and graphical editors, giving support for such essential editing functionalities as syntax coloring, code assist, refactoring, and quick fixes.

- **J2EE Artifacts Model**: This model represents J2EE source and deployment artifacts like JSPs, EJBs, deployment descriptors, etc., that can be created and managed within a project together with other artifacts such as image resources, text files, and various other files that may be packaged into a deployable module. The model further represents the deployment modules in their archival state, i.e., WAR, EJB JAR, EAR, and RAR files. Natures, builders, validators, and EMF models associated with a project will also be represented by this model.

- **J2EE Server Model**: The server model provides the abstractions required to support the deployment of modules to many different types of application servers. It additionally provides a unified control mechanism to start, administer, and stop these J2EE application servers. The model also provides the means for managing the configuration details of these servers including environment parameters, JVM parameters, and classpaths.

J2EE module management such as packaging, deployment, debugging, removal, import, and export of the J2EE modules are managed by the model.

J2EE Standard Tools

We will now examine the tools resulting from the JST project. As stated earlier, these tools are of use in creating J2EE source artifacts or providing supporting functions for the creation of J2EE applications. The tools are an exemplar implementation of the JCM described previously and were created by extending the models and the APIs made available by the JCM. The resulting product of this activity is an integrated set of tools, views, perspectives, and wizards useful for various J2EE development activities.

JST provides several tools for enterprise application development, with each tool targeted at aiding in a specific domain of activities related to developing a J2EE application. Servlet Tools for instance are useful for creating servlet components that are deployed within the web container of an application server, while EJB Tools are used to create EJBs that are deployed within the EJB container. We discuss the tools of the JST in this section.

J2EE Project and Module Tools

The J2EE Project Tools support the creation of a J2EE project as a collection of source artifacts that each constitute a deployment module of a J2EE application. The project also contains important configuration information that is stored and managed within the project workspace but excluded from the deployable module resulting from the project. These tools support the creation of five types of projects:

- **EJB Project**: Consists of Enterprise JavaBean components and supports source artifacts that would be compiled and deployed within the EJB container of an application server.

- **Dynamic Web Project**: Consists of servlets, JSPs, and additional Web Tier components such as taglibs, HTML documents, images, etc. that are targeted for deployment inside the web container of an application server.

- **Application Client Project**: Consists of application client components often designed for the consumption of services provided by an enterprise application.

- **Connector Project**: Consists of source files for the creation of connector applications to integrate legacy systems with J2EE applications as specified by JSR 112 (J2EE Connector Architecture 1.5).

- **Enterprise Application Project**: Consists of modules that represent a complete enterprise application. This project provides the ability to reference several EJB, Web, Application Client, and Connector Projects whose products will be deployed together.

The J2EE Module Tools additionally provide multiple useful features in the creation of a J2EE project. These features include the ability to create and manage artifacts within each of the J2EE projects described earlier and also provide a module structure that represents the deployable artifacts within the project. The module structure can then be packaged into a suitable J2EE deployable archive.

Figure 4-1 shows a dialog box of the Project Creation wizard and displays some of the valid choices for an Enterprise Application Project. Additional dialog boxes are provided to developers, allowing them to include further details specific to the project type chosen on this initial project creation page. Figure 4-2 shows the screen provided when an Enterprise Application Project (which is highlighted in Figure 4-1) is being created.

Figure 4-1. *Project Creation wizard*

Figure 4-2. *Enterprise Application Project dialog box*

The project tool provides support for validating the deployment module within projects, editing its deployment descriptor, as well as packaging the contents within the module. The tool also provides the ability to create projects through the importation of modules. We will provide a more in-depth discussion of project structures in Chapter 7.

J2EE Server Tools

J2EE applications need to be deployed into a web or EJB container as we discussed in Chapter 1, and these containers exist within a J2EE application server. In JST, management of servers to which J2EE applications would be deployed is handled by the J2EE Server Tools. The Server Tools provide a mechanism for the definition of server runtime environments and the creation of instances of an application server from this definition. They also ensure that when a project of a particular type is being created, it can be deployable to the server chosen for the project. Tomcat, for instance, being an application server consisting only of a web container, would not be available as a choice for the creation of an EJB Project. Table 4-2 shows the application servers that are supported as well as the project type and version that they support.

Table 4-2. *Project Types and Supported Application Servers*

Web Version	EJB Version	Application Server
2.2, 2.3, and 2.4	1.1, 2.0, and 2.1	Apache Geronimo 1.0
2.2		Apache Tomcat version 3.2
2.2 and 2.3		Apache Tomcat version 4.0
2.2 and 2.3		Apache Tomcat version 4.1
2.2, 2.3, and 2.4		Apache Tomcat version 5.0
2.2, 2.3, and 2.4		Apache Tomcat version 5.5
2.2, 2.3, and 2.4	1.1, 2.0, and 2.1	BEA WebLogic Server version 8.1
2.2, 2.3, and 2.4	1.1, 2.0, and 2.1	BEA WebLogic Server version 9.0
2.2, 2.3, and 2.4	1.1, 2.0, and 2.1	IBM Websphere 6.0.x
2.2, 2.3, and 2.4	1.1, 2.0, and 2.1	JBOSS 3.2.3
2.2, 2.3, and 2.4	1.1, 2.0, and 2.1	JonAS 4.1.4

The tool is also capable of managing the definition of multiple server runtime environments, thereby allowing deployable modules from different J2EE projects within the workbench to be deployed to their own specific target deployment servers. Figure 4-3 shows an example of the Installed Server Runtime Environments Preferences page where definitions of J2EE server runtime environments can be configured.

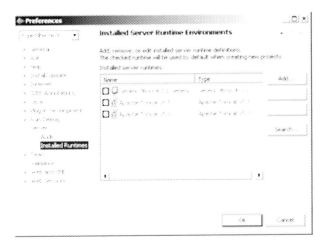

Figure 4-3. *Server runtime definition*

Additional configuration is available for each defined server runtime environment, allowing you to provide such items as environment variables and classpaths for the runtime instance, as well as modify the default startup and VM arguments of the server. J2EE Server Tools additionally provide a mechanism to create instances of servers from these definitions and control execution of the server runtime instances through the Servers View. The Servers View provides the ability to start, stop, debug, and profile each application server. Output generated from each of these processes is written to the Console View.

Tip The Servers View is available as a part of the J2EE Perspective, discussed in its own section later in this chapter. It can also be accessed by selecting Window ➤ Show View ➤ Other ➤ Server ➤ Servers. The Console View, which is not a part of the J2EE Perspective, can be accessed by selecting Window ➤ Show View ➤ Other ➤ Basic ➤ Console.

Servlet Tools

Servlets provide J2EE with the ability to dynamically process requests and provide responses to invocations that support a request/response model. They are most commonly used with HTTP, which expectedly supports the request/response model, and is therefore an important part of most J2EE web applications. The J2EE Servlet Tools include support for servlets in JST by providing such functions as wizard-assisted creation of servlet classes. It additionally automates the insertion of configuration information about each created servlet such as the <servlet> and <servlet-mapping> elements into the deployment descriptor of the web project that references the servlet. Figure 4-4 shows the Create Servlet wizard page available during the creation of a servlet, which prompts for the servlet name, description, initialization parameters, and URL mappings that are needed by the servlet.

Figure 4-4. *Create Servlet wizard*

Additional wizard pages allow the user to specify the associated package for this servlet as well as choose access modifiers for the servlet class and method stubs that should be generated in the new servlet. Figure 4-5 displays one of these wizard pages showing the default modifiers, implemented interfaces, and method stub choices preselected by the tool. As with all wizards, these choices can easily be altered to suit the needs of your project.

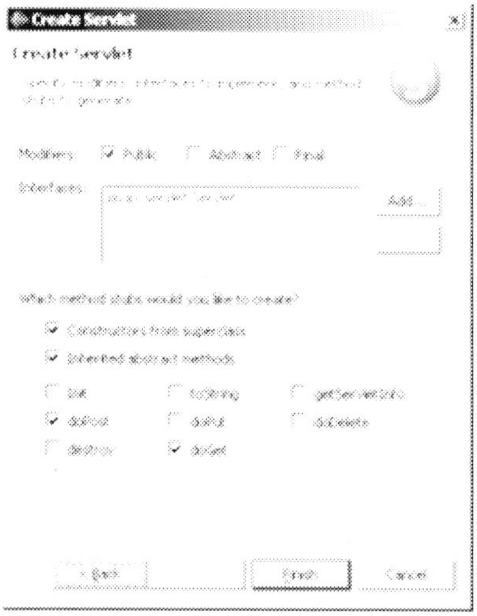

Figure 4-5. *Selection of methods to insert into servlet*

For each of the methods chosen from Figure 4-5, an appropriate method signature is inserted into the generated servlet source file with a TODO task tag statement included that denotes where user-based implementation is required. The text associated with these task tags is immediately reflected in the Tasks View, providing a cohesive location for the developer to track uncompleted tasks. Listing 4-1 shows the servlet file generated by the wizard, including the XDoclet annotations that would be used to insert configuration details into the web.xml deployment descriptor.

Listing 4-1. *Generated Servlet File*

```
package com.projst.ticket.web;

import java.io.IOException;
import javax.servlet.ServletException;
import javax.servlet.http.HttpServletRequest;
import javax.servlet.http.HttpServletResponse;

/**
 * Servlet implementation class for Servlet: ChartTickets
 *
 * @web.servlet
 *    name="ChartTickets"
 *    display-name="ChartTickets"
 *    description="Servlet to create a chart of existing trouble tickets"
 *
 * @web.servlet-mapping
 *    url-pattern="/ChartTickets"
 *
 * @web.servlet-init-param
 *      name="status"
 *      value="open"
 *      description="Ticket type to include in chart"
 *
 */
public class ChartTickets
        extends javax.servlet.http.HttpServlet
        implements javax.servlet.Servlet {
    /**
     *
     */

    /* (non-Java-doc)
     * @see javax.servlet.http.HttpServlet#HttpServlet()
     */
    public ChartTickets() {
        super();
    }
```

```
    /* (non-Java-doc)
     * @see HttpServlet#doGet(HttpServletRequest arg0, HttpServletResponse arg1)
     */
    protected void doGet(HttpServletRequest arg0, HttpServletResponse arg1)
                    throws ServletException, IOException    {
        // TODO Auto-generated method stub
    }

    /* (non-Java-doc)
     * @see HttpServlet#doPost(HttpServletRequest arg0, HttpServletResponse arg1)
     */
    protected void doPost(HttpServletRequest arg0, HttpServletResponse arg1)
                    throws ServletException, IOException    {
        // TODO Auto-generated method stub
    }
}
```

USING TASK TAGS

Eclipse provides *task tags* to serve as markers within documents being edited. When included, comments defined as tasks immediately show up in the Tasks View, providing you with information about additional tasks that need to be completed within your application. These tags can be defined within the Task Preferences page, which can be accessed by selecting Window ➤ Preferences ➤ Java ➤ Compiler ➤ Task Tags. Tags can then be added or edited on this Preferences page.

The TODO tag is the default task tag, and it additionally defaults to a priority of normal. To use the TODO tag, a line like the following is included within your source code file:

```
// TODO Auto-generated method stub
```

You will notice that the TODO task tag is inserted as a Java comment tag, ensuring that your code can be compiled in any IDE without causing errors, since comment tags are universally ignored. Figure 4-6 shows an example of the Tasks View when the servlet file shown in Listing 4-1 is being edited.

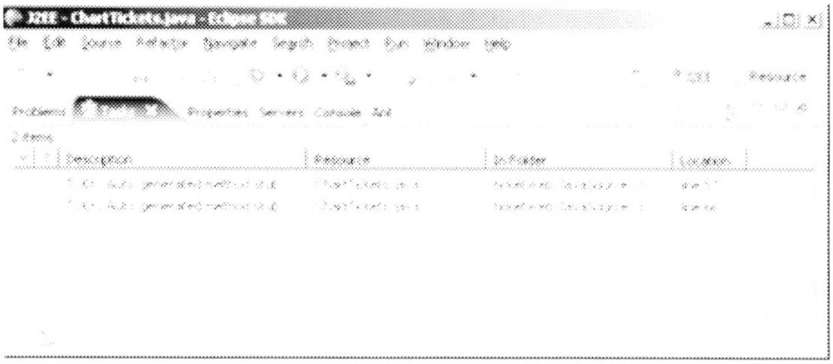

Figure 4-6. *Tasks View displaying task tags from the servlet in Listing 4-1*

You may notice that XDoclet tags are being used in Listing 4-1. These tags provide annotations that can easily be modified to manage information included within the web.xml deployment descriptor about this servlet. Listing 4-2 shows the values inserted into the web.xml file based on the content of the XDoclet annotations in Listing 4-1.

Listing 4-2. *Servlet Tag Generated into the web.xml Deployment Descriptor*

```
<servlet>
    <servlet-name>ChartTickets</servlet-name>
    <display-name>ChartTickets</display-name>
    <description>
        <![CDATA[Servlet to create a chart of existing trouble tickets]]>
    </description>
    <servlet-class>com.projst.ticket.web.ChartTickets</servlet-class>

    <init-param>
        <param-name>status</param-name>
        <param-value>open</param-value>
        <description><![CDATA[Ticket type to include in chart]]></description>
    </init-param>
</servlet>

<servlet-mapping>
    <servlet-name>ChartTickets</servlet-name>
    <url-pattern>/ChartTickets</url-pattern>
</servlet-mapping>
```

It should be noted that servlets are not edited with special editors, but instead with a standard Java editor that is used in creating a Java class. Due to the servlets' nature of being Java source files, creation of specialized editors for servlets is not required. In Chapter 13, we have provided an extended discussion of the use and creation of servlets with JST.

JSP Tools

JavaServer Pages are an integral part of the presentation layer of many enterprise applications, providing access to programmatic functions through a web interface. JST provides a mechanism for the creation and management of JavaServer Pages source files through the JSP Tools. The JSP Tools rely heavily on WST to provide a core foundation for its functions. This is because a JSP file can contain code based on HTML, JavaScript, and CSS technologies in combination with Java expressions and custom tags. Formatting and content assist for the technologies based on open standards are managed by WST, while JST manages the same for Java-related content within the page. For a JSP page, important features such as syntax coloring of the different elements within the JSP file like Java code, JSP tags, HTML tags, and JavaScript code is supported. Figure 4-7 shows the JavaServer Page wizard used for the initial creation of JSP documents.

Figure 4-7. *JavaServer Page wizard*

Creation of JSPs is template based, and these templates can be managed through the JSP Templates Preferences page by selecting Window ➤ Preferences ➤ Web and XML ➤ JSP Files ➤ JSP Templates. We provide additional information about the creation and management of these templates in Chapter 12. Listing 4-3 shows the JSP source file generated from choosing one of the default templates shown in Figure 4-7 earlier.

Listing 4-3. *A Generated JSP File*

```
<!DOCTYPE HTML PUBLIC "-//W3C//DTD HTML 4.01 Transitional//EN">
<html>
<head>
<%@ page language="java" contentType="text/html; charset=ISO-8859-1"
pageEncoding="ISO-8859-1"%>
<meta http-equiv="Content-Type" content="text/html; charset=ISO-8859-1"/>
<title>Insert title here</title>
</head>
<body>

</body>
</html>
```

JSP Tools also provide debugging support for JSP source artifacts as specified by JSR-45 with the ability to set breakpoints in the JSP editor as well as step through code execution.

EJB Tools

JST greatly simplifies the process of creating Enterprise JavaBeans through the inclusion of the EJB Tools. These tools provides wizard-assisted mechanisms for the creation of entity, session, and message-driven beans, thereby automating the process of creating these artifacts and greatly reducing the possibility of error that could occur if they are directly created by a developer. One such wizard, in this case a wizard page for the creation of a message-driven bean, is shown in Figure 4-8.

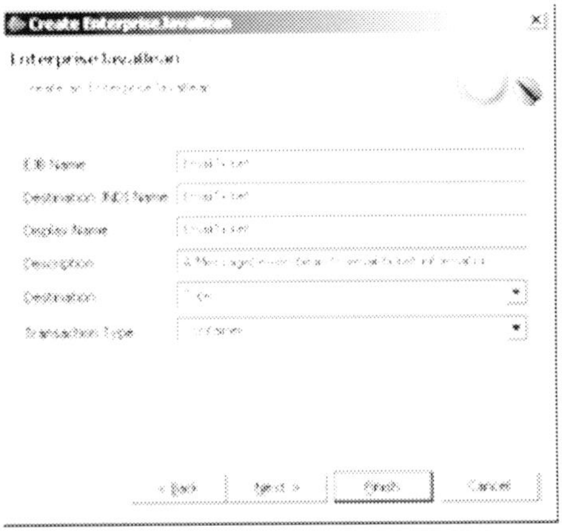

Figure 4-8. *EJB Creation wizard*

Beyond the provision of wizards, J2EE tools additionally provide annotation support for the source file generated in the form of XDoclet attributes. These attributes automate certain mechanical tasks that are part of the process of creating an EJB such as the creation of home and remote interfaces for the EJB or the inclusion of appropriate values for such properties as JNDI names and EJB type within the deployment descriptor of the module. Listing 4-4 shows the annotated source file generated by Eclipse from the wizard shown in Figure 4-8.

Listing 4-4. *A Generated Stateless Session Bean Including XDoclet Annotations*

```
/**
 *
 * <!-- begin-user-doc -->
 * A generated session bean
 * <!-- end-user-doc -->
 * *
 * <!-- begin-xdoclet-definition -->
 * @ejb.bean name="Facility"
 *       description="A session bean named Facility to manage information about the "
```

```
*           display-name="Facility"
*           jndi-name="Facility"
*           type="Stateless"
*           transaction-type="Container"
*
* <!-- end-xdoclet-definition -->
* @generated
*/

public abstract class FacilityBean implements javax.ejb.SessionBean {

    /**
     *
     * <!-- begin-xdoclet-definition -->
     * @ejb.interface-method view-type="remote"
     * <!-- end-xdoclet-definition -->
     * @generated
     *
     * //TODO: Must provide implementation for bean method stub
     */
    public String foo(String param) {
        return null;
    }
}
```

We have provided extended descriptions of the J2EE EJB Tools in Chapter 8, Chapter 9, and Chapter 10.

Java Web Services Tools

JST provides the Java Web Services Tools, which allow users to automate the process of creating and consuming a Web Service. Built upon Apache Axis (http://ws.apache.org/axis/), a widely used platform that simplifies the process of creating and accessing Web Services, the tools provide wizard-assisted creation of Java Web Services from EJBs, JavaBeans, or WSDL files. It also provides wizards for the creation of Java clients that consume Web Services made available by others. Figure 4-9 shows the initial creation screen during the creation of a Web Service client.

Figure 4-9. *Web Service Client Creation wizard*

The Web Services Tools integrates into the context menu available within the Project Explorer to provide a mechanism for the creation of Web Services whenever servlet or stateless session beans are selected within the Project Explorer. Facility to test the Web Service created is also provided by the tool through the automated generation of JSP pages that can invoke each selected Web Service method or by using the Web Services Explorer.

Web Services Explorer

A significant addition to Eclipse is the inclusion of the Web Services Explorer as part of the Web Services Tools. This tool, which is available from the Run ➤ Launch Web Services Explorer menu selection, allows you to browse UDDI registries for available Web Services that can then be used within you application. It provides a facility to query these registries for available Web Services and additionally automates the generation of clients to connect to any available Web Service. Figure 4-10 shows a sample of the Web Services Explorer execution.

The Web Services Explorer tool provides the additional benefit of being able to test any Web Service that is available from a UDDI registry providing a useful evaluation tool to test out the functioning of a Web Service before referencing it within an application. This tool can also test Web Services that exist within the workbench in a similar fashion.

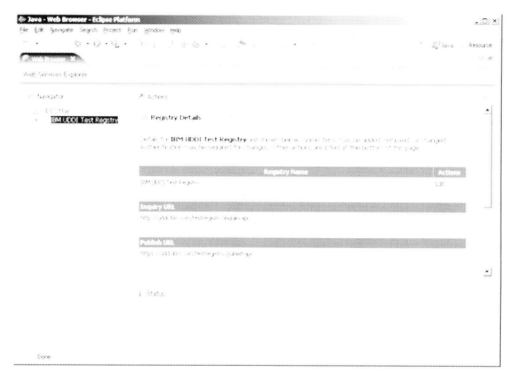

Figure 4-10. *Web Services Explorer*

Navigation Tools

The Navigation Tools comprise a series of views that are useful during the development phases of a J2EE application. These include the ability to navigate through the projects within the current workspace, view hierarchical contents of open resources, monitor problems with the module artifacts, track uncompleted tasks, monitor properties of module artifacts, view and manage instances for all servers defined for the project, observe the console messages generated by these servers, and also view the results of queries executed against data sources.

The J2EE Perspective and the Module View provides access to some of these navigation functionalities within Eclipse.

J2EE Perspective

A collection of several views useful for J2EE development activity make up the J2EE Perspective. Eclipse provides the concept of a perspective as a visual set of views and editors relating to a project type. This supplies the user with the ability to easily open up a series of related views that have relevance to a project being worked on. A J2EE web application, for instance, will often include multiple files that need to be modified, a server to deploy packaged artifacts to, and a console to view the output of the server. The J2EE Perspective provides instant accessibility to these useful views; Table 4-3 lists the available views.

Table 4-3. *Views from the J2EE Perspective*

View	Description
Project Explorer	A navigator provided to browse through the contents of open project. The Project Explorer is aware of J2EE components and denotes the different component types with appropriate icons.
Outline View	Displays the structural elements contained within a document being edited using a tree view structure, providing users with the ability to see what elements within the document relate to each other.
Problems View	A list of the problems existing with the current project being modified such as compilation and validation errors. The view contains a reference to the document and the specific line in which the error exists.
Tasks View	Provides a listing of items that have been delegated as *tasks*, which are often reminders to the developer. Task tags are defined in the Preferences window and support the ability to specify a priority level. Inclusion of this tag inside the comment of a document generates a reference within the view.
Properties View	Provides the ability to inspect and modify the properties of the current element selected within a document. The properties available differ based on the type of document being edited and the element type selected within such a document.
Servers View	Provides a mechanism to control the operations of all configured runtime instances of application servers.

It should be noted that in addition to the views that make up a perspective, additional views can be opened by selecting Window ➤ Show View ➤ Other and then choosing the needed view. The new view then opens alongside existing views from the J2EE Perspective, resulting in a customized perspective. Any such customized perspective can be saved by selecting Window ➤ Save Perspective As for later access.

Synchronization automatically occurs between each view and the source document in the editor. The Outline View, for instance, will immediately show the hierarchical outline of a document being edited, while the Properties View would show the property settings of the actual tag selected within the document.

Module View

This tool is available within the Project Explorer, providing a navigable representation of all the deployable J2EE artifacts that are available within a project. The contents available within the Module View match the elements specified within the deployment descriptor of a deployable module, and the deployment descriptor is in turn specific to a type of project. This means that a module for a Web Project will contain references for servlets, servlet mappings, etc., while a module for an EJB Project will contain references for session, entity, and message-driven beans. Figure 4-11 shows the Module View for a J2EE Web Project.

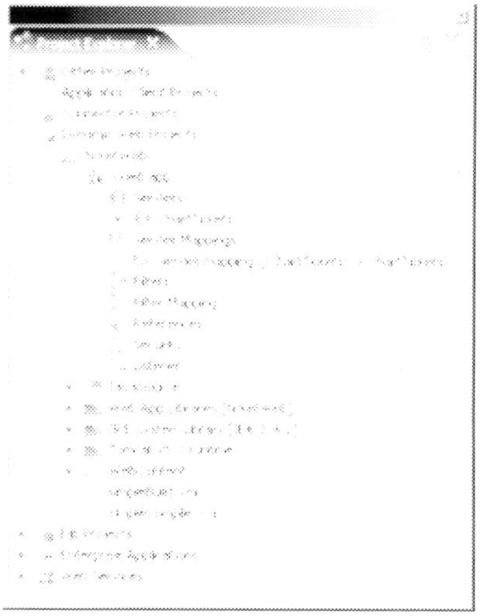

Figure 4-11. *Module View for a Web Project within the Project Explorer*

Summary

We began this chapter by providing an introduction to JST and describing its usefulness to both the enterprise application developer and tool extender. Next, we examined the scope of JST and discussed the criteria that determined which standards and technologies would be supported. The J2EE Core Model, or JCM, was next described, including details on its abstraction of core J2EE functionality and the APIs it exposes. This foundation, as we stated, is of great value to anyone, such as third-party vendors or open source developers interested in extending Eclipse to provide support for currently unsupported technologies.

Finally, we provided an introduction to the different useful tools that are included in JST and briefly discussed some of their uses and benefits. This discussion is expanded in later chapters of this text, providing detailed examples of using these tools in the context of implementing a project.

CHAPTER 5

Introduction to WST

The Web Standard Tools (WST) project is the other subproject of the Eclipse Web Tools Platform (WTP) project and a sibling project to the J2EE Standard Tools (JST) project described in the preceding chapter. The WST project aims to provide a set of tools for the creation of applications in Eclipse-based development environments with a specific focus on web applications. You may remember that JST is focused on the development of enterprise applications based on the J2EE Specification.

The WST project supports web application development by providing multiple tools that are useful to developers in the creation of artifacts that exist within web applications such as HTML files, XML documents, and JavaScript code. The provided tools are also useful in the management, monitoring, debugging, and testing of web applications and additionally present a myriad of supporting functions such as the ability to manage database connections, and view objects within the connection such as tables and modify their contents. The scope of the WST project covers management of artifacts created from a large number of open standards and technologies, such as XML and HTML; it understandably cannot support all available standards, and some standards such as PHP are unsupported. Since only open technologies are candidates for support, no proprietary technology such as ASP.NET is supported. We will provide in Table 5-1, later in this chapter, a comprehensive listing of the technologies that are supported by WST.

It should be noted that a deployable J2EE web module, as described in Chapter 1, is also referred to as a web application. Indeed, a J2EE web module can, and often does, contain artifacts from the many open standards and technologies supported by the WST project as well as include support for JCP standards that are supported by the JST project. It is therefore clear to see that the features supported by WST are greatly beneficial to J2EE developers. This relationship between the WST and JST projects is further explained later in this chapter in the section "WST and JST Relationship."

We will start the chapter by describing the goals that drove the creation of the WST project; we will further describe the foundation provided from this project that can be useful in building additional web-centric tools. Then, we will cover the scope of the tools resulting from the WST project for the creation and management of web applications, and finally we will conclude the chapter by introducing you to these tools.

WST Goals

Among the goals of the WST project was an attempt to significantly grow the user base of the Eclipse IDE and increase usage of the Eclipse Platform by filling a void in the capabilities of the platform. With Java Development Tools (JDT), many people adopted the Eclipse Platform for use in the creation of their Java applications and applets; however, without the existence of bundled tools for the creation of web or enterprise applications, adoption of Eclipse in the area of server-side development has been slower. It has already been stated that there are several Eclipse plug-ins for web development available to individuals who seek to use the platform. But, we have also highlighted some of the difficulties involved in finding and assembling the right set of plug-ins for a project. Often, it is a time-, effort-, and cost-intensive exercise.

To help remedy this situation, the WST project was created to provide users of the Eclipse Platform with readily available tools that can be used for the creation of their web-centric applications. This means that Eclipse now provides a standardized set of tools that can be used to view, manage, and edit the many different types of artifacts that are found within a web application. Additional tools that are provided can be used to manage such important tasks like Internet connection settings, network traffic monitoring, and even the configuration and management of datasources that the application will use for persistence. It is hoped that the existence of this readily available set of useful tools would draw web developers to the platform just as the availability of J2EE tools would draw enterprise Java developers to the platform.

Beyond simply providing a set of tools though, the WST project has also created a framework from which additional web-focused tools can be built. This mechanism is provided to allow third-party developers to extend the Eclipse Platform to support additional languages and technologies. It is hoped that vendors would be encouraged by the availability of this framework to adopt Eclipse as the foundation of any development environment that they may wish to create or as a platform that they need to support for whatever tools they might be offering. An example of this is that Microsoft may choose to provide Eclipse plug-ins that would allow the management of its Internet Information Server (IIS) from within Eclipse. By utilizing the framework provided by WST, the ability to configure IIS would become available within the server configuration page that currently supports the configurations of such servers as Apache Tomcat and JBoss. Management of IIS would also become possible in the Eclipse Server View. We will describe the framework provided later in this chapter in the section "Web Core Model" and also talk about the tools built from them and released as part of the WST project.

It is probably inevitable that comparisons will be made between the WST tools and the favorite tools that a developer has become used to working with. However, this does not fit into any of the goals of the WST project. What is being provided is an expansion of the available choices of ways to manage web artifacts and related components as well as a standardized framework to aid in future extensions of the platform. Developers who might have grown used to a specific set of plug-ins still retain the ability to use these tools for their development, while newer users to the platform could start working right away with the WST-provided tools.

In a nutshell, WST provides a *standardized* way of managing web applications components for users of the Eclipse IDE and a *framework* for creating web-focused application tools for developers who seek to extend the Eclipse Platform. This supplies an overall increase in *choices* available to users of Eclipse and results in a more *robust* development platform.

Table 5-1 lists the technologies that are supported by the WST project.

Table 5-1. *WST-supported Standards and Technologies*

Standards Bodies	Standards
World Wide Web Consortium (W3C)	HTTP, HTML, XHTML, CSS, XML, DTD, and XSD
European Computer Manufacturers Association (ECMA)	JavaScript (ECMAScript)
Internet Engineering Task Force (IETF)	TCP/IP
American National Standards Institute (ANSI)	SQL
Organization for the Advancement of Structured Information Standards (OASIS)	Web Services
Web Services Interoperability Organization (WS-I)	Web Services interoperability

Web Core Model

We have mentioned that development tools are not the only resulting product of the WST project—a framework for the development of additional tools is also provided. The existence of this framework cannot be overemphasized because the tools that we will describe later in this chapter are in fact an exemplar implementation of this framework. We will discuss here this framework and how it is of use to individuals trying to create their own Eclipse plug-ins.

The framework that is provided consists of a set of object models that supplies an abstraction of groups of functionalities within the Eclipse Platform and also includes concrete classes that implement these abstractions. Such functionalities could encompass the ability to configure a server definition for a project on the Preferences page, deploy a project to the server in the Navigator View, manage the server in the Servers View, and monitor the server output in the Console View. In these instances, a model would exist that manages all aspects of the server from definition to maintenance activities and would provide APIs through which these views can access information about the server as well as run commands against it.

The public methods of the concrete classes that implement the model's abstraction comprise the APIs through which plug-in developers can access the underlying model. So, if a developer were attempting to create a plug-in to support the Jetty application server from within Eclipse, that developer would have a starting point to begin this exercise from and be able to fit his or her new tool within the existing server definition window.

This infrastructure, along with the exposed APIs, makes up the Web Core Model (WCM). WCM contains a collection of models that provide object representation for specific activities that can be performed against web applications and that serve as the foundation for plug-ins that can be generated for the platform. There are four models available within WCM:

- **Project model**: The project model manages web application projects within Eclipse and provides the platform with a mechanism to reference all artifacts that constitute a project. It also provides the project with the ability to perform builds and package the contents of the project in deployment units.

- **Editor model**: This provides the foundation for managing the editing of documents within the Eclipse IDE. Editors created from this model can provide different forms of textual or graphical views of a single document, additionally synchronizing edits across these views.

An XML document, for instance, can be displayed in a tree structure and also as a textual document. This model additionally provides support for document mixing such as the inline editing of JavaScript code within HTML documents.

- **Web artifacts model**: This model provides a representation of the different forms of web artifacts supported by the Eclipse Platform, allowing developers to manipulate artifacts based on any of the supported open standards and technologies. For example, the HTML model will provide information about the tag types and attributes that exist in HTML.

- **Server model**: The server model provides a representation of the server and allows the definition of multiple server types and versions for each web application. It also serves as a centralized mechanism to control the execution of these application servers.

The tools of the WST projects were created from these models, and it is hoped that many commercial entities would also provide support for their products within Eclipse by extending the same models. The benefit to developers becomes the existence of a single, comprehensive platform that integrates all the tools that are useful for their development activity.

WST and JST Relationship

Before we introduce the WST tools, we must briefly clarify the scope of WST and how it relates to the JST project. As we have discussed earlier, the WST project provides tools that are of use in the creation and management of multitiered web applications based upon various open standards and technologies. Many of the tools provided are useful for creating artifacts that web applications often depend upon such as SOAP documents and SQL scripts. WST, however, does not provide tools for the creation of web application elements that are specifically based on any JCP standards, since support for these standards falls within the scope of the JST project.

To illustrate the close interrelation between these two projects, we will use the editing of a JSP document as an example. JSR 152 defines the JavaServer Pages 2.0 Specification, and so this web artifact falls within the scope of JST. However, JSP pages sometimes contain JavaScript code within them for use in client-side logic processing. JavaScript, an ECMA standard, falls within the scope of the WST project, and so the JSP editor that needs to support inline editing of JavaScript code has a dependency on the appropriate WST component. Figure 5-1 provides a listing of the libraries required by the JSP editor.

You will note from this figure that a JSP editor utilizes functionality from multiple WST libraries including the `org.eclipse.wst.sse.*`, `org.eclipse.wst.html.*`, `org.eclipse.wst.css.*`, `org.eclipse.wst.xml.*`, and `org.eclipse.wst.common.*` libraries that define the model and editors for many web artifacts.

Another example of this relationship beyond the library interdependence level can be seen in the management of the deployment descriptor of a WAR deployment module. The deployment descriptor of a WAR file is named `web.xml` and it is created as part of a J2EE project, covered by the JST project. However, the `web.xml` file is in XML format, which is a technology supported by the WST project.

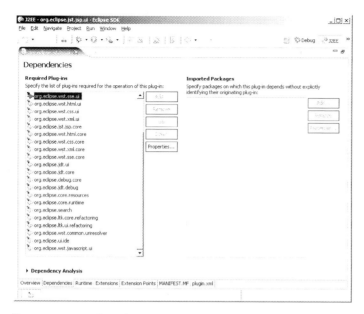

Figure 5-1. *JSP editor dependencies*

WST Tools

Now that we have discussed WCM, the WST scope, and how the project relates to JST tools, we will now describe the tools that were provided with the WST project. You will remember from our earlier discussions that these are an implementation of WCM and that they provide the Eclipse IDE with the ability to support web-centric development efforts.

The tools provided fall into several groups, and we have provided the following description of them in a manner with which users would expectedly interact with them.

Web Projects

The WST tools are available for the development of web applications and this is represented in the Eclipse IDE by Web Projects. A Web Project references the collection of artifacts that makes up a web application including those that are deployable, e.g., HTML files and XML documents, and those that are useful for maintenance of the web application, e.g., SQL script files and server configurations. There are two types of Web Projects supported by WST: WST supports the creation of Simple Projects for web applications that specifically contain static content such as HTML, JavaScript, and images and it provides support for Dynamic Web Projects that are web applications that, in addition to static content, support the ability to generate content in response to user input. Dynamic content can be generated from server-side J2EE components like JSPs and servlets or other such open technologies like CGI or PHP. Figure 5-2 shows the choices for the creation of a new Web Project.

Figure 5-2. *Web Projects available in Eclipse*

Though J2EE-specific components are out of the scope of the WST project, many of the web artifacts that are within the scope of WST often feature prominently in J2EE web module deployments. For example, it is quite common to see a J2EE web application that contains HTML pages that submit form data to a Java servlet for processing. In these instances, non-J2EE-specific content within a Dynamic Web Project is supported by the WST tools, while J2EE-specific content is supported by the JST tools.

Note Creating a project is available through several means including selecting File ➤ New ➤ Project on the menu or pressing Alt+Shift+N and then selecting Project from the context menu.

Server Tools

For occasions where a Dynamic Web Project is being created, deployment to an application server is required to allow testing. The Server Tools provide a mechanism for managing the definition of various commercial and open source servers. It additionally supports the configuration of multiple versions of a server. Figure 5-3 shows the configuration page for selecting among the multiple versions of the Apache Tomcat server.

Figure 5-3. *Selection between multiple versions of Tomcat server*

Additionally, multiple server runtime environments can be created for a project as shown in Figure 5-4, allowing the developer to make a choice during the deployment of the application.

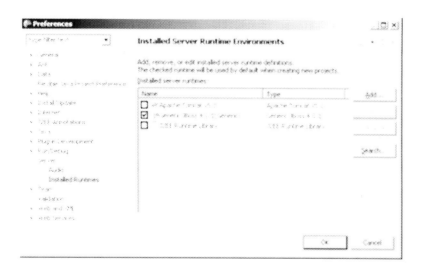

Figure 5-4. *Multiple server runtime definition*

Other useful functions such as the usage of audio prompts to indicate the completion of a task by the server is also supported by the Server Tools. Management of the server associated with a project is performed through the Servers View, providing the developer with the ability to perform such activities as starting, pausing, stopping, publishing, and debugging. Output generated by the server is available in the Console View, including such valuable information as server state messages and log statements printed to the console.

It should be remembered that a J2EE web application is packaged into a WAR file as a web module, or into an EAR file, and deployed within the web container of an application server. Configuration and management of the application server for all J2EE-related activities is performed through these same views.

Note All views within the platform are available to you at any time by navigating to Window ➤ Show View and selecting the desired view. Based on the task being performed, certain views may not contain any information.

Internet Tools

Many web applications often require access to other Internet sites either by linking the contents of these sites or utilizing services that these other sites might have made available. The Internet Tools provide a mechanism for configuring and managing most Internet-related functions required by a web application. Configuration of the Internet Tools is done through the Preferences page, accessible by selecting Windows ➤ Preferences ➤ Internet for the configuration of proxy settings and managing the Cache Resolver. Managing the TCP/IP Monitor used to monitor request/response traffic from a server is available by selecting Windows ➤ Preferences ➤ Run/Debug ➤ TCP/IP Monitor.

Proxy Settings

Some network environments utilize proxy servers to referee Internet access in a bid to ensure that the local network is secure. In such cases, for the web application being created in Eclipse to communicate properly with the Internet, these proxy settings must be properly configured. Without the correct settings, HTML links within the embedded web browser tool, for example, will fail to load a requested page, while such items as the Web Services Explorer and the database Server Explorer would be unable to connect to destinations that do not exist within the local network. Figure 5-5 provides a view of the configuration settings for the Proxy Settings tab within the Internet Tools component.

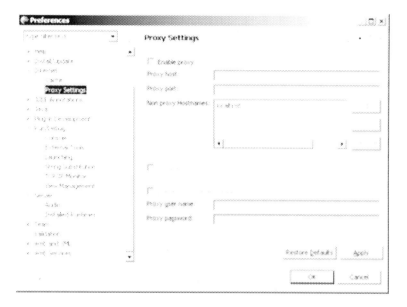

Figure 5-5. *Proxy settings*

The page accepts the configuration of the proxy host and port settings as shown in Figure 5-5, as well as the option of providing a username/password if the proxy server in use requires authentication. See the "Setting Proxy Configuration" sidebar for instructions on configuring Internet Tools to work in an environment that utilizes a proxy server.

SETTING PROXY CONFIGURATION

In most corporate environments, Internet access is funneled through a proxy server to help ensure the security of the internal corporate network. In these instances, all Internet access will be managed through the designated proxy server, and without proper configuration of the Internet Tools to use the proxy server features like the integrated web browser, Web Service invocations, etc., will not work properly. To configure the proxy, the developer will have to configure the following settings:

- **Enable proxy**: Check this checkbox to inform Eclipse that a proxy server is being utilized in your corporate environment. This action will allow values to be entered in the proxy host and port fields.

- **Proxy host and Proxy port**: Enter the address of the proxy server the port made available on this server. This information would need to be provided to you by someone that is within your corporate network.

- **Non proxy Hostnames**: Enter all hostnames that are resolved within the internal network and as such do not need to be processed through the proxy server. This list can be managed by using the Add, Edit, and Remove buttons.

- **Use SOCKS**: Check this checkbox if you wish to use the SOCKS networking proxy protocol.

- **Enable proxy authentication**: Some environments authenticate users on the proxy server to provide an extra layer of security. In such instances, a user name/password pair is provided for access through the proxy server. This user name/password could be unique to the user or to a group of users according to organizational policies. If proxy authentication is being used, this checkbox would need to be checked, which enables username and password info to be provided.

- **Proxy user name and Proxy password**: Enter the user name and password pair provided to you for access through the proxy server.

TCP/IP Monitoring

It is also very useful to monitor TCP/IP traffic between web browsers and application servers to help debug communication problems that might be occurring with a web application. For instance, if invocations of a specific Web Service is not resulting in the expected output values being displayed within the application, it might be helpful to monitor the outgoing/incoming traffic between the application client and the Web Service host to determine where within the chain of communication the erroneous values are originating from. The Internet Tools provide the capability to configure the monitoring on specific ports where an application server has been started as well as manage the monitoring process. Figure 5-6 shows the configuration of this monitoring capability from within the Preferences page as well as the ability to manage the monitoring.

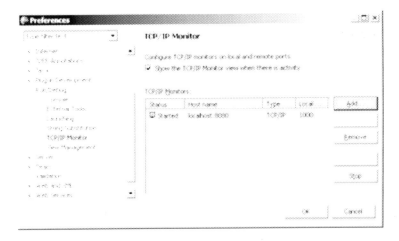

Figure 5-6. *TCP/IP Monitor settings*

Eclipse supports the creation of multiple monitors, with each of the monitors capable of being managed from the settings page as shown in Figure 5-6, and allows the ability to start and stop the monitoring session. Results generated from these monitoring sessions are available through the TCP/IP Monitor View, allowing the user to view HTTP request and response communications as well as additional statistics about the data packet such as time, type, and size of transmission. See the "Monitoring TCP/IP Traffic" sidebar for information on how to create TCP/IP monitoring sessions.

Note TCP/IP Monitors can only monitor traffic between two endpoints with at least one endpoint being on the local machine.

MONITORING TCP/IP TRAFFIC

As we have discussed, it is often useful as a debugging tool to view the request/response data traffic being sent between two components in an application. To facilitate this, Eclipse has provided the TCP/IP Monitor. For each monitoring session, a separate monitor has to be set up, and this can be done by clicking the Add button on the TCP/IP Monitor Preference page. The New Monitor dialog box that appears can be configured as follows:

- **Local monitoring port**: An unused port on the local machine. Though many monitors can be configured to use the same port, only one monitor session can be started on each port.

- **Host name**: Address of the server you intend to communicate with.

- **Port**: The port on the server you intend to connect to.

- **Type**: Choices include HTML and TCP/IP. Choosing HTML separates multiple requests that are made in loading an HTML document such as retrieval of image files and style sheets. Choosing TCP/IP provides the byte traffic between the local and remote machine without any translation.

After creation, TCP/IP Monitors need to be started before use. It should be noted that the TCP/IP Monitor functions like a proxy. Accessing `http://localhost:<local port>` would process your request through the monitor and redirect the request to `http://<remote host>:<remote port>`. The response provided by the remote host will also be directed through the proxy, and the contents of this traffic will be made available in the TCP/IP Monitor View. Note that accessing `http://<remote host>:<remote port>` directly bypasses the monitor, and therefore no data will be recorded for the specific request/response transaction.

Cache Resolver

XML documents rely on a schema to specify what elements are valid content within the XML document. The schemas specify rules for the contents of the XML file and help ensure the validity of the XML documents. This way, anyone using the XML file does not have to worry about validity of content. Expectedly, multiple XML documents are based on a similar schema. An example of this would be that deployment descriptors of EJB 2.1 modules would reference a schema found at `http://java.sun.com/xml/j2ee/ejb-jar_2_1.xsd`. Within the workbench, multiple EJB projects, and thus deployment modules, can exist simultaneously.

In each of these instances, documents being accessed exist on a remote location and have to be downloaded to the local machine whenever access is needed. The Cache Resolver optimizes this effort by caching a copy of these resources within the local machine and uses this cached instance for repeated accesses to the resources.

Access to the Cache Resolver is available by selecting Window ➤ Preferences ➤ Internet ➤ Cache. The Preferences page as shown in Figure 5-7 provides the user with the ability to control caching as well as remove some, or all, of the cached resources.

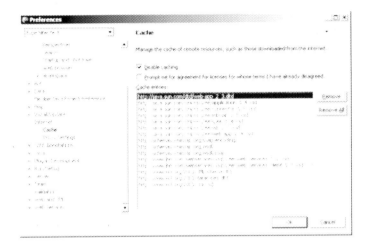

Figure 5-7. *Cache Resolver Preferences page*

Web Browser

A web browser is a useful part of developing a web application as it provides the ability to view and debug the resulting HTML document that would be presented to users of the application. Eclipse 3.1 introduced an embedded browser that can be used for rendering web artifacts within the Eclipse environment. If other browsers are installed on the system, any one of these can be used as an alternative browser for files being edited. This allows developers to render pages specifically in the browser versions their applications are expected to support.

Configuration of the web browser within which to view web artifacts in the workbench is available by selecting Window ➤ Preferences ➤ General ➤ Web Browser. Figure 5-8 shows the configuration page that allows the selection of the appropriate browser for use during the development of a web application. The ability to search for and select any browser existing on the system is also provided through this configuration page. The choice of browsers made here allows the developer to view artifacts such as image files that are associated with most web applications but that do not have an associated editor in Eclipse.

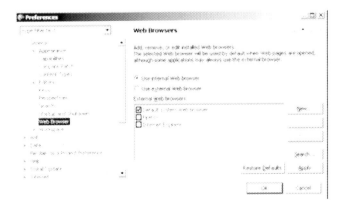

Figure 5-8. *Web browser settings*

Web Tools

Tools used in creating and manipulating web artifacts that are processed within a web browser are collectively supported by the Web Tools. In fact, the Web Tools component is itself a collection of components, each of which provides services to a specific supported technology. Such services include the provision of appropriate wizards to assist in the creation of web artifacts, managing preference settings for each of the different web artifacts and providing appropriate viewers for the specific type of document being created. This means that the services provided to a CSS document such as validation of content and management of templates may differ from the services provided to a JavaScript file, which does not include template management.

Web Tools also manage viewers and editors within which a web artifact can be either viewed or edited. One of the editor types that includes a rich set of features useful to the artifact creation and manipulation is derived from the Structured Source Editor Framework, which we describe later in the chapter. A web artifact can, however, be edited, or viewed, in a plurality of editors and viewers. An HTML page, for instance, can be viewed using a browser integrated into the workspace in WYSIWYG format or instead edited in source view. In the source view, the HTML tags are appropriately recognized and syntax highlighting is employed for the document. Appropriate syntax highlighting is additionally provided for such items as CSS styles and JavaScript that can exist inline within an HTML document. The appropriate tag hierarchy for these items would be available in the Outline View as shown in Figure 5-9 where an HTML document is being edited using the HTML Source Page Editor.

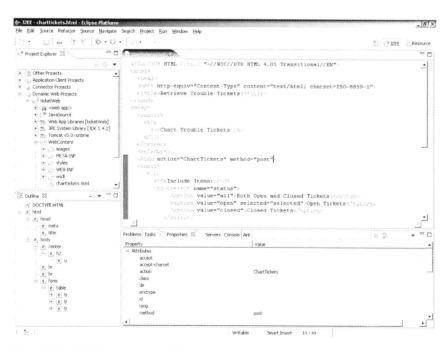

Figure 5-9. *HTML Source Page Editor*

Opening this same document in a standard text editor, an option that is provided by the Web Tools, results in the tags within the documents not being recognized as HTML tags. This would allow the developer that prefers to edit documents in this format to easily and quickly make their changes.

A similar situation occurs for items such as Cascading Style Sheet (CSS) documents and JavaScript files that Web Tools provide creation and management support for. Other artifacts such as image files and multimedia content, which are also found within web applications, can be browsed within the Project Explorer and launched using appropriate viewers found on the system.

XML Tools

The ability to create and edit XML files is a welcome addition to the Eclipse Platform, and this is supported in the WST project by the XML Tools. This component also supports the creation and modification of XML-related documents such as XML Schema Definitions (XSD) and Document Type Definition (DTD) files that define a structure for the content of XML documents and would serve as the base for extending Eclipse to provide support for such XML-centric technologies as XPath and XQuery. The ubiquity of XML makes this tool a very important development tool, as a majority of configuration files for enterprise applications (such as deployment descriptors for web and EJB modules) as well as configuration files of web frameworks (such as Struts and Tiles) utilize the XML format.

The XML Tools manage preference settings for each of the supported document types and also provide an XML catalog that helps with the creation of XML documents by eliminating the need to change the URIs of schema documents that are referenced within by an XML document if these schema documents change location. Figure 5-10 shows the XML Catalog Preferences page that is accessible by selecting Window ➤ Preferences ➤ Web and XML ➤ XML Catalog.

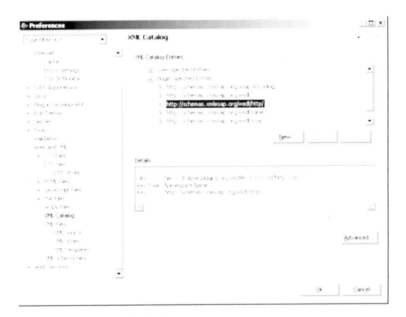

Figure 5-10. *XML Catalog Preferences page*

Validation, an important part of ensuring that an XML document is both well formed and conforms to the related schema definitions, is also supported by this tool and is easily available to the developer through the context menu in the Project Explorer. Validation of DTD files and XSD schemas is also supported, and validation for other XML-based technologies such as WSDL and XML-based stylesheets in the form of Extensible Stylesheet Language Transformation (XSLT) documents is managed by the XML Tools.

The XML Tools also provide the ability to view and edit XML documents in several formats including a graphical tree view and text-based editors.

Tip Files within the workspace can be viewed by selecting them and choosing Open from the context menu. To define the editor to open the file in, you must choose Open With from the context menu and specify the menu you want from the available choices in the provided submenu.

Structured Source Editor Framework Tools

Structured Source Editor Framework Tools are exceedingly useful for the management of the Web and XML components we have described previously. This component consists of a framework for the creation of editors, and though it is not directly of use to web application developers, the editors built upon it are a vital part of web application development activity. Source editors that we have described in the "Web Tools" and "XML Tools" sections previously are based upon this framework. The usage of the framework as a base for editors of multiple artifacts allows for consistency across these editors. The Structured Source Editor Framework provides a host of useful functionalities that is available to anyone extending it to create an editor. Table 5-2 provides a list of the features supported by this tool and a description of its usefulness to the developer.

Table 5-2. *Features Provided by the Structured Source Editor Framework*

Feature	Description
Syntax highlighting	Different categories of keywords within a language or technology are highlighted with different colors, providing immediate visual cues to the developer about the appropriateness of their usage.
Content assist	Context-sensitive help is provided for the technology in use, showing the developer the list of valid options available for use. In editing an HTML document, for instance, content assist would suggest the available tags in the language and then the available attributes for the selected tag.
Error highlighting	Errors are immediately highlighted with the insertion of red squiggly lines under incorrect code insertions.
Delimiter matching	Matching of respective start and end delimiters is often a difficulty, especially in files where sections of code are deeply nested. This feature provides the ability to quickly match an opening delimiter with its corresponding closing delimiter.
Linking to referenced files	Files referenced within a source file being edited can quickly be opened for viewing using the hyperlink feature provided. This feature allows the immediate viewing of contents of these referenced files through the employment of a preconfigured keystroke combination, allowing the developer to modify/verify the contents of the file as needed.

(Continued)

Table 5-2. *(Continued)*

Feature	Description
Source formatting	Support is provided for the automatic indentation of source files based on patterns defined in a template for the language type. This aids the readability of the source code being edited.
Inline editing of languages	While web artifacts such a JavaScript and CSS can be separated into files distinct from the HTML pages that utilize them, they can also be embedded into the HTML file. Support is provided for recognizing different languages within a single document and providing the correct syntax highlighting and appropriate content assists for each of these different languages.
Context-based actions	Actions available for a document are matched to the type of document being edited. Selection of an XML document, for instance, will include an action to validate the XML document, while an HTML document will expectedly not include this.
Context-based preferences	Allows the selection of preferences during the editing of a document to bring up the Preferences page for the type of document currently being edited.

These features are immediately available to developers who wish to create plug-ins to support the editing of a new language within the Eclipse Platform, allowing the editing of documents of the language type to fit in seamlessly with the existing supported languages. Listing 5-1 shows the `plugin.xml` file for the HTML Source Page Editor plug-in, highlighting its dependency on the Structured Source Editor (SSE) component.

Listing 5-1. *The plugin.xml File for the HTML Editor Showing Dependency on the SSE Component*

```xml
<requires>
    <import plugin="org.eclipse.ui.ide"/>
    <import plugin="org.eclipse.ui.views"/>
    <import plugin="org.eclipse.jface.text"/>
    <import plugin="org.eclipse.ui.workbench.texteditor"/>
    <import plugin="org.eclipse.ui.editors"/>
    <import plugin="org.eclipse.ui"/>
    <import plugin="org.eclipse.wst.sse.ui"/>
    <import plugin="org.eclipse.wst.xml.ui"/>
    <import plugin="org.eclipse.wst.css.ui"/>
    <import plugin="org.eclipse.wst.sse.core"/>
    <import plugin="org.eclipse.wst.css.core"/>
    <import plugin="org.eclipse.wst.html.core"/>
    <import plugin="org.eclipse.wst.javascript.common.ui"/>
    <import plugin="org.eclipse.wst.xml.core"/>
    <import plugin="org.eclipse.wst.common.contentmodel"/>
    <import plugin="org.eclipse.core.resources"/>
    <import plugin="org.eclipse.core.runtime"/>
    <import plugin="org.eclipse.wst.common.encoding"/>
    <import plugin="org.eclipse.jdt.ui"/>
    <import plugin="org.eclipse.wst.common.uriresolver"/>
    <import plugin="org.eclipse.wst.validation"/>
</requires>
```

You will also notice from Listing 5-1 the other libraries that are depended upon by the HTML editor such as wst.javascript, wst.xml, and wst.css. These libraries support the inline editing of their respective base languages within an HTML document. Figure 5-11 shows the editing of an HTML document with inline JavaScript and CSS code.

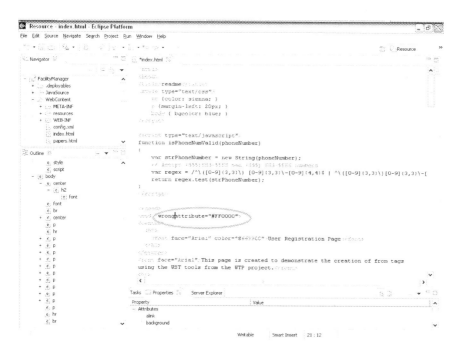

Figure 5-11. *HTML editor with inline editing of JavaScript and CSS code*

Appropriate syntax highlighting is applied to the different technologies (namely CSS, JavaScript, and HTML) combined within this document. Additionally, we have included a syntax error within the body tag of the HTML page. This error is promptly highlighted by the editor by underlining the perceived syntax problem with red squiggly lines as shown in Figure 5-11.

Web Service Tools

Creation and consumption of Web Services is managed within WST by the Web Service Tools. This toolset provides support for the creation and management of WSDL files, which are used to either expose Web Services or to consume them. The toolset provides a wizard for the creation of WSDL files, allowing the developer to choose between SOAP and HTTP and any appropriate bindings supported by these protocols. The generated WSDL file can then be further edited in the WSDL editor provided by WST. This editor supports the modification of WSDL documents in either textual or graphical mode. Figure 5-12 shows a WSDL file being edited in graphical mode using this editor. It should be noted that the automatic generation of WSDL files from Java sources belongs within the scope of JST and not WST, and JST does provide a wizard to automate this generation process. As you might expect, the wizard utilizes libraries from WST.

Figure 5-12. *WSDL file being edited using the Graph View*

A major provision of the Web Service Tools is the creation of foundation libraries useful for working with WSDL, UDDI, and WSIL files. For instance, the Web Services Explorer, which we described in the previous chapter, depends heavily on libraries created by WST for its functions. We will describe all the Web Services Tools originating from both WST and JST in greater detail in Chapter 15.

RDB Tools

RDB Tools provide web applications with the ability to connect to relational databases and execute statements against these databases. The necessity of data persistence extends beyond web applications alone, being a core part of the enterprise application architecture, therefore this function is also used extensively in J2EE applications. (You may review this discussion in Chapter 1.) RDB Tools support the editing and managing of SQL documents used to create object structures within a database such as tables, sequences, and views, as well as connecting to and viewing the contents of the relational database.

Connection to the database and modification of the contents during the runtime of the application is often done in Java using the JDBC API or through other technologies such as PHP that are not supported by WST. What the data tools provide are a mechanism with which data utilized by a web or J2EE application can be directly viewed and/or modified by the developers. More details on this will be provided in Chapter 16.

WST RDB Tools provide the SQL Scrapbook, Server Explorer, and DB Output View.

SQL Scrapbook

The SQL Scrapbook is used for the creation of SQL statements that can be used to define the structure of a database schema. The development process of enterprise applications often requires a persistence layer in which data gathered by the application will be stored. The creation of the database elements such as tables and sequences that will be used as part of the storage of data often needs to be done using SQL. Although many databases provide graphical tools to manage this activity, usage of SQL statements is the single method that ensures the portability of the structure across different DBMS products whenever necessary.

The SQL Scrapbook provides an editor for managing such an SQL document as this, together with complete support for syntax highlighting and content assist for the SQL commands. Additionally, it integrates into the Eclipse workbench and provides the ability for the contained statement to be executed against a defined database connection.

Database Explorer View

This tool provides a mechanism to define and manage multiple connections to different databases. Once connected, it provides the ability to browse the element contained within the databases and additionally integrates with the SQL Scrapbook to support the execution of the SQL statements contained with the file. Figure 5-13 shows the Connection wizard provided for the creation of connections within the Database Explorer View. You will note the existence of multiple database managers defined within this dialog box. Examples in this book will utilize the Apache Derby DBMS. See Appendix A for more information about Apache Derby, including installation instructions.

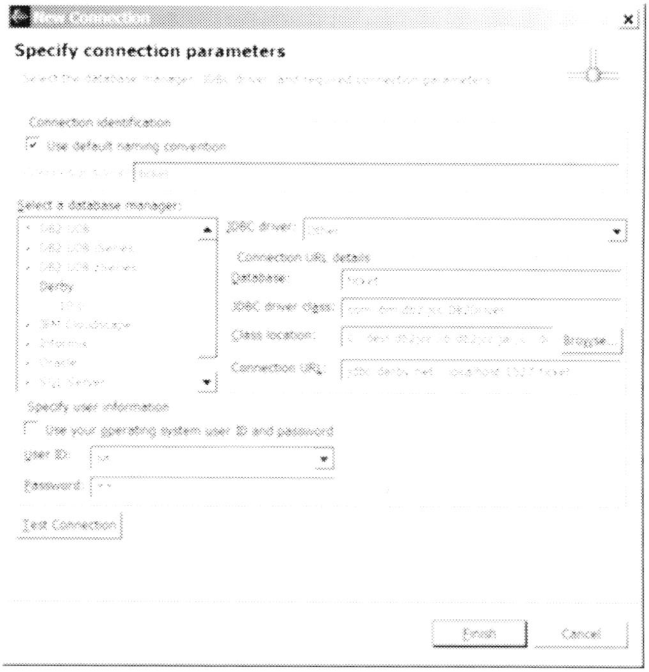

Figure 5-13. *DBMS Connection dialog box*

Data Output View

The Data Output View provides a mechanism to view messages, parameters, and results generated from the execution of stored procedures and scripts from within SQL Scrapbooks against an open database connection. Connections can be managed through the Database Explorer View previously discussed. The ability to view extended information about the execution of statements against a connection is a valuable feature for developers, especially in the debugging process. Additional information provided by the tool includes status information about the action being performed, type of action, and the object involved in the action.

A majority of the tools discussed in this chapter will be seen multiple times throughout the rest of the book as we go through the creation of a project using many of them. This additional interaction with the tools will hopefully help you gain familiarity with them.

Summary

In this chapter, we have provided an introduction to the WST project and discussed the goals of the project as well as its relationship to the JST project. We additionally introduced you to WCM, which lies at the foundation of the tools created by the WST project and can be used by plug-in developers to create additional web-focused tools for the Eclipse Platform. We concluded by discussing the different tools that are provided by WST and the benefits many of these tools provide to the web application developer.

CHAPTER 6

Eclipse Web Tools Installation

Installing most Eclipse plug-ins is relatively easy. Small plug-ins usually come packaged as a zip file with instructions to either unpack them in the Eclipse root directory or the Eclipse `plugins` directory. Plug-in providers may also provide a URL to an update site. Given a URL, the Eclipse Update Manager can install, configure, and update a plug-in when new releases are made available.

The Eclipse Web Tools Platform (WTP) project, however, is quite a large plug-in and has several dependencies on other large Eclipse projects, the Eclipse Modeling Framework (EMF/SDO/XSD), the Graphical Editor Framework (GEF), and the Java Edit Model (JEM). In addition, if you want to have multiple versions of Eclipse use the same version of WTP, you don't have to install WTP and its dependencies multiple times. This chapter will explain how to install WTP and its dependencies as an Eclipse extension. Extensions are commonly used by large commercial plug-ins such as Genuitec's MyEclipse or Borland's Together. In addition to explaining how to install WTP as an extension, this chapter will explain the build types offered by Eclipse-managed projects so you know which build best fits your needs. The examples in this book are dependent on JBoss 4.0.1. Unfortunately, JBoss 4.0.1 support is not included with WTP, so we will show you how to install an application server–specific extension using the Update Manager. WTP is also dependent on an external annotation engine, XDoclet. We will conclude the chapter with instructions for installing XDoclet.

Eclipse Build Types

All Eclipse-managed projects including WTP, the Eclipse Platform, and WTP's dependencies provide multiple versions or builds. The build types, which range from production ready to may not even compile, are as follows:

- **Release**: Stable tested version ready to be used for day-to-day development. It is considered certified and to contain no major bugs.

- **Stable**: Generally considered stable and usable.

- **Integration**: Inclusion of a new stable component and generally becomes a stable build if no major bugs are discovered.

- **Nightly**: Version built straight from the CVS repository.

If you want a production-ready version, you should stick with the release build. It will have the fewest defects and the fewest headaches. For those wanting a good ratio of stability and the newest features, the stable build is what the doctor ordered. Anyone wanting to live on the edge with unexpected results and lots of bugs can use either the integration or nightly builds.

Note The versions of Eclipse, WTP, and WTP dependencies are likely to change over time. Visit `http://download.eclipse.org/webtools/downloads/` for the current versions of WTP. Select your desired WTP build to see its current dependency versions and links to download them.

Installing Eclipse 3.1

WTP requires Eclipse SDK 3.1 or higher as well as a Java Developer Kit (JDK). If you already have Eclipse SDK 3.1 or higher installed and a JDK, feel free to skip to the next section.

Installing JDK

The Eclipse SDK 3.1 requires a Java Runtime Environment (JRE) of 1.4.2 or higher be installed. However, we will demonstrate installing the JDK because J2EE application servers require it to compile JavaServer Pages (JSP). By installing a JDK 1.4.2 or higher that is compatible with your application server and Eclipse, you may be able to kill two birds with one stone and at the same time save some disk space. See your application server documentation for its required JDK.

Installing a JDK can vary depending on your operating system. For example, Red Hat Package Manager (RPM) and self-extracting versions are available for Linux. Most other Unix platforms have a self-extracting or tar version available. Microsoft Windows, on the other hand, has an offline and online installation program available.

To download and install the JDK, complete the following steps:

1. Visit `http://java.sun.com/j2se/downloads/`.

2. Select the appropriate J2SE version.

3. On the page containing all the J2SE-related downloads, make sure you select the Download J2SE SDK and not the JRE, documentation, or J2EE 1.4 SDK.

4. Read and accept the license agreement.

5. To begin downloading, select the operating system and package most appropriate for your development environment.

6. Install the JDK in your `~/devl` or `C:\devl` directory, depending on your operating system, according to the instructions included with the download.

Once you have completed the download and installation, you can verify the JDK installed correctly by opening a command prompt and typing `java -version`. If the installation was successful, you will see the JDK version number displayed. With a successful JDK installation, you are ready to install Eclipse.

Installing Eclipse SDK 3.1

The Eclipse SDK 3.1 installation consists of downloading a zip or tar file and uncompressing it. You can download Eclipse SDK 3.1 from http://www.eclipse.org/downloads/. Select the build and operating system bundle you wish to install. The zip or tar file will automatically start downloading. Once the download is complete, uncompress the archive to the location you would like to install Eclipse. The recommended location to install Eclipse on Unix, Linux, or OSX is ~/devl/eclipse-3.1 or C:\devl\eclipse-3.1 on Windows. However, your location may vary based on your operating system or preferences. So for the remainder of this chapter, Eclipse's installation directory will be referred to as <eclipse>.

Tip We often have multiple versions of Eclipse installed on our computer, so we like to uncompress the contents of the zip file in a directory that denotes the version of Eclipse. For example, Eclipse 3.1 would be installed in the eclipse-3.1 directory. You may also find yourself in a similar situation, so you might want to get in the habit now. This can be especially true if you are brave enough to use the integration builds.

In order to make Eclipse easier to start up, you may want to create a shortcut to the Eclipse executable on your desktop or Start menu.

That's all there is to installing Eclipse. Now you are able to start developing basic Java applications. However, if you want to start building enterprise Java applications using the J2EE specification, keep reading. You still need to install WTP and its dependencies.

Creating the Extension

An *extension* is a technique used to install a collection of related plug-ins and features sometimes referred to as an *Eclipse-based product*. WTP fits the definition of a product, so we will use this technique to install WTP. By using an extension, you will be able to take advantage of the following:

- **Clear separation**: WTP and dependent plug-ins will not pollute the Eclipse plug-ins directory. This is helpful because the WTP and dependent plug-ins all begin with org.eclipse, just like the Eclipse Platform.

- **Easy uninstall**: Having WTP and dependent plug-ins in a separate directory makes it easy to uninstall WTP without accidentally removing critical Eclipse Platform plug-ins or to upgrade to a new version of Eclipse without having to copy the WTP plug-ins to the new plug-in directory.

- **Reuse**: If you have multiple versions of Eclipse, they can use the same WTP installation.

In order to create an extension, Eclipse requires a directory structure like the one shown in Figure 6-1 along with an .eclipseextension file.

Figure 6-1. *WTP extension directory structure*

For an extension, the root directory should be something descriptive. The eclipse-wtp-0.7 directory name makes it clear this is version 0.7 of the WTP Eclipse plug-in. Create this directory at the same level as the <eclipse> directory. In other words the directory will be ~/devl/eclipse-wtp-0.7 or C:\devl\eclipse-wtp-0.7 depending on your operating system. For the remainder of the book, this directory will be referred to as <eclipse-wtp>. Within the <eclipse-wtp> directory, there must be an eclipse directory. The eclipse directory must contain a features and plugins directory much like Eclipse itself.

The other requirement is the <eclipse-wtp>\eclipse directory must include an .eclipseextension file. Think of this file as a deployment descriptor for Eclipse extensions. You must create this file using a standard text editor, and it must contain the extension's name, ID, and version. Listing 6-1 shows the contents of the file.

Listing 6-1. *Contents of WTP's .eclipseextension File*

```
name=Eclipse Web Tools
id=org.eclipse.wtp
version=0.7
```

Because the extension is for the Eclipse Web Tools Platform project, it makes sense to make the name Eclipse Web Tools. The org.eclipse.wtp ID is descriptive because it identifies the Eclipse domain and the common Web Tools abbreviation much like a Java package. The version number is likely to be the version in which you install, in this case version 0.7.

Tip The extension concept is so powerful, we routinely include an extension called eclipse-experiment that contains experimental plug-ins we don't want to have pollute our <eclipse>\plugins directory until we are sure they work.

In order to tell Eclipse about the extension, choose Help ➤ Software Updates ➤ Manage Configuration from the main menu. Next, select Add an Extension Location from the right pane and browse to the <eclipse-wtp> directory. Eclipse will prompt you to restart the workbench. This is a good idea. After the restart, the Product Configuration dialog box should contain the WTP extension as shown in Figure 6-2.

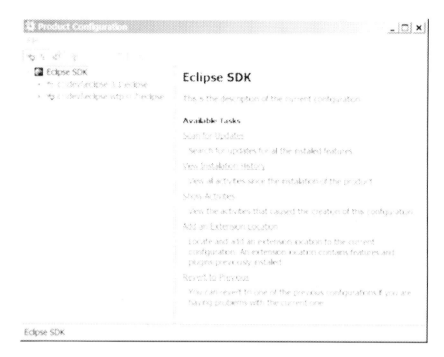

Figure 6-2. *Completed installation of the WTP extension*

Once the WTP extension is installed, you can install the WTP plug-ins and dependent plug-ins into the `<eclipse-wtp>\eclipse` directory just like you would install a plug-in into the `<eclipse>` directory.

Installing Dependencies

WTP is dependent on several Eclipse managed projects: the Eclipse Modeling Framework, Graphical Editing Framework, and Java Edit Model, all subprojects of the Eclipse Tools project. The goal of the Eclipse Tools project is to foster a diverse set of development tools including additional language support. It includes support for C/C++ as well as COBOL.

Installing EMF/SDO/XSD

The Eclipse Modeling Framework is a code generator that can generate Java classes from XML Metadata Interchange (XMI), Annotated Java Interfaces, or XML Schema. EMF includes Service Data Objects (SDO), a specification currently traveling through the Java Community Process as JSR 235. SDO defines core infrastructure APIs for heterogeneous data access using common J2EE design patterns. EMF also includes the XML Schema Infoset Model (XSD), for creating, reading, and modifying XML Schemas.

Fortunately, the EMF project provides a bundle that includes all three projects, so you don't have to install each of them separately and worry about conflicting versions. WTP depends on the 2.1.0 release build, which you can download from `http://download.eclipse.org/tools/emf/scripts/downloads.php`. Make sure you select ALL SDK, highlighted in Figure 6-3, which includes EMF, SDO, and XSD.

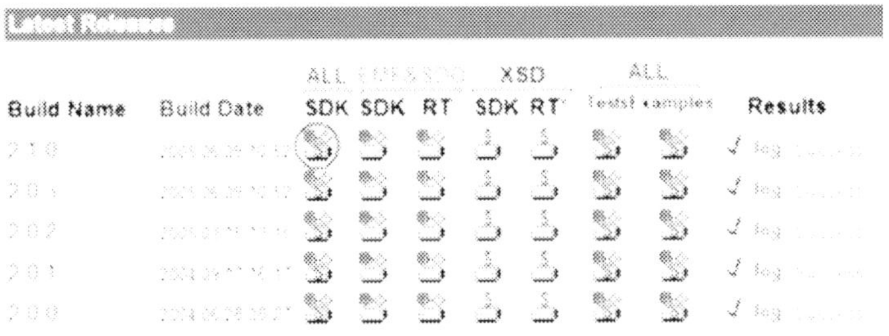

Figure 6-3. *Download page of EMF with the required ALL SDK highlighted*

Once the emf-sdo-xsd-SDK-2.1.0.zip file is downloaded, uncompress it in the <eclipse-wtp> directory.

Installing GEF

The Graphical Editor Framework is a framework for providing functionality similar to Microsoft Visio. It can be used to render and manipulate UML diagrams. WTP depends on version 3.1. The GEF zip file, GEF-SDK-3.1.zip, can be downloaded from http://download.eclipse. org/tools/gef/downloads/. Once it has been downloaded, it too can be uncompressed in the <eclipse-wtp> directory.

Installing JEM

Java EMF Models are used to simplify interactions with EMF. JEM is itself a stand-alone framework, but it also comes as part of the Visual Editor (VE), a GUI builder for Swing/JFC and SWT. In the future, VE hopes to include builders for other widgets and languages such as C/C++. WTP depends on version 1.1.0 of JEM. To download JEM, visit the VE download page at http://download. eclipse.org/tools/ve/downloads/. Select the 1.1 build and on the build page select JEM-SDK-1.1.zip. To install, uncompress the JEM-SDK-1.1.zip file in the <eclipse-wtp> directory.

Installing Web Tools

The last step in the process of installing WTP is to actually install WTP. It is available from http://download.eclipse.org/webtools/downloads/ as either just WST or a combination of WST and JST. Because JST is built on top of WST, it is not possible to install just JST.

Just like the previous dependencies, after downloading wtp-sdk-0.7.zip, uncompress it in the <eclipse-wtp> directory. If Eclipse is currently running, it will need to be restarted. To confirm the installation, select File ➤ New ➤ Other and look for the J2EE and Server folders. If they exist, everything installed correctly.

Tip When installing large plug-ins like WTP, it is a good idea to restart Eclipse with the -clean option. This will clean out the workspace cache. It is not a good idea to use the -clean option for normal use since it can take a long time to clean.

Installing JBoss 4.0.1 Extension

WTP comes with support for a couple of application servers out of the box, including BEA Weblogic 8.1, JBoss 3.2.3, and JOnAs 4.1.4. However, WTP developers want to focus on building the foundational tools for building J2EE applications in an application-server agnostic manner. WTP developers don't want to get stuck maintaining support for every possible application server on the market. If that were to happen, they would never have time to focus on the application development tools. Therefore, WTP has created extension points for vendors and individuals to create their own application server plug-ins.

Note To learn more about the JBoss application server and how to install it, see Appendix B.

All the examples explained in this book were tested and developed on JBoss 4.0.1. As the previous paragraph stated, WTP does not include JBoss 4.x support. So we have created an extension to support JBoss 4.x to enable starting, stopping, and deploying WAR, EJB-JAR, and EAR files to a JBoss 4.x server. This plug-in has been made available on the website that accompanies this book, at http://www.projst.com. The plug-in can be installed using the Eclipse Update Manager.

To install the JBoss 4.0.1 plug-in, complete the following steps:

1. Select Help ➤ Software Updates ➤ Find and Install from the Eclipse main menu.

2. Select Search for new features to install and click Next.

3. Click New Remote Site and enter a name for the Pro Eclipse JST update site and URL of http://www.projst.com/eclipse/updates/ as shown in Figure 6-4, and click OK.

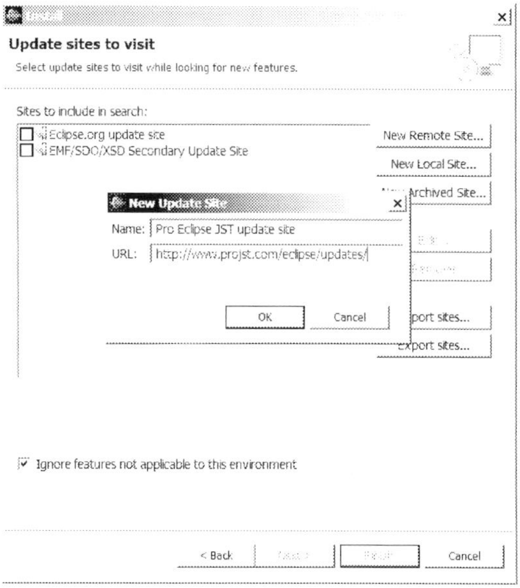

Figure 6-4. *New Update Site dialog box*

4. With the Pro Eclipse JST update site checked, click Finish.

5. On the Search Results page, check the Pro Eclipse JST update site and click Next.

6. On the Feature License page, read and accept the license.

7. On the Installation page, change the location to be `<eclipse-wtp>` and click Finish.

8. On the Feature Verification page, you will be prompted that the plug-in has not been signed. Disregard the warning and click Install.

9. When prompted, restart Eclipse.

Chapter 7, Chapter 11, and Chapter 14 will use the JBoss 4.0.1 extensions.

Installing XDoclet

As you will learn in Chapter 8, WTP uses XDoclet annotations to generate classes, interfaces, and deployment descriptors for EJBs and servlets. Here we will cover the installation of XDoclet to make sure you are ready to use it in Chapter 8.

To download and install XDoclet, complete the following steps:

1. Visit `http://sourceforge.net/projects/xdoclet/`.

2. In the Lastest File Releases section, select xdoclet.

3. In the xdoclet package list, select Download `xdoclet-bin-1.2.2.tgz` or `xdoclet-bin-1.2.2.zip` depending on your operating system.

4. Select a mirror close to your geographical location, and the file should immediately begin downloading.

5. When the file has completed downloading, uncompress it in your `~/devl/` or `C:\devl` directory depending on your operating system.

Chapter 8 will cover how to configure and use XDoclet in WTP.

Summary

In this chapter, you learned WTP is not your average plug-in due to its size and dependency on EMF, SDO, XSD, GEF, and JEM. Therefore, we explained how WTP can be installed as an extension. You also learned where to find each of the plug-ins for download and that after downloading them you just need to uncompress them in the `<eclipse-wtp>` directory.

CHAPTER 7

J2EE Standard Tools Projects

J2EE applications are the resulting product of multiple compiled Java source files, non-Java source artifacts, and resource files of various formats. These different artifacts work together to provide the logic and functionality that make the application useful to approaching a particular domain of problems. Most J2EE applications are composed of one or more J2EE components, and these J2EE components are in turn composed of one or more Java source files. Session EJBs, for instance, require separate compiled class files to define their home interface, remote interface, and bean classes. JSP files are another example of components that rely on multiple files to function properly. JSPs often rely on several non-Java-based files such as JavaScript source files and additional resource files like stylesheets and image files in order to display properly within a browser.

During the development process, it is useful to manage the collection of the source files and resources that constitute a J2EE component in a way that all the files are readily accessible to the developer. This way, changes to files that are related to work being done can be easily implemented, and the resulting deployable artifact from the project can then be easily tested. Extending this approach beyond individual components to groups of components that compose a J2EE application is immediately apparent. The structure that is used to manage this within Eclipse is a J2EE project. *Projects* are special structures created within the file system and referenced by the Eclipse Workbench that associate multiple files that are related to a J2EE component. Several types of projects are supported by JST, and we will discuss these in this chapter.

To be clear, projects are not a new feature introduced to Eclipse by the WTP project. Projects have always existed in Eclipse for use in managing myriad activities such as creating Java applications or Eclipse plug-ins. What has been introduced by JST is the capability to create J2EE projects of various kinds, including web and EJB applications, connectors, application clients, and enterprise applications.

In this chapter, we will be discussing the different types of projects that are supported by JST, the contents of each of these projects, as well as how to create J2EE projects. Several options have also been provided for use in customizing a project, and we will discuss these options at length.

JST Project Types

JST provides Eclipse with the ability to create different types of J2EE application components. Each J2EE application component being created must be defined within a project type that can support such an application component. This means that EJBs must be created within an EJB Project because the EJB project type contains the logic to properly package and deploy the EJBs. A servlet, which is a Web Tier component and exists within a Dynamic Web Project, can therefore not be created within an EJB Project.

The five types of project introduced by JST are the following:

- **Dynamic Web Project**: This project is used to create a J2EE web application that is targeted and deployed within the web container of an application server. Projects of this type contain web components and static resources that are often accessed through the use of a web browser. These components include JSP pages, servlets, and Java objects. Static resources such as image files, HTML pages, stylesheets, and JavaScript files are also often created within this project type.

- **EJB Project**: This project type is used to create EJB deployment modules that are targeted for deployment within the EJB container of an application server. An EJB Project is used to create session, entity, and message-driven EJB components. Additionally, this project typically contains Java objects that were created to support the functionality of the EJB components.

- **Application Client Project**: This project type is used to create clients that can be employed to access either web or EJB components. Application client modules do not need to be deployed within an application server and only require a Java Virtual Machine (JVM) within which to execute. This project type is often composed of Java objects and additional resources such as image files that are used by these objects.

- **Connector Project**: This project type is used to create resource adapters that can access resources from back-end legacy systems known as Enterprise Information Systems (EISs).

- **Enterprise Application Project**: Projects of this type are created to hold references to one or more modules from EJB, Web, Application Client, or Connector Projects. While each of the projects described previously can represent a portion of an enterprise application, an Enterprise Application Project is often used to represent a complete enterprise-wide solution to a problem. The Trouble Ticket application we look at in this book is an example of an enterprise application. The web component within this project provides a mechanism to add to and view a ticket, while the EJB component provides a mechanism to add, update, and delete tickets. Together, both the web and EJB deployable modules constitute the Trouble Ticket enterprise application.

In addition to these project types, WST provides support for the creation of a *Simple Project*. This project is created as an empty structure within which different static web artifacts such as HTML files and CSS documents can be stored. This works well for the creation of static web pages, which, unlike JST projects, do not need to be packaged into a deployable module.

We will discuss the different project types provided by JST throughout the rest of the book as well as describe the deployable components and artifacts that are available within these projects. To do this, from this point on we will demonstrate the creation of a J2EE application that manages trouble ticket information and show you how to use the tools available within JST to create and maintain enterprise applications.

Flexible Projects

Most IDEs available today limit each project structure to containing only a single deployment module. This means that, for instance, when a J2EE web application is being created in the form of a Web Tier project, there can be only one module managed within this project, with the module contents being packaged into a WAR file for deployment of the web application. To create many WAR file structures that are perhaps targeted at different subdomains of a large problem set will require the creation of multiple project structures to hold each of the deploy-abable modules. In short, most IDEs only support the creation of a single deployable asset from each project that is managed within them.

By default, JST similarly operates in this default mode of a single module per project. However, it is possible to unleash the full flexibility of the platform to allow the creation of multiple modules within each project. Doing this simply requires setting an option in the Preferences page. This option is available by choosing Window ➤ Preferences ➤ Flexible Java Project Preference. On the provided Preferences page, you should check the Allow multiple modules per project checkbox.

Once this option is activated, you will be allowed to create multiple modules, and thus multiple deployment artifacts, from within a single project.

Creating a J2EE Project

Before you can begin with creating projects, you must define the runtime environment that the workbench will use for the compilation of your source artifacts. In JST, a J2EE project requires the existence of both a Java Runtime Environment and a J2EE Runtime Environment. The Java Runtime Environment consists of classes provided by the Java 2 Standard Edition (J2SE) class library as well as the JVM supplied by this installation. The J2EE Runtime Environment provides support for the enterprise features that will be used in this project. Because J2EE is an extension of J2SE, you will begin with creating a configuration of the Java Runtime Environment. This will next be followed by the definition of a J2EE Runtime Environment.

It is required that these activities be completed at least once, after which multiple projects can be defined that make use of the configured Java and J2EE Runtime Environment. Expect-edly, JST supports the definition of multiple Java and J2EE Runtime Environments, allowing you to create projects that are deployable on different versions of the Java virtual machine as well as within different versions of an application server.

JRE Wizard

We will begin by demonstrating the creation of a Java Runtime Environment. This is necessary as the first step, because the creation of a J2EE Runtime Environment depends on the existence of the Java Runtime Environment. Eclipse has provided a configuration page within which the information about the installed runtime environment is entered. This page, accessible by selecting Window ➤ Preferences ➤ Java ➤ Installed JREs, shows all the Java Runtime Environments configured within Eclipse, and you can edit the configurations that they are based on by selecting any one of them and clicking the available Edit button.

To add a Java Runtime Environment definition to this page, you would then click the available Add button, and this brings up a dialog box that allows you to provide the configuration details for the desired Java Runtime Environment. Figure 7-1 shows an example of the dialog box that is presented when you are adding a JRE configuration.

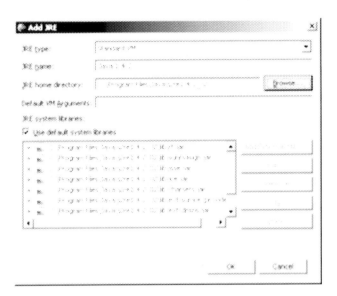

Figure 7-1. *JRE configuration dialog box*

This dialog box prompts for details about the JRE that you intend to use for your projects. You must already have at least one installation of the J2SE Runtime on your machine prior to getting to this step. This is a safe assumption because Eclipse is a Java application and requires the existence of a JVM to run. You could conceivably have multiple JRE installations on your machine.

To begin, you must indicate the type of JRE that you are planning to use. The available options include

- **Standard VM**: This should be chosen in all instances where a Java 1.2 or higher JRE is being used.

- **Standard 1.1.x VM**: This should be chosen when the JRE type uses Java 1.1, or when the target application that would be created using this application would need to run on a Microsoft JVM.

Other details prompted for by this dialog box include a JRE name, a descriptive name that will be used to reference this configuration within Eclipse. The location of the JRE home directory is also prompted for, and valid choices for this include either the location of a JRE within your file system or the location of a JDK. Using a JDK here is acceptable because a JDK is always installed together with a JRE.

Tip If you do not know the location of your JRE, you may be able to find it if the JAVA_HOME environment variable is set on your system. To check this, if you are using a Windows system, you should run echo %JAVA_HOME% at a command prompt. In Unix, at the shell prompt you should run echo $JAVA_HOME instead. If the variable is set within your environment, the location of your JRE will be displayed.

Selecting the JRE home directory instantly loads all the libraries available within the JRE and displays this in the appropriate section of the dialog box. To add additional JAR files to this list, you will need to uncheck the Use default system libraries checkbox option. This will then provide you with the ability to add your external JAR files to the list of libraries, which is accomplished by clicking the Add External JARS button and selecting the JAR files from the file system. Care should be taken whenever you opt to include additional JAR files, because applications created with your configured runtime environment will require the additional library files that were manually added to the configuration in order to run properly. Therefore, you must make sure to provide these JAR files in your deployment environment.

Finally, this dialog box prompts for VM arguments that will be passed to the environment whenever this runtime environment is initiated.

Note A JDK is composed of a JRE and additional tools that are useful in the development of a Java application.

Server Creation Wizard

Once the JRE is configured, you next create a J2EE Runtime Environment. As we indicated, the J2EE Runtime Environment provides support for the enterprise features that will be used within your J2EE application. A J2EE application that is created must be targeted at an instance of this J2EE runtime library.

Unlike with the configuration of a JRE, where the installed JRE is often provided by Sun Microsystems (the creator of the Java language), J2EE Runtime Environments are available from a wide variety of vendors. This is because the J2EE Specification as we have described in Chapter 1 merely provides a blueprint for the creation of J2EE applications. Different vendors then create their own application servers and dependent libraries that conform to this blueprint. This is the reason why you may see the terms *J2EE Runtime Environment* and *server runtime environment* used interchangeably within JST.

A J2EE application must therefore be targeted at a specific implementation of the J2EE Specification that is contained within a J2EE Runtime Environment supplied by a vendor. This J2EE Runtime Environment is often included as a part of a J2EE application server available from the vendor. It is best to define a runtime environment based on the application server that you eventually plan to deploy your application in, though if great care is taken during the development process to only use standard J2EE classes rather than application server–specific libraries, the resulting deployable module from the project can be easily deployed onto any J2EE application server.

Configuring a J2EE Runtime Environment is a two-step wizard-assisted process. This process can be initiated by selecting Window ➤ Preferences ➤ Server ➤ Installed Runtimes ➤ Add. This loads the New Server wizard displayed in Figure 7-2.

Figure 7-2. *New Server wizard*

This wizard prompts for the application that you will be using for your J2EE Runtime Environment. The supported application servers available in this page can be sorted by name, vendor, version, and module support.

The choice of application server made on this page determines the next page of the server wizard that is presented. We have shown in Figure 7-3 the page that is loaded when JBoss 4.0.1 is chosen in the first step of the wizard.

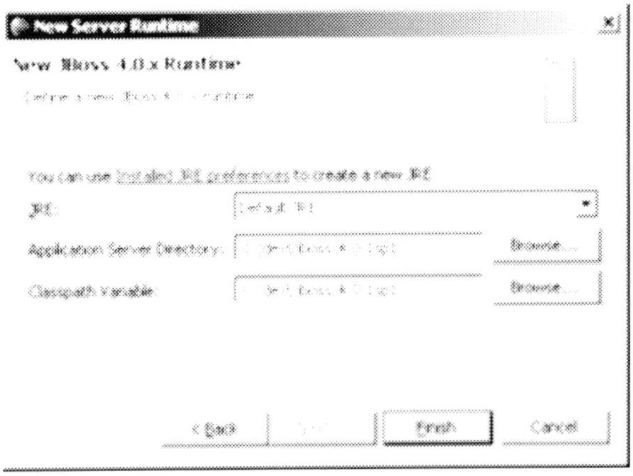

Figure 7-3. *Server runtime definition dialog box*

The dialog box provided prompts for the location of a configured JRE (which you have just created) and also the location of the application server within the file system. It also prompts for a classpath variable, which can be set to the same location as the application server directory. This immediately makes all the JAR file libraries available within this directory available to your J2EE project.

Eclipse supports the creation of multiple J2EE Runtime Environments, with each environment based upon a different application server installed on the system. Multiple runtime configurations can also be created based on a single installation of an application server. This might be useful if you intend to test your application using the same application server but different versions of a JRE. Figure 7-4 shows an example of the Preferences page that contains all the installed server runtime environments on the system.

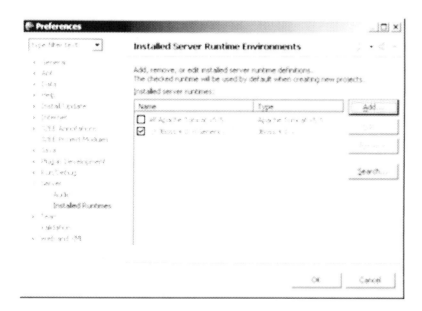

Figure 7-4. *Installed server runtime environments*

J2EE Runtime Library

In certain instances, you may have as a target deployment environment an application server that is not supported by JST. In this situation, you will still find it preferable to compile against the J2EE classes provided by the creators of your target application server. JST supports this scenario by providing you with the option of defining a generic J2EE runtime library. This choice of J2EE server runtime configuration allows you to select libraries provided by any installed application server to compile against even when such an application server is not directly supported by JST.

To create this server runtime definition, you will need to invoke the New Server wizard as we have shown in Figure 7-2. From the presented page, you will select J2EE Runtime Library and click Next. This will then present you with a dialog box that allows you to choose the location of your desired J2EE library files as well as the JRE to compile these against.

Project Creation Wizard

Once you have completed the creation of the Java and J2EE Runtime Environments, you can now create a J2EE project. JST provides wizards to ease the creation of projects, and this is especially helpful because different projects require different details during their creation. The New Project wizard eases this process by presenting different pages to enter details based on the project type being created. The items prompted for on the presented page are of relevance to the type of project being created. To launch the New Project wizard, begin by selecting File ➤ New ➤ Project. This loads the New Project wizard shown in Figure 7-5. Alternatively, selecting File ➤ New ➤ Other presents a generic New wizard dialog box that allows you to create new components of many types. The supported J2EE projects are some of the components included within this dialog box.

Figure 7-5. *New Project wizard*

The next page of the wizard differs based on the type of project being created. For each of the project types, the following information is prompted for:

- **Name**: This is a name that will be used to reference the project within the workbench. Eclipse uses this name to create a directory structure within the workspace. All the files created within this new project will be stored and managed within this directory structure.

- **Target server**: The name of the J2EE Runtime Environment that this project will be compiled against. The choices available for selection in this step include the J2EE Runtime Environments that have been configured within the workbench. We have shown the process for creating these target servers earlier in this chapter.

- **Version**: This specifies the version of the J2EE project being created. Each of the supported project types map to a specific version of a J2EE artifact. The continued growth of J2EE is quite evident with the revisions to the components that exist within the technology. Many J2EE application servers specify the versions of components they support, and so you are limited to creating an application that is based on that version. Tomcat 5.0, for instance, supports web application versions 2.2, 2.3, and 2.4, while Tomcat 4.1 only supports the 2.2 and 2.3 versions of web applications. For a project being deployed in Tomcat 4.1, the additional features provided in the 2.4 web application version will not be available for use.

As you might expect, the New Project wizard prompts for more information than what has been listed previously during the creation of your J2EE project. The additional information requested is useful not to all project types, but to the specific type of project being created. Table 7-1 lists the additional information for each J2EE project type the New Project wizard may ask for. These additional settings, as well as the target server and version settings, are only available when the advanced options mode is selected by clicking the Show Advanced button on the New Project wizard.

Table 7-1. *Additional Details Requested During Project Creation*

Item	Project Type	Description
Context root	Web	Provides a virtual path within which the contents of the web application will be accessed on the server
Annotated class support	EJB, Web	Specifies whether annotation support should be provided for components created within this project
EAR application	Web, EJB, Connector, Application Client	Specifies whether the module within the project being created should be added to a new or an existing J2EE Enterprise Application Project

Additionally, the New Project wizard dialog box that is provided looks different depending on whether support for Flexible projects has been selected or not. Specifically, when Flexible projects are in use, you are allowed to use the New Project wizard to select an existing project from a provided list and add a new module to the project.

Tip JST provides the J2EE Perspective, which contains views that are useful in the development of any J2EE application. We have described the contents of this perspective in Chapter 4. You can switch to the J2EE Perspective by selecting Window ➤ Open Perspective ➤ Other ➤ J2EE.

Working with Existing Projects

In addition to the creation of new projects, JST provides support for working with existing projects that may have been created using different development tools. The tools provided can be used to import files in various formats into your workspace for development. Also included are tools that you can use to share your project and project artifacts with other developers.

Importing Projects

To edit the artifacts within a project, the project must be referenced within the workbench and must be in an *open* state. Eclipse already provides the capability to import different types of items into the workbench, including complete projects or a group of artifacts from within these projects. JST extends this feature to support the importation of J2EE artifacts into the workbench. These artifacts are then referenced as Eclipse projects within the workbench and made available for edits. The import feature does not require the project being imported to be developed using the Eclipse Platform, thereby providing the ability for users to use whatever development tool suits them best during the development of an application.

The Import wizard that is used in this process can be launched by choosing File ➤ Import from the Eclipse IDE menu. This loads the dialog box shown in Figure 7-6. The Import action is also available in the context menu of the Project Explorer.

Figure 7-6. *Import wizard dialog box*

You can see in Figure 7-6 that there are multiple source methods from which to import a J2EE project. As we have stated, some of these import methods are provided by the base Eclipse Platform, while some have been provided by JST. We have included here a list of methods that are provided by JST for importing projects:

- **App Client JAR file**: Imports an Application Client Project into the workspace from an Application Client JAR file.

- **EAR file**: Imports a J2EE enterprise application into the workspace as an Enterprise Application Project and converts the modules available within the EAR file into suitable projects. The new Enterprise Application Project would contain references to these projects.

- **EJB JAR file**: Imports an EJB JAR file into the workspace as an EJB Project.

- **RAR file**: Creates a Connector Project within the workbench from the selected RAR file.

- **WAR file**: Imports a WAR file into the workspace as a Dynamic Web Project.

Tip For projects developed within Eclipse, choosing the Existing Projects into Workspace import source launches a dialog box that allows you to select the root folder of an existing Eclipse-created project, or alternatively to choose an archive file that contains the project and load this project into the workbench. Because this is a feature provided by the base Eclipse Platform and not specifically by JST, you can use this to import any project type into the workbench.

Exporting Projects

Just as projects can be imported into the workbench, so they can be exported into several different archival forms. These forms can then in turn be imported into the workbench using the process we described in the preceding section. To begin the process of exporting a project, you must select File ➤ Export from the Eclipse menu or alternatively select Export from the context menu in the Project Explorer.

This loads the Export wizard, which provides a selection of different types of items to export. From the available options in this wizard dialog box, the choices that can be used to export a J2EE project include App Client JAR file, EAR file, EJB JAR file, RAR file, and WAR file. For each of these choices, the second dialog box of the Export wizard presents options through which you can select what project to export from and also specify the name of the exported file. The option to include source files within the exported archive file is also provided. Figure 7-7 shows an example of the dialog box that is presented when an EJB Project is being exported to an EJB JAR file.

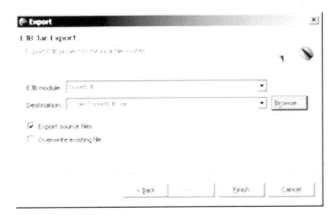

Figure 7-7. *Exporting an EJB Project to an EJB JAR file*

When exporting a project that you expect others to import into their workbench for further modification, you should make sure the Export source files checkbox is checked. This will include the source files from your project within the artifact being exported.

Project Properties

J2EE projects are created with default properties set by the New Project wizard. These default properties are often suitable for many projects being developed; however, in certain instances you may find the need to alter these properties to suit the goals of your application. JST provides you with the ability to modify the settings within your project; this is done through the Properties dialog box available by selecting Project ➤ Properties from the Eclipse menu. Alternatively, you can launch the same Properties dialog box by selecting your project within the Project Explorer and choosing Properties from the context menu. Figure 7-8 shows the Properties dialog box that is launched when any of these actions are taken.

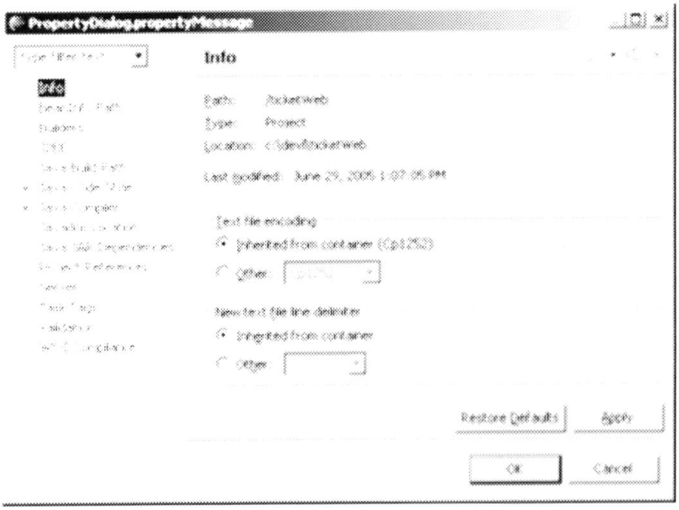

Figure 7-8. *Project Properties page*

The Properties dialog box shown in Figure 7-8 is for the web module that is a part of the Trouble Ticket enterprise application that we will be constructing throughout the rest of this book. A Properties dialog box with the same set of properties is launched for all the five types of supported J2EE projects; however, you will find that some of the items may not be configurable for the project type you are working on. In Table 7-2, we provide a description of the properties that can be read or set using this dialog box.

Table 7-2. *Configurable Properties for a J2EE Project*

Property	Description
Info	Provides general information about the project including its location on the file system, encoding type, and end-of-line delimiter.
BeanInfo Path	Enables the use of BeanInfo introspection and manages the packages and location of BeanInfo classes to search when providing bean information.
Builders	Lists builders for building the project.
Java Build Path	Indicates location of additional files, projects, and libraries to include when building the project. It additionally manages the order of reference for these items.
Java Code Style	Provides extensive Java coding options including support for defining templates, formatting code, and organizing imports.
Java Compiler	Provides extensive options for the Java compiler including options for building determining errors and creating Javadoc files.
Javadoc Location	Specifies location of Javadoc files for the project.
Java JAR Dependencies	Indicates JAR files that the project is dependent on.
Project References	Provides management of projects within the workspace to create a reference to.
Server	Provides information about the target runtime environment for the provided project and the server instances that the project will be deployed in.
Task Tags	Specifies tags that can be used to denote tasks when they appear as comments as well as the priority associated with these tasks.
Validation	Lists validators that will run during the validation of the project.
WS-I Compliance	Specifies the Web Services Interoperability Organization (WS-I) compliance levels for Attachments Profile and Simple SOAP Binding Profile.

Project Folder Contents

As we have indicated, a project created in Eclipse is represented within the file system in a directory structure. This directory structure holds all the source files and resource files that are a part of your project.

As part of the creation and management of your J2EE project, Eclipse also creates certain files within this project directory, which it uses to manage information about your project. These files are created using the XML document format, meaning that they are text-formatted documents that you can easily view and edit. Great care should be taken while editing these documents, however, as they could impact how Eclipse loads your project.

Table 7-3 describes four important files that are created for every J2EE project. Each of these files can be found on the file system within the root path of your project directory. Remember that the project directory is located within the workspace directory.

Tip An easy way of finding the location of the project on the file system is by bringing up the project's Properties page and clicking the Info list item.

Table 7-3. *Configurable Properties for a J2EE Project*

File Type	Description
`.runtime`	Contains information about the J2EE Runtime Environment that this project will be compiled against
`.classpath`	Contains entries stating the location of directories and JAR files that will be used in compilation of the project
`.project`	Contains information about the nature, builder, and additional properties that have been defined within the project
`.wtpmodules`	Describes all the modules found within the project

Caution If you choose to edit the content of these files, we strongly recommend that you create a backup copy of the files.

.deployables Directory

In addition to the files described in Table 7-3, Eclipse also creates a `.deployables` directory within the root directory of the project the first time a build operation is invoked on a project. This directory represents a deployment structure for the project that is in use, and Eclipse inserts into the directory all the compiled class files and deployable artifacts that are managed within the J2EE project.

Note The files described in Table 7-3 together with the `.deployables` directory are not visible within the workbench and can only be viewed by browsing the project on the file system.

We will describe in later chapters how some of the deployable artifacts of a project are automatically generated using such tools as XDoclet. In such cases, the resulting artifact generated by the XDoclet process will be compiled and placed into this `.deployables` directory. We will discuss the deployment structure for EJB components in Chapter 11 and for web applications in Chapter 14.

Working with Projects

After a project is created, new artifacts can be added to it. These artifacts include such items as servlets, JSP pages, and EJBs. Many of these components have complex rules regarding their creation that must be followed for the artifact to be properly included in a project for deployment. JST provides the J2EE Perspective for use in the management of J2EE projects and the different artifacts contained within them. As we discussed in Chapter 4, perspectives are a collection of views, natures, and builders that are useful for the completion of a particular set of tasks. We have also described in Chapter 4 the views that are available as part of the J2EE Perspective. You may wish to refer to that chapter for a refresher on these items.

In certain instances, a project you are working on might require the use of certain views that are not included as a part of the J2EE Perspective. An example of this is a situation where you need to connect to a database and run SQL queries against it. Database connections in WTP are managed through the use of the Database Explorer, and the Data Output View is used for viewing the results of SQL queries run against the database. However, neither of these views are a part of the J2EE Perspective. Eclipse provides the ability to alter a perspective and, importantly, save and later load this altered version of the perspective. By saving the perspective, the selected views and the layout of these views are saved and easily retrieved for subsequent usage.

To use this feature, begin by selecting an existing perspective. You can then add any new views to this perspective by using the View dialog box accessible by selecting Window ➤ Show View ➤ Other. Close any views that you do not wish to include in your updated perspective and modify the layout as you like. At this point, you can then save the perspective to preserve your modifications. To do this, select Window ➤ Save Perspective As from the Eclipse menu. The dialog box shown in Figure 7-9 will then be displayed on your screen.

Figure 7-9. *Saving perspectives*

The dialog box provided allows you to save the perspective under a new name or replace an existing perspective. Saved perspectives can be loaded by selecting Window ➤ Open Perspective ➤ Other from the IDE menu.

Additional customization of a perspective can also be achieved by selecting Window ➤ Customize Perspective. This loads the Customize Perspective dialog box, which can be used to modify the toolbar and menu items displayed in the editor.

Tip Always remember to save your perspective after making changes to it.

Summary

We have provided in this chapter information about the different types of J2EE application projects that can be created within JST. We described how each of the five available project types is used to manage a specific type of J2EE component. We will provide more in-depth discussion about each of these components in later chapters of this book.

The process of creating a Java Runtime Environment as well as a J2EE Runtime Environment were described in this chapter. These environments are essential to any J2EE project because the project requires the classes that exist within these environments. Finally, we discussed the contents of a J2EE folder that you might find when looking at your project directory.

CHAPTER 8

Session Beans

Session beans are the most commonly used of the Enterprise JavaBeans (EJB). Their popularity has grown even more in recent years due to the market shift toward Service-Oriented Architectures (SOAs). Organizations wanting to implement SOAs built on the Java platform but not necessarily Web Services are exposing business services using stateless session beans.

This chapter begins with an overview of the session bean technology. In order to simplify the creation of Enterprise JavaBeans, JST has adopted the annotation paradigm in order to manage some of the complexity. Because this is the first chapter on Enterprise JavaBeans, we will explore how JST uses annotations. Then we will show you how to use the wizards and annotations to create stateless and stateful session beans.

Session Beans Overview

Session beans are a critical part of the J2EE 1.4 specification. They are the distributed server-side business components that expose the business logic to the Web Tier and Client Tier typically through service-oriented interfaces. Session beans can also be used to hide the details or aggregation of legacy systems in the Enterprise Information Tier.

Often session beans are used in a common J2EE design pattern called the *Session Façade*. The goal of the Session Façade pattern is to wrap fine-grain access, commonly to entity beans (discussed in the next chapter), into coarse-grain access to reduce network traffic and improve performance. The details of the Session Façade pattern are explained in the "Session Façade Pattern" sidebar.

Session beans come in two types: stateful and stateless. *Stateful session beans* maintain conversational state across methods calls. Therefore, each stateful session bean is dedicated to a single client and is not pooled by the application server. An example of a stateful session bean would be a shopping cart that remembers what has been added to the cart between calls. Due to the overhead of managing state, stateful session beans are not known for their performance and are seldom used.

A *stateless session bean*, on the other hand, does not maintain state between calls and requires the state to be passed to the bean as parameters with each call. Because the stateless session beans contain no state, multiple clients can reuse the same bean instance. This enables the beans to be pooled by the application for better performance.

SESSION FAÇADE PATTERN

Early usage patterns of EJBs, specifically entity beans, led to poorly performing J2EE applications. During this time the Web Tier and Client Tier interacted directly with remote entity beans. As discussed in Chapter 1 and further detailed in the next chapter, entity beans represent persistable business objects. Entity beans consist mostly of getters and setters. Each call to the getters and setters had to incur the overhead of marshaling the data and making a network call. This is referred to as *fine-grain access*.

To improve performance and reduce fine-grain access, the Session Façade and Data Transfer Object (DTO) patterns evolved. The Session Façade pattern exposes a stateless session bean with course-grain service methods to the client. Its implementation would perform the fine-grain getter and setter calls to the entity bean. The data is transferred back and forth using the Data Transfer Object pattern. The DTO pattern uses regular JavaBeans to contain the data as it flows between the client and session bean.

To read more about the Session Façade pattern, visit `http://java.sun.com/blueprints/corej2eepatterns/Patterns/SessionFacade.html`, and to read more about the Data Transfer Object pattern, visit `http://java.sun.com/blueprints/corej2eepatterns/Patterns/TransferObject.html`.

Both stateful and stateless session beans have an implementation class referred to as the *bean*. Then depending on whether the session bean is exposing functionality to a remote client (client in another JVM) or a local client (client in the same JVM), the session bean requires some additional interfaces.

If the session bean is exposing functionality to a remote client, it requires a remote interface. This is an interface that extends `javax.ejb.EJBObject` (see Listing 8-4 later in this chapter). The remote interface typically has the same method signatures of the business methods the bean class wants to expose with one caveat: each of the methods must throw the `java.rmi.RemoteException`. This notifies the client developer that something could happen in the process of interacting with the remote server and he or she should handle it appropriately. A remote interface also requires a home interface. The home interface (see Listing 8-3 later in this chapter) exposes one or more create methods for getting a reference to the remote session bean. The home interface must extend `java.ejb.EJBHome`. A home interface for a stateless session bean may only have a single create method that passes no parameters. A stateful session bean, on the other hand, may have multiple create methods and can optionally include parameters to set up the initial state. The home interface must be looked up via JNDI. The JNDI lookup returns a application server–specific proxy implementation that implements the home interface.

Exposing functionality to a local client follows the same pattern as exposing functionality to a remote client. You have both a home interface referred to as a *local home* (see Listing 8-6 later in this chapter) and a service interface referred to as a *local interface* (see Listing 8-5 later in this chapter). The local home interface must extend the `javax.ejb.EJBLocalHome` interface, while the local interface must extend the `javax.ejb.LocalObject` interface. One other difference besides the inheritance between remote and local is that local interfaces do not require the remote exception to be thrown.

A session bean can support both a remote and local interface at the same time. If it does, that is a minimum of five files that must be kept in sync. Add to that the standard EJB deployment descriptors and possible application server–specific deployment descriptors and that is a lot of files. This is one of the reasons J2EE development is considered complicated. In the next section, you learn how JST uses annotations to glue all these files together.

Tip If you want to learn more about session beans, we suggest you read *Beginning J2EE 1.4: From Novice to Professional* by James L. Weaver, Kevin Mukhar, and Jim Crume (Apress, 2004) or *Pro J2EE 1.4: From Professional to Expert* by Meeraj Kunnumpurath and Sue Spielman (Apress, 2004).

Annotations Overview

Having to keep the bean, remote, local, and home interfaces as well as deployment descriptors in sync by hand is not very fun. It can lead to hours of frustration debugging deployment exceptions or runtime obscurities. Therefore, most J2EE development tools take one of two approaches to simplify the problem: they either provide visual editors or use metadata described in annotations to generate and manage the complexity.

JST chose the route of annotations. JST was designed to plug in different annotation providers. In its first release, JST includes XDoclet, a popular open source framework available at `http://xdoclet.sourceforge.net`, as its reference implementation. XDoclet extends the Javadoc framework by using a custom Doclet to gather metadata from Javadoc tags as well as class, method, and field information from the class itself. The XDoclet framework can be used to generate EJB classes, servlet mappings, Struts configurations, and much, much more.

Note Future versions of JST might include support for J2SE 5.0 metadata (annotations), also known as JSR 175.

XDoclet support is implemented as an XDoclet Builder, which executes one of two Ant scripts at points when a project rebuilds. This includes when a project is explicitly built by invoking the Clean, Build All, or Build Project commands from the Project main menu or when specific files are saved if Build Automatically is enabled.

The Ant scripts are found in the `eclipse\plugins\org.eclipse.jst.j2ee.ejb.annotations.xdoclet_1.0.0\templates\builder` directory. `xdoclet.xml` is used to generate EJB artifacts discussed later in this chapter. `xdocletweb.xml` is used to generate web application–related artifacts discussed in Chapters 12 and 13. If the task configurations do not meet your needs, you can modify these Ant scripts to customize your output.

Before creating J2EE applications, you must install XDoclet and configure JST to point to its location. Chapter 6 explains how to install XDoclet. The XDoclet configurations can be located by selecting Window ➤ Preferences ➤ J2EE Annotations from the main menu. On the initial J2EE Annotations page (see Figure 8-1), you must set the Active Annotation Provider. As mentioned before, there is not much choice since JST only supports XDoclet at this time.

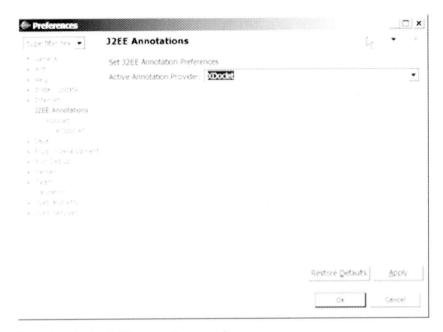

Figure 8-1. *Active J2EE annotation provider*

Next, the location and version of XDoclet must be configured, as shown in Figure 8-2.

Figure 8-2. *XDoclet location and version configuration*

In Figure 8-2, JST is configured to use the current version of XDoclet version 1.2.2. The version is installed outside of Eclipse and JST in the `~/devl/xdoclet-1.2.2` or `C:\devl\xdoclet-1.2.2` directory, respectively.

Lastly, the Ant ejbdoclet task can be configured to generate application server–specific deployment descriptors for JBoss, JOnAS, WebLogic, or WebSphere (see Figure 8-3).

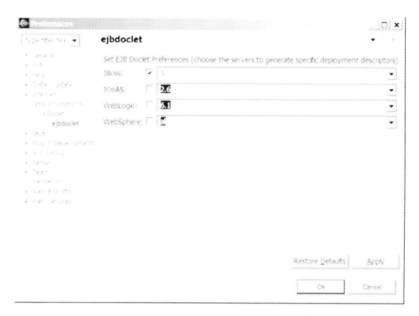

Figure 8-3. *XDoclet application server–specific deployment descriptor configuration*

In Figure 8-3, XDoclet is configured to generate deployment descriptors for the JBoss application server version 4.0.

Writing Session Beans

The JST includes an EnterpriseJavaBean wizard for creating session beans, entity beans (the focus of Chapter 9), and message-driven beans (the focus of Chapter 10). For each of these types of beans, the wizard uses a template to generate the bean class and some basic annotations. XDoclet takes care of the rest by generating and maintaining all the glue classes including the remote, local, and home interfaces, as well the J2EE deployment descriptors and application server–specific deployment descriptors. By default, XDoclet also includes a utility class for simplifying the lookup of the home interface.

Session Bean Wizard

Assuming you are working in a Flexible project containing a J2EE EJB module and are using the J2EE Perspective, you can invoke the EnterpriseJavaBean wizard using the project's context menu and choosing New ➤ EnterpriseJavaBean. Alternatively, you can use File ➤ New ➤ Other ➤ EJB ➤ EnterpriseJavaBean.

Using this wizard to create a session bean is a four-step process. It begins by prompting for the type of EJB to create and an annotation provider (see Figure 8-4). The wizard includes support for creating a session or message-driven bean by selecting the appropriate radio button. Using the drop-down list, you may choose your preferred annotation provider. At this time, there is not a lot of choice. WTP only includes support for XDoclet annotations.

Figure 8-4. *The first step in the EnterpriseJavaBean wizard defines the type of bean and annotations to use.*

Underneath the covers, this first step identifies the code templates for generating the initial bean class. WTP uses the Java Emitter Templates (JET) from the Eclipse Modeling Framework (EMF) as the template engine. So a combination of SessionBean and XDoclet options will cause the templates in the `eclipse/plugins/org.eclipse.jst.j2ee.ejb.annotations.xdoclet_1.0.0/` `templates/ejb/session` directory to be used. The combination of MessageDrivenBean and XDoclet will cause the templates in the `eclipse/plugins/org.eclipse.jst.j2ee.ejb.annotations.` `xdoclet_1.0.0/templates/ejb/message` directory to be used.

Note If you don't like the way the source code is generated from the EnterpriseJavaBean wizard, you can modify the templates in the directories mentioned previously. These files are read every time the wizard is executed so you won't have to restart Eclipse. However, in a team environment, managing template changes in the JST plug-in would be difficult. Therefore, it is not recommended. Instead, you could implement your own plug-in using the JST `org.eclipse.jst.j2ee.ejb.annotations.emitter.template` extension point and control your plug-in versioning with an internal Eclipse update site.

The second step in the EnterpriseJavaBean wizard (see Figure 8-5) collects information about where the bean source code will be placed as well as standard class information including the package, class name, and class it inherits from.

Figure 8-5. *The second step in the EnterpriseJavaBean wizard is used to identify where the output of the wizard goes.*

The first aspect of determining where to put the generated session bean code is deciding which project it belongs in. Depending on how your projects are organized, you may have multiple projects representing different partitions of your application. For example, you may have a separate EJB, Web, and Enterprise Application Projects. Or you may have one project with different modules representing your partitions, for example, an Application Project with an EJB module, Web module, and Enterprise Application module. So the Project drop-down menu lists all the open projects in the workspace. Once a project is selected, the modules in the project will be displayed in the Module Name drop-down menu. If the selected project does not contain a module, a warning message of "The source folder cannot be empty" will appear along the top of the dialog box. The folder must be the source folder of the EJB module. By default, it will contain the correct folder if the wizard is invoked from a Flexible project containing an EJB module. Unfortunately though, the field is not tied to the module name or project. So if either of them is changed, the folder is not automatically updated. Therefore, it is a good idea to use identifiable module names to make them easier to find.

Note The Generate an annotated bean class checkbox does not make a difference in the output of the wizard, since either way it uses the same template, and there is no conditional logic in the template to exclude annotations.

The next step in the Session Bean wizard (see Figure 8-6) prompts for information that initially will populate the annotations. When XDoclet processes the annotations, the information will be used to update the standard EJB deployment descriptors to describe the EJB.

Figure 8-6. *The third step in the EnterpriseJavaBean wizard gathers information for the deployment descriptors.*

The EJB name is used to uniquely identify an EJB within the context of an ejb-jar. It is primarily used for defining the relationships between the EJB and other elements in the deployment descriptors. The JNDI name is used to look up the home or local home interface from the JNDI context. The mechanism for mapping EJBs to JNDI names is not described in the EJB specification and is therefore not included in the standard EJB deployment descriptors. Most application servers include a vendor-specific deployment descriptor that contains the implementation-specific JNDI element. Some application servers, for example JBoss, default to the EJB name if the JNDI name is not explicitly defined. It is not uncommon to see JNDI names that match the EJB names as in Figure 8-6, where both the EJB name and JNDI name are TicketService. It is also not uncommon to see JNDI names that provide additional context like ejb/TicketService, ejb/service/Ticket, or service/Ticket.

Note Because the JNDI name is a vendor-specific setting and some application servers can work without a vendor-specific deployment descriptor, it is easy to create an EJB with a JNDI name other than the default and have it appear in the application server JNDI tree as the default. Or worse, you could try to look up the EJB and get a `javax.naming.NamingException` thrown even though you are looking up the JNDI name in the bean's annotations. To resolve this issue, make sure the vendor-specific deployment descriptor is being generated by going to Window ➤ Preferences ➤ J2EE Annotations ➤ XDoclet ➤ ejbdoclet and choosing the correct application server checkbox and the appropriate version from the drop-down menu. Before redeploying, you will need to regenerate the deployment descriptors by modifying and saving the bean class or explicitly rebuilding.

The display name and description are both optional elements of the EJB standard deployment descriptors. Some development tools and application servers may optionally display this additional information.

At this point, you also get to choose what type of state and transactions you want for your session bean. For the state type, you get to choose between stateful and stateless, which were covered earlier in the chapter. For transaction type, you determine whether your session bean transactions will be managed by the container (by choosing Container), or you will manage transactions yourself in code (by choosing Bean).

The final step in the EnterpriseJavaBean wizard (see Figure 8-7) is the standard Java Class page. It collects information about the class's modifiers, interfaces, and methods you want stubbed.

Figure 8-7. *The fourth step in the EnterpriseJavaBean wizard is the Eclipse standard Class page.*

At this time, the last step in the process is more informational than useful. All the settings on this page are ignored. If you completely do the opposite by reversing the checkmarks and removing the interface, you will still get the same results because the templates do not do anything with this information. This is not a problem because the generated session bean has the configuration you are most likely to need. For example, I have never seen an EJB that contains a main method. In addition, according to the EJB specification, it must not be final because one implementation an application server may choose is to add the container management functionality by extending the bean classes.

Depending on how familiar you are with the EJB specification, you may be looking at Figure 8-7 and asking yourself, "Doesn't the EJB specification also state the EJB cannot be abstract?" And the answer is, "Yes it does." As you will discover in just a moment when we review the output of the wizard, XDoclet subclasses your bean classes with a session class that implements all the javax.ejb.SessionBean required methods. It is this session class that the application server will require not to be abstract.

Upon completing the wizard, a session bean similar to the one shown in Listing 8-1 will be generated complete with XDoclet annotations.

Listing 8-1. *Generated Session Bean*

```
/**
 *
 */
package com.projst.ticket.service;


/**
 *
 * <!-- begin-user-doc -->
 * A generated session bean
 * <!-- end-user-doc -->
 * *
 * <!-- begin-xdoclet-definition -->
 * @ejb.bean name="TicketService"
 *           description="A session bean named TicketService"
 *           display-name="TicketService"
 *           jndi-name="TicketService"
 *           type="Stateless"
 *           transaction-type="Container"
 *
 * <!-- end-xdoclet-definition -->
 * @generated
 */

public abstract class TicketServiceBean implements javax.ejb.SessionBean {

    /**
     *
```

```
 * <!-- begin-xdoclet-definition -->
 * @ejb.interface-method view-type="remote"
 * <!-- end-xdoclet-definition -->
 * @generated
 *
 * //TODO: Must provide implementation for bean method stub
 */
public String foo(String param) {
    return null;
}
}
```

Listing 8-1 is the bean implementation. This is the class where the business logic of the session bean should be placed. In order to demonstrate this pattern, the template code includes the stubbed foo method, which would represent a business logic method.

Notice in Listing 8-1 that the class includes a Javadoc. The first part of the Javadoc identifies where you should put a description of your bean. The second part contains XDoclet annotations. Specifically, it contains the XDoclet ejb.bean annotation. The annotations here contain the EJB name, JNDI name, display name, description, state type, and transaction type entered on the third page of the wizard. XDoclet will use these annotations to generate the EJB standard and vendor-specific deployment descriptors.

Tip Removing the <!--begin-user-doc--> improves the readability of the hover-over Javadoc help, or tooltip. It does not have any effect on the HTML produced by Javadoc because the browser treats it as an HTML comment.

The foo method also contains some Javadocs with an XDoclet annotation. This Javadoc does not contain the general reminder to describe the message like the class Javadoc does, but it is still a good idea and standard practice to document the intent of the method. It does, however, contain a single XDoclet annotation. The ejb.interface-method annotation is used to define which interfaces this method will appear in based on the value of the view-type attribute. Historically, the view-type could contain local to include the method in the session bean's local interface, remote to include the method in the session bean's remote interface, or both to include the method in both the session bean's remote and local interfaces.

As of the EJB 2.1 specification, EJBs can now expose methods as Web Services using a service-endpoint element in the deployment descriptor. To support this EJB enhancement, XDoclet has added the service-endpoint, remote-service-endpoint, local-service-endpoint, and all values to view-type. The service-endpoint exposes the method as a Web Service. The remote-service-endpoint includes the method in the Remote interfaces as well as a Web Service. Therefore it is pretty logical that the local-service-endpoint includes the method in the Local interfaces as well as exposing the method as a Web Service. The all exposes the method in both interfaces as well as a Web Service.

Note Don't forget to remove the TODO comment after you add your own implementation.

If Build Automatically is enabled, within seconds of completing the wizard, the XDoclet Builder will launch and generate a bunch of additional files. You will probably notice the XDoclet Builder running because the output is displayed in the console window. This process will produce a session class that extends the bean classes in the EJB module (see Listing 8-2 later in this chapter). In addition, it will generate a home, remote, local, local home, and utility class (shown later in this chapter in Listings 8-3 through 8-7, respectively) in the EJB client module. It will also update the `ejb-jar.xml` file and possibly vendor-specific deployment descriptors (depending on your J2EE annotation configurations) if they exist or create them if they don't. The deployment descriptors are found in the EJB module's `META-INF` directory.

Note Having Build Automatically enabled while working with a JST EJB and/or Web Project may cause XDoclet to run frequently.

The class in Listing 8-1 is not a true session bean yet because it does not implement all the life cycle methods (`ejbActivate`, `ejbPassivate`, `setSessionContext`, `unsetSessionContext`, `ejbRemove`, `ejbCreate`) required by the `javax.ejb.SessionBean` interface. This is the reason the class is declared as abstract. In order to complete the session bean, the XDoclet Builder generates a descendent of the bean class (see Figure 8-8 and Listing 8-2).

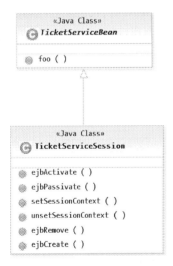

Figure 8-8. *Inherited relationship between the bean and generated session classes*

Figure 8-8 shows the relationship of the bean class and the generated session class. The session class extends the bean class and implements life cycle methods. Looking at Listing 8-2, you can see the implementations of the life cycle methods are simply empty blocks.

Listing 8-2. *Session Class That Extends the Bean Class*

```
/*
 * Generated by XDoclet - Do not edit!
 */
package com.projst.ticket.service;

/**
 * Session layer for TicketService.
 * @generated
 * @wtp generated
 */
public class TicketServiceSession
    extends com.projst.ticket.service.TicketServiceBean
    implements javax.ejb.SessionBean
{
    public void ejbActivate()
    {
    }

    public void ejbPassivate()
    {
    }

    public void setSessionContext(javax.ejb.SessionContext ctx)
    {
    }

    public void unsetSessionContext()
    {
    }

    public void ejbRemove()
    {
    }

    public void ejbCreate() throws javax.ejb.CreateException
    {
    }

}
```

As you can see from the UML class diagram in Figure 8-8, the separation of the bean and session classes makes for a clean separation of business logic and what are typically just boilerplate life cycle methods. The business methods like foo in this example belong in the bean class, and the life cycle methods are located in the session class.

Notice in Listing 8-2 that the file begins with a comment stating this file was generated by XDoclet and should not be edited. If you do decide to edit this file to provide functionality to the life cycle methods, your implementation will be overwritten the next time the XDoclet Builder runs. So, if you need to add functionality to the life cycle methods, implement the specific life cycle method in the bean class. When the session class gets regenerated, it will include a call to the superimplementation, which is the bean class.

Depending on the value of the ejb.bean view-type, XDoclet generates home, remote, local, and local home interfaces (see Listings 8-3 through 8-6 for these interfaces). By default, XDoclet generates all four of these. These files are all generated in the EJB client module because the client will need access to them at compile time and runtime. Just like the session class, these classes should not be modified because XDoclet will just overwrite them.

Listing 8-3 shows the generated home interface. This interface is used by clients running outside the application server in order to get a reference to a remote session bean. Like all home interfaces, this interface contains a create method for getting the reference to a remote session bean. It also provides two convenience constants. The COMP_NAME constant is the bean's component name, and the JNDI_NAME is the bean's JNDI name. These constants should be used by the client when looking up the bean. This way, if the names ever change, the client code does not need to be updated because XDoclet will change the values of the constants. These constants are also used by the utility class discussed later.

Listing 8-3. *Generated Home Interface*

```
/*
 * Generated by XDoclet - Do not edit!
 */
package com.projst.ticket.service;

/**
 * Home interface for TicketService.
 * @generated
 * @wtp generated
 */
public interface TicketServiceHome
    extends javax.ejb.EJBHome
{
    public static final String COMP_NAME="java:comp/env/ejb/TicketService";
    public static final String JNDI_NAME="TicketService";

    public com.projst.ticket.service.TicketService create()
       throws javax.ejb.CreateException,java.rmi.RemoteException;

}
```

Listing 8-4 shows the generated remote interface. This interface is used by clients running outside of the application server to invoke methods on the session bean. This interface will expose any methods declared in the bean's method annotation to have a view-type of remote, both, or all. In this example, the exposed business method is the foo method.

Listing 8-4. *Generated Remote Interface*

```
/*
 * Generated by XDoclet - Do not edit!
 */
package com.projst.ticket.service;

/**
 * Remote interface for TicketService.
 * @generated
 * @wtp generated
 */
public interface TicketService
   extends javax.ejb.EJBObject
{
   /**
    * <!-- begin-xdoclet-definition -->
    * @generated //TODO: Must provide implementation for bean method stub    */
   public java.lang.String foo( java.lang.String param )
      throws java.rmi.RemoteException;

}
```

Listing 8-5 shows the generated local interface. This interface is used by clients running inside the application server to invoke methods of the session bean. Typically, these clients are web applications or other EJBs. This interface will expose any methods declared in the bean's method annotation to have a view-type of local, both, or all. By default, the foo method is marked as remote so the interface contains no methods and is therefore not very useful. Later in the chapter when we finish the implementation, we will expose a method to both the remote and local interfaces.

Listing 8-5. *Generated Local Interface*

```
/*
 * Generated by XDoclet - Do not edit!
 */
package com.projst.ticket.service;

/**
 * Local interface for TicketService.
 * @generated
 * @wtp generated
 */
public interface TicketServiceLocal
   extends javax.ejb.EJBLocalObject
{

}
```

Listing 8-6 shows the generated local home interface. This interface is used by clients running inside the same container to create an instance of the session bean. Just like the home interface, this interface contains a `create` method and two constants for looking up the bean.

Listing 8-6. *Generated Local Home Interface*

```
/*
 * Generated by XDoclet - Do not edit!
 */
package com.projst.ticket.service;

/**
 * Local home interface for TicketService.
 * @generated
 * @wtp generated
 */
public interface TicketServiceLocalHome
   extends javax.ejb.EJBLocalHome
{
   public static final String COMP_NAME="java:comp/env/ejb/TicketServiceLocal";
   public static final String JNDI_NAME="TicketServiceLocal";

   public com.projst.ticket.service.TicketServiceLocal create()
      throws javax.ejb.CreateException;

}
```

XDoclet also generates a utility class (see Listing 8-7). The utility class contains methods for looking up both home and local home interfaces. In addition, it includes a utility method for generating globally unique identifiers (GUIDs).

Listing 8-7. *Generated Utility Class*

```
/*
 * Generated file - Do not edit!
 */
package com.projst.ticket.service;

/**
 * Utility class for TicketService.
 * @generated
 * @wtp generated
 */
public class TicketServiceUtil
{
   /** Cached remote home (EJBHome). Uses lazy loading to obtain its value
    *  (loaded by getHome() methods).
    */
```

```java
private static com.projst.ticket.service.TicketServiceHome
    cachedRemoteHome = null;

/** Cached local home (EJBLocalHome). Uses lazy loading to obtain its value
 * (loaded by getLocalHome() methods).
 */
private static com.projst.ticket.service.TicketServiceLocalHome
    cachedLocalHome = null;

private static Object lookupHome(java.util.Hashtable environment,
    String jndiName, Class narrowTo)
  throws javax.naming.NamingException {
   // Obtain initial context
   javax.naming.InitialContext initialContext =
       new javax.naming.InitialContext(environment);
   try {
      Object objRef = initialContext.lookup(jndiName);
      // only narrow if necessary
      if (narrowTo.isInstance(java.rmi.Remote.class))
         return javax.rmi.PortableRemoteObject.narrow(objRef, narrowTo);
      else
         return objRef;
   } finally {
      initialContext.close();
   }
}


// Home interface lookup methods

/**
 * Obtain remote home interface from default initial context
 * @return Home interface for TicketService. Look up using JNDI_NAME
 */
public static com.projst.ticket.service.TicketServiceHome getHome()
    throws javax.naming.NamingException
{
   if (cachedRemoteHome == null) {
        cachedRemoteHome = (com.projst.ticket.service.TicketServiceHome)
            lookupHome(null,
                     com.projst.ticket.service.TicketServiceHome.JNDI_NAME,
                     com.projst.ticket.service.TicketServiceHome.class);
   }
   return cachedRemoteHome;
}


/**
 * Obtain remote home interface from parameterized initial context
 * @param environment Parameters to use for creating initial context
```

```
 * @return Home interface for TicketService. Look up using JNDI_NAME
 */
public static com.projst.ticket.service.TicketServiceHome getHome(
    java.util.Hashtable environment )
    throws javax.naming.NamingException
{
    return (com.projst.ticket.service.TicketServiceHome) lookupHome(
        environment,
        com.projst.ticket.service.TicketServiceHome.JNDI_NAME,
        com.projst.ticket.service.TicketServiceHome.class);
}

/**
 * Obtain local home interface from default initial context
 * @return Local home interface for TicketService. Look up using JNDI_NAME
 */
public static com.projst.ticket.service.TicketServiceLocalHome getLocalHome()
    throws javax.naming.NamingException
{
    if (cachedLocalHome == null) {
        cachedLocalHome = (com.projst.ticket.service.TicketServiceLocalHome)
            lookupHome(null,
                com.projst.ticket.service.TicketServiceLocalHome.JNDI_NAME,
                com.projst.ticket.service.TicketServiceLocalHome.class);
    }
    return cachedLocalHome;
}

/** Cached per JVM server IP. */
private static String hexServerIP = null;

// initialize the secure random instance
private static final java.security.SecureRandom seeder =
    new java.security.SecureRandom();

/**
 * A 32-byte GUID generator (Globally Unique ID). These artificial keys SHOULD
 * <strong>NOT </strong> be seen by the user,
 * not even touched by the DBA but with very rare exceptions, just manipulated
 * by the database and the programs.
 *
 * Usage: Add an id field (type java.lang.String) to your EJB, and add
 * setId(XXXUtil.generateGUID(this)); to the ejbCreate method.
 */
public static final String generateGUID(Object o) {
    StringBuffer tmpBuffer = new StringBuffer(16);
    if (hexServerIP == null) {
```

```
            java.net.InetAddress localInetAddress = null;
            try {
                // get the inet address

                localInetAddress = java.net.InetAddress.getLocalHost();
            }
            catch (java.net.UnknownHostException uhe) {
                System.err.println("TicketServiceUtil: Could not get the local " +
                    "IP address using InetAddress.getLocalHost()!");
                // todo: find better way to get around this...
                uhe.printStackTrace();
                return null;
            }
            byte serverIP[] = localInetAddress.getAddress();
            hexServerIP = hexFormat(getInt(serverIP), 8);
        }

        String hashcode = hexFormat(System.identityHashCode(o), 8);
        tmpBuffer.append(hexServerIP);
        tmpBuffer.append(hashcode);

        long timeNow     = System.currentTimeMillis();
        int timeLow      = (int)timeNow & 0xFFFFFFFF;
        int node         = seeder.nextInt();

        StringBuffer guid = new StringBuffer(32);
        guid.append(hexFormat(timeLow, 8));
        guid.append(tmpBuffer.toString());
        guid.append(hexFormat(node, 8));
        return guid.toString();
    }

    private static int getInt(byte bytes[]) {
        int i = 0;
        int j = 24;
        for (int k = 0; j >= 0; k++) {
            int l = bytes[k] & 0xff;
            i += l << j;
            j -= 8;
        }
        return i;
    }

    private static String hexFormat(int i, int j) {
        String s = Integer.toHexString(i);
        return padHex(s, j) + s;
    }
```

```
    private static String padHex(String s, int i) {
        StringBuffer tmpBuffer = new StringBuffer();
        if (s.length() < i) {
            for (int j = 0; j < i - s.length(); j++) {
                tmpBuffer.append('0');
            }
        }
        return tmpBuffer.toString();
    }

}
```

Notice in Listing 8-7 that the lookup methods of getHome and getLocalHome perform a basic JNDI lookup using javax.naming.InitialContext. There is one caveat, though: they cache the interfaces to improve performance. In addition, the getHome method is overloaded. The getHome with no parameters uses the default InitialContext configuration usually configured in a jndi.properties file. The getHome with the java.util.Hashtable parameter provides the opportunity to supply an explicate JNDI environment configuration.

The generateGUID method on the utility class generates a 32-bit guaranteed unique identifier. This method can be helpful when the client, especially a remote client, creates instances of an object such as a DTO that must be uniquely identifiable before the instance is passed to the remote session bean.

XDoclet will also update or create the ejb-jar.xml deployment descriptor and possibly an application server–specific deployment descriptor based on the bean class's annotations. Listing 8-8 shows an example of the ejb-jar.xml and Listing 8-9 shows the generated jboss.xml file.

Tip There is a shortcut to open the ejb-jar.xml file in the J2EE Perspective. Right-click the EJB node in the J2EE Perspective and select Open.

Listing 8-8. *Generated ejb-jar.xml File*

```xml
<?xml version="1.0" encoding="UTF-8"?>

<ejb-jar  xmlns=http://java.sun.com/xml/ns/j2ee
 xmlns:xsi=http://www.w3.org/2001/XMLSchema-instance
 xsi:schemaLocation="http://java.sun.com/xml/ns/j2ee
http://java.sun.com/xml/ns/j2ee/ejb-jar_2_1.xsd" version="2.1">

    <description>
      <![CDATA[ticketEJB generated by eclipse wtp xdoclet extension.]]>
    </description>
    <display-name>ticketEJB</display-name>

    <enterprise-beans>
```

```xml
    <!-- Session Beans -->
    <session >
        <description><![CDATA[A session bean named TicketService]]></description>
        <display-name>TicketService</display-name>

        <ejb-name>TicketService</ejb-name>

        <home>com.projst.ticket.service.TicketServiceHome</home>
        <remote>com.projst.ticket.service.TicketService</remote>
        <local-home>com.projst.ticket.service.TicketServiceLocalHome</local-home>
        <local>com.projst.ticket.service.TicketServiceLocal</local>
        <ejb-class>com.projst.ticket.service.TicketServiceSession</ejb-class>
        <session-type>Stateless</session-type>
        <transaction-type>Container</transaction-type>

    </session>

    <!--
        To add session beans that you have deployment descriptor info for, add
        a file to your XDoclet merge directory called session-beans.xml that contains
        the <session></session> markup for those beans.
    -->

    <!-- Entity Beans -->
    <!--
        To add entity beans that you have deployment descriptor info for, add
        a file to your XDoclet merge directory called entity-beans.xml that contains
        the <entity></entity> markup for those beans.
    -->

    <!-- Message Driven Beans -->
    <!--
        To add message driven beans that you have deployment descriptor info for, add
        a file to your XDoclet merge directory called message-driven-beans.xml that
        contains the <message-driven></message-driven> markup for those beans.
    -->

</enterprise-beans>

<!-- Relationships -->

<!-- Assembly Descriptor -->
    <!--
        To specify your own assembly descriptor info here, add a file to your
        XDoclet merge directory called assembly-descriptor.xml that contains
        the <assembly-descriptor></assembly-descriptor> markup.
    -->
```

```
<assembly-descriptor >
  <!--
    To specify additional security-role elements, add a file in the merge
    directory called ejb-security-roles.xml that contains them.
  -->

<!-- method permissions -->
  <!--
    To specify additional method-permission elements, add a file in the merge
    directory called ejb-method-permissions.ent that contains them.
  -->

<!-- finder permissions -->

<!-- transactions -->
  <!--
    To specify additional container-transaction elements, add a file in the merge
    directory called ejb-container-transaction.ent that contains them.
  -->

<!-- finder transactions -->

  <!--
    To specify an exclude-list element, add a file in the merge directory
    called ejb-exclude-list.xml that contains it.
  -->
</assembly-descriptor>

<ejb-client-jar>ticketEJBClient.jar</ejb-client-jar>

</ejb-jar>
```

Listing 8-8 is the new ejb-jar.xml file containing a reference to the new TicketService session bean in the enterprise-beans section. Notice how the TicketService's description, display-name, ejb-name, session-type, and transaction-type all match the values from the TicketServiceBean's annotations. Also notice the home, remote, local-home, local, and ejb-class elements are the classes generated by XDoclet.

The ejb-jar.xml file is generated and overwritten each time XDoclet is run. So, XDoclet provides a merge feature for including configurable deployment descriptors that are not specific to an EJB and therefore cannot logically be annotated with an EJB as well as include existing EJBs not containing annotations. The XDoclet merge injects or copies specifically named and formatted XML files from a merge directory into the appropriate locations of the standard and vendor-specific deployment descriptors. Throughout the generated deployment descriptors are XML comments about the files that are merged. The JST-configured merge directory is the same directory containing the ejb-jar.xml file, the EJB module's META-INF directory.

Depending on your configurations, you may also get a vendor-specific deployment descriptor. Listing 8-9 shows an example of a JBoss-specific deployment descriptor, jboss.xml.

Listing 8-9. *Generated jboss.xml File*

```xml
<?xml version="1.0" encoding="UTF-8"?>
<!DOCTYPE jboss PUBLIC "-//JBoss//DTD JBOSS 4.0//EN"
 "http://www.jboss.org/j2ee/dtd/jboss_4_0.dtd">

<jboss>

   <unauthenticated-principal>nobody</unauthenticated-principal>

   <enterprise-beans>

     <!--
        To add beans that you have deployment descriptor info for, add
        a file to your XDoclet merge directory called jboss-beans.xml that contains
        the <session></session>, <entity></entity>, and
        <message-driven></message-driven> markup for those beans.
     -->

     <session>
        <ejb-name>TicketService</ejb-name>
        <jndi-name>TicketService</jndi-name>
        <local-jndi-name>TicketServiceLocal</local-jndi-name>

        <method-attributes>
        </method-attributes>
     </session>

   </enterprise-beans>

   <resource-managers>
   </resource-managers>

   <!--
     | for container settings, you can merge in jboss-container.xml
     | this can contain <invoker-proxy-bindings/> and <container-configurations/>
   -->

</jboss>
```

Once XDoclet has finished and all the files have been generated, the Session Beans node in the J2EE Perspective will be updated to include the new session bean (see Figure 8-9).

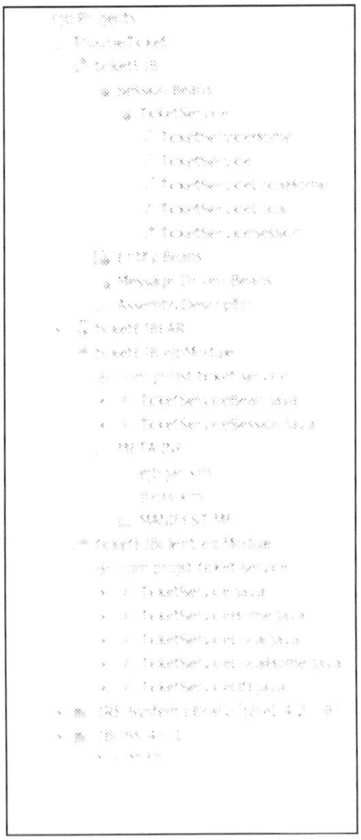

Figure 8-9. *J2EE Project Explorer after XDoclet completes*

Figure 8-9 shows an expanded view of the TroubleTicket project after the TicketService session bean has been added. Notice the new TicketService bean is under the Session Beans node. Underneath the TicketService are the related TicketService interfaces as well as the TicketService session bean. Within the source folders, you can see generated files including TicketServiceBean.java, TicketServiceSession.java, ejb-jar.xml, jboss.xml, TicketService.java, TicketServiceHome.java, TicketServiceLocal.java, and TicketServiceHome.java.

> **Note** It is important to use version control with your source code so you can guarantee repeatable builds at different points in time and consistent builds amongst a team of developers. Technically, you only need to use version control with the bean class because everything related to that class will be regenerated.

XDoclet Session Bean Annotations

In order to generate the interfaces and deployment descriptors in JST, you must be familiar with your chosen annotation tool. Since XDoclet is the only option at this point, this section will introduce you to some of the session bean–specific XDoclet annotations. This is not an exhaustive list. For a complete list, check out the XDoclet documentation at http://xdoclet.sourceforge.net/xdoclet/index.html.

Tip The JST has XDoclet code assist. It can be invoked using Ctrl+space after @. Unfortunately, it does not include all XDoclet annotations.

Session beans have many class-, method-, and field-level annotations. Because there are so many, we will limit ourselves to a couple of tables identifying the most common class-level tag, @ejb.bean (see Table 8-1) and the most common method-level tag, @ejb.interface-method (see Table 8-2).

Table 8-1. *XDoclet Session @ejb.bean Class Parameters*

Parameter	Type	Description	Required
name	Text	Enterprise bean name (ejb-name) and must be unique within an ejb-jar file	True
description	Text	Description of bean	False
display-name	Text	Short name	False
small-icon	Text	16×16 icon image	False
large-icon	Text	32×32 icon image	False
generate	Boolean	Generate bean deployment description	False
jndi-name	Text	Remote JNDI name	False
local-jndi-name	Text	Local JNDI name	False
view-type	Text	Whether bean is local, remote, Web Service, or all	False
type	Text	Whether bean is stateless or stateful	True
transaction-type	Text	Container or bean transaction	False

Table 8-2. *XDoclet Session @ejb.interface-method Class Parameters*

Parameter	Type	Description	Required
view-type	Text	Whether method is local, remote, Web Service, or all	False

Note Visit http://xdoclet.sourceforge.net/xdoclet/index.html for application server–specific session bean annotations.

Finishing the Session Bean Implementation

The session bean generated by the EnterpriseJavaBean wizard does not do much by default. In this section, we will show you how to add some basic functionality to the TicketServiceBean.java file. We will change the foo method into a ping method (see Listing 8-10) and expose it as both a remote and local method. The ping method can be used to make sure the bean is alive. In the next two chapters, we will add an addTicket service method to this session bean, but for now we will keep it simple.

Listing 8-10. *Implementation of the ping Method*

```
/**
 * Method used to ensure session bean is available by providing an echo message.
 * <!-- begin-xdoclet-definition -->
 * @ejb.interface-method view-type="both"
 * <!-- end-xdoclet-definition -->
 * @generated
 */
public String ping(String param) {
    return "pong: " + param + " at " + new Date();
}
```

In Listing 8-10, notice the TODO comment reminding us to provide an implementation has been removed. Next, the Eclipse refactoring tools come in handy for renaming the foo method to ping. For the ping method to appear both on the remote and local interface, the @ejb. interface-method view-type must be changed to both. It is always a good idea to include relevant documentation, so the Javadoc was updated with a comment as well.

The implementation for the ping method is not very fancy. It appends the parameter passed in to a String containing the word "pong" and then appends the current date and time to the end of the entire String and returns it back to the client.

Once this file is saved, XDoclet will run, and the remote and local interfaces will immediately reflect the changes made.

In the next section, we will be invoking the ping method from a remote client application.

Writing a Remote Session Bean Client

Now that our session bean has a ping method exposed, we will call it from a remote client. In Chapters 12 and 13, we will show you how to invoke the session bean as a local service.

This client application will be a simple application that looks up the remote session bean and invokes the ping method. Once the client gets the response, it will write the response to system out.

Note Chapter 11 discusses how to deploy the session bean to the application server. The application will need to be deployed for the client application to work.

Create a Remote Client Project

Typically, a remote Java client will have its own Eclipse project. JST does not have any special client projects. Either a regular Eclipse Java Project or JST Flexible Java Project will work. The project just needs to include the application server–specific client jars and the EJB Project in its build path.

One advantage of starting with a Flexible project is it is already application server–specific client-JAR aware. However, it does not include a default source path or prompt for dependent projects, so these steps have to be done by hand.

To create a remote client project using the Flexible project, choose File ➤ New ➤ Project ➤ Java ➤ Flexible Java Project. When prompted (see Figure 8-10), give the project a meaningful name and click the Show Advanced button to display the available target servers. Select your target server. This will add the server library to your project.

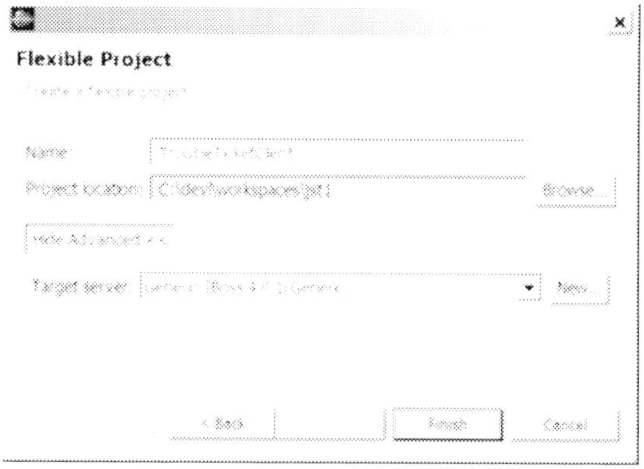

Figure 8-10. *Flexible Java Project wizard for the remote client application*

Notice in Figure 8-10 the name of the project is set to TroubleTicketClient and the target application server is JBoss 4.0.1.

Next, the source folder (see Figure 8-11) and dependency on the project containing the EJB application client module (see Figure 8-12) must be added to the project build path. This can be done using the project property Java Build Path. To configure the build path, first select the project. Then choose Project ➤ Properties ➤ Java Build Path ➤ Source starting from the main menu.

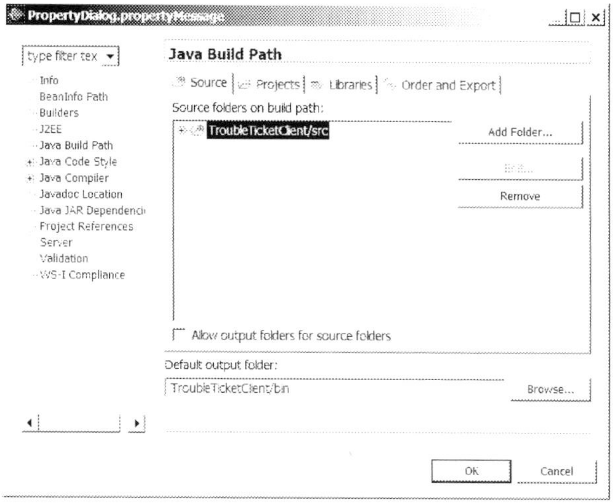

Figure 8-11. *Client project source folder*

As shown in Figure 8-12, on the Source tab, press the Add Folder button. At the prompt, enter src for the source folder.

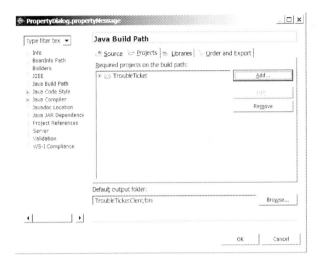

Figure 8-12. *Client dependency on project containing the EJB application client module*

As shown in Figure 8-12, on the Projects tab, press the Add button. At the prompt, select the project containing the EJB application client module.

Call Remote Session Bean for Class

A remote session bean client may be a Swing, SWT, AWT, or, in this case, a simple command-line Java application. Because the client we are creating will be a command-line client, we can use the standard Eclipse Class wizard to generate a class with a `main` method.

To create the class, select File ➤ New ➤ Other ➤ Class from the main menu (see Figure 8-13). Give the class a name and a package. In addition, make sure you check the public static void main(String[] args) checkbox. The wizard will generate a simple class stub.

Figure 8-13. *Java Class wizard for the remote session bean client*

To invoke the remote session bean, you must look up the home interface. With the home interface, you can call its create method to get the remote interface. Then with the remote interface, you can invoke the ping method. See Listing 8-11 for the client source code.

Listing 8-11. *Remote Client Source Code*

```java
package com.projst.client;

import java.rmi.RemoteException;

import javax.ejb.CreateException;
import javax.naming.NamingException;

import com.projst.ticket.service.TicketService;
import com.projst.ticket.service.TicketServiceHome;
import com.projst.ticket.service.TicketServiceUtil;

/**
 * Remote TicketService (Session Bean) client.
 * @author cjudd
 */
public class Main {

  /**
   * Application main entry point.
   * @param args command-line arguments
   */
  public static void main(String[] args) {
      try {

          TicketServiceHome home = TicketServiceUtil.getHome();
          TicketService service = home.create();
          String result = service.ping("ping");
          System.out.println(result);

      } catch (NamingException e) {
          e.printStackTrace();
      } catch (RemoteException e) {
          e.printStackTrace();
      } catch (CreateException e) {
          e.printStackTrace();
      }
      System.out.println("\nDone");
  }
}
```

Notice in Listing 8-11 that the main method uses the TicketServiceUtil class generated by XDoclet to get a reference to the home interface. Then it uses that home interface to get a reference to the remote interface `TicketService`. With the remote interface reference, it calls the `ping` method and prints the result.

If you run the application at this point, you will receive a `javax.naming.NoInitialContextException` because JNDI does not know which implementation of JNDI it should use to look up the home interface, and it does not know where the JNDI server is. The easiest way to resolve this problem is to create a `jndi.properties` file in the source folder. The contents of your `jndi.properties` file may vary based on the application server or location of the server. Listing 8-12 shows an example of a `jndi.properties` file for JBoss. See your application server documentation for specifics.

Listing 8-12. *JBoss jndi.properties File*

```
java.naming.factory.initial=org.jnp.interfaces.NamingContextFactory
java.naming.provider.url=jnp://localhost:1099
java.naming.factory.url.pkgs=org.jboss.naming:org.jnp.interfaces
```

The JNDI configuration in Listing 8-12 tells the JNDI initial context to use the JBoss implementation. It also says the server is running on the same machine as the client.

When the application is executed, you should see a message that says `pong: ping at` followed by the current date and time. This proves the client was able to make a remote call to the TicketService session bean and get the result back.

Summary

In this chapter, we reviewed JST's support for the most common type of EJBs, the stateless session bean, as well its cousin, the stateful session bean. In order to generate all the interfaces and deployment descriptors, we showed you how JST uses annotations, specifically XDoclet annotations, to manage the complexities of keeping all the files in sync. In the next two chapters, we will demonstrate how to create entity and message-driven beans. Then in Chapter 11, we will discuss how to package, deploy, and debug EJBs in a J2EE application server.

CHAPTER 9

Entity Beans

Entity beans are the most controversial aspect of the Enterprise JavaBeans (EJB) and J2EE Specifications. They are responsible for managing persistence of business objects to a datasource, usually a relational database. Due to performance and scalability problems, entity beans have given EJBs a bad name. But unfortunately, unless you want to hand-code SQL and JDBC calls, entity beans are the only means defined in the EJB 2.1 and J2EE 1.4 specifications for persisting objects. That is not to say there are no other options outside the specifications for persisting Java objects. In fact, Java has another persistence specification called Java Data Objects (JDO); see http://java.sun.com/products/jdo/ for more information. There are also a number of open source and commercial object-to-relational mapping frameworks available, including the popular open source Hibernate framework (http://www.hibernate.org/) from the JBoss group.

The Java persistence space is rapidly changing. As of this writing, the finishing touches are being placed on the EJB 3.0 Specification (JSR 220), which will change Java persistence once again. One of the EJB 3.0 Specification goals is to merge EJB and JDO into a common persistence model that works within a J2EE application server as well as for a simple J2SE application.

This chapter begins with an overview of the entity bean technology. Unfortunately, at the time of this writing, the JST does not have wizard support for entity beans. However, it does have annotation support for them. So, we will use the session bean wizards to create the base entity bean and then modify the bean to become an entity bean.

Note Entity 2.1 support is scheduled to be added to the WTP 1.0 release due in December 2005. After the WTP 1.0 release, support for entity 3.0 is scheduled to begin.

Entity Beans Overview

As mentioned in the introduction, entity beans are the primary abstract method of persistence in the EJB 2.0 Specification. Rather than managing connections, writing select and update statements, or interacting directly with a database through JDBC, you interact with an object using its getters and setters. This object represents a business entity such as an employee, ticket, or customer. Typically, each entity bean instance represents a row in the database. Each attribute (getter and setter) maps to a column of the database as shown in Figure 9-1.

Figure 9-1. *Mapping between entity bean attributes and columns in a database*

Figure 9-1 shows the relationship between the entity bean's (TicketBean's) attributes, and the columns of the ticket table. Notice the database columns of SUMMARY, SUBMITTED, and DETAIL map directly to the getters and setters of the same name on the bean. You may also notice the ID column only maps to a getter. There is no setter for the ID column because according to the ticket table definition, the ID column is automatically generated by the database and therefore can never be set.

Note If you don't have a relational database available, we recommend using Apache Derby. We will be using it throughout this chapter. See Appendix A for Apache Derby installation and configuration instructions.

Each entity bean must define a primary key to uniquely identify an instance of the entity. The primary key can be a specialized class or a standard Java class such as java.lang.String or java.lang.Integer. Specialized primary key classes may represent a single or compound field in the database and by convention have a class name that ends in PK. For example, the TicketBean in Figure 9-1 could have a TicketPK class as its primary key rather than java.lang.Integer. Specialized primary keys must override the equals and hashcode methods so they can be used to look up entity beans from internal caches. They must also be serializable and contain a zero argument constructor so they can be sent across the network. In addition, it is a good idea to override the toString method to print out something descriptive. This can make debugging easier because the application server will call it when throwing exceptions.

There are two types of entity bean persistence mechanisms: container-managed persistence (CMP) and bean-managed persistence (BMP). For CMP, the EJB container or application server is responsible for managing the persistence and all the entity bean life cycle methods. When the bean is deployed, the application server generates the SQL code for the mapping between the

CHAPTER 9 ENTITY BEANS 121

table and bean attributes. The mapping is defined in the deployment descriptors, both standard and container specific.

The developer does not have to allow the container to manage persistence. If a developer prefers, he or she can code the SQL in the bean life cycle methods. This is referred to as BMP and is commonly practiced when the datasource has a schema that does not map well to the entity. For example, an entity may have its attributes defined in multiple tables. This often happens in nonrelational legacy datasources. To implement BMP, you must write and execute SQL in the entity life cycle methods of `ejbCreate`, `ejbRemove`, `ejbFind`, `ejbLoad`, and `ejbStore`. Table 9-1 shows the type of SQL statement that should be executed in each of the life cycle methods.

Table 9-1. *Entity Life Cycle Method to SQL Statement Mapping*

Life Cycle Method	SQL Statement
ejbCreate	INSERT
ejbRemove	DELETE
ejbFind	SELECT
ejbLoad	SELECT
ejbStore	UPDATE

CMP is generally preferred over BMP by the EJB 2.1 Specification and application server vendors. This is because CMP provides more independence from the datasource. With CMP, it is not possible for database vendor-specific SQL to accidentally be introduced. This makes migrating an application to a new database easier. In addition, CMP commonly has better performance because the application server vendor can take advantage of special optimizations. Because of the CMP preference, the remainder of this chapter focuses on CMP rather than BMP.

Like session beans, entity beans can expose their getters and setters to both remote and local clients. Remember from Chapter 8 that remote clients are clients that live in a different VM from the bean, whereas local clients live in the same VM as the bean. However, unlike with session beans, exposing entity bean getters and setters remotely is never a good idea. This is referred to as *fine-grain access* and is the primary reason entity beans suffer from performance problems. The performance problems stem from each call to a getter or setter being a separate remote method call, which incurs all the network overhead. For example, if a client wanted to display the ID, summary, details, and submitted date of a trouble ticket, it would require five remote calls. One remote call would be made to find the entity and four others to call the getter methods. Instead, only *course-grain access* should be used for remote EJBs using the Session Façade and Data Transfer Object patterns (see the "Session Façade Pattern" sidebar in Chapter 8). Fortunately, XDoclet helps implement this pattern by generating a data object that represents our entity bean. It even provides a convenience method on the entity bean to get the data object.

Like a local session bean, a local entity bean requires a local interface, a local home interface, a bean class, and some deployment descriptors. The local interface must extend the `javax.ejb.EJBLocalObject` (see Listing 9-11 later in this chapter). The local interface contains getters and setters for each of the entity bean attributes.

A local entity bean also requires a local home interface (see Listing 9-10 later in this chapter). The local home interface must extend `javax.ejb.EJBLocalHome`. The local home interface contains methods for controlling the life cycle of an entity bean. For example, it typically contains one or more create methods, finder methods, and a remove method. The create methods are called when a new entity is required. Under the covers it performs an insert in the datasource with the data it is provided. All columns in the table that have a `NOT NULL` constraint should be passed into the create method and set on the entity bean or defaulted in the create method. Otherwise, when the record is inserted, an exception will be thrown stating the table constraints have been violated. The finder methods are used to locate and load the entities into memory. They may return a single local interface or a collection of local interfaces. At a minimum, there is a `findByPrimaryKey` method required, which the application server implements on your behalf. Other finder methods may require a specialized SQL syntax called EJB Query Language, or EJB QL, to be set in the deployment descriptors. Lastly, the remove method permanently removes the entity by deleting the row in the datasource. The home interface must be looked up via JNDI. The JNDI lookup returns an application server–specific proxy implementation that implements the home interface.

In addition to the standard `ejb-jar.xml` deployment descriptor and a container-specific EJB deployment descriptor, CMP entity beans also require a container-specific CMP deployment descriptor. The CMP deployment descriptor defines the bean-to-table mappings as well as the field-to-column mappings. Depending on the application server, it may also contain optimization hints, generated key hints, and instructions to create the tables if they do not exist. See your application server documentation for specifics.

Tip If you want to learn more about entity beans, we suggest you read *Beginning J2EE 1.4: From Novice to Professional* by James L. Weaver, Kevin Mukhar, and Jim Crume (Apress, 2004) or *Pro J2EE 1.4: From Professional to Expert* by Meeraj Kunnumpurath and Sue Spielman (Apress, 2004).

Writing Entity Beans

As mentioned in the introduction of this chapter, JST does not provide any wizard support for creating entity beans. However, it does include XDoclet support for entity beans. So, we will use the EnterpriseJavaBean wizard to create a session bean and then change it to an entity bean. You could alternatively use the standard Eclipse Class wizard to generate the entity stub and then add the XDoclet annotations if you wish. However, be aware that the XDoclet Builder that runs XDoclet whenever there is a change to the bean class is added to the project at the end of the EnterpriseJavaBean wizard. Therefore, if the first bean you create is an entity bean using the standard Eclipse Class wizard, the glue classes that XDoclet creates will not include the local and local home interfaces as well as the standard deployment descriptors and application server–specific deployment descriptors.

Session Bean Wizard

Assuming you are working in a Flexible project containing a J2EE EJB module and are using the J2EE Perspective, you can invoke the EnterpriseJavaBean wizard using the project's context menu and choosing New ➤ EnterpriseJavaBean. Alternatively, you can use File ➤ New ➤ Other ➤ EJB ➤ EnterpriseJavaBean.

> **Tip** If you are using the EnterpriseJavaBean wizard to create a session bean that will later be modified to become an entity bean, you may want to turn off automatic builds so unnecessary files will not be generated by XDoclet until the session bean has been modified to become an entity bean. To turn off automatic builds, select Project ➤ Build Automatically.

Using this wizard to create an entity bean is a four-step process. It begins by prompting for the type of EJB to create and an annotation provider (see Figure 9-2). The wizard includes support for creating session or message-driven beans by checking the appropriate radio button. Because entity beans are not supported at this time, we will demonstrate generating a session bean. Using the drop-down list, you may choose your preferred annotation provider. At this time, there is not a lot of choice, as WTP only includes support for XDoclet annotations.

Figure 9-2. *The first step in the EnterpriseJavaBean wizard defines the type of bean and annotations to use.*

Underneath the covers, this first step identifies the code templates for generating the initial bean class. WTP uses the Java Emitter Templates (JET) from the Eclipse Modeling Framework (EMF) as the template engine. So a combination of SessionBean and XDoclet options will cause the templates in the `eclipse/plugins/org.eclipse.jst.j2ee.ejb.annotations.xdoclet_1.0.0/templates/ejb/session` directory to be used.

Note If you don't like the way the source code is generated from the EnterpriseJavaBean wizard, you can modify the templates in the directories mentioned previously. These files are read every time the wizard is executed, so you won't have to restart Eclipse. However, in a team environment, managing template changes in the JST plug-in would be difficult. Therefore, it is not recommended. Instead, you could implement your own plug-in using the JST `org.eclipse.jst.j2ee.ejb.annotations.emitter.template` extension point and control your plug-in versioning with an internal Eclipse update site.

The second step in the EnterpriseJavaBean wizard, shown in Figure 9-3, collects information about where the bean source code will be placed as well as standard class information including the package, class name, and class it inherits from.

Figure 9-3. *The second step in the EntpriseJavaBean wizard is used to identify where the output of the wizard goes.*

The first aspect of determining where to put the generated entity bean code is deciding which project it should go in. Depending on how your projects are organized, you may have multiple projects representing different partitions of your application. For example, you may have separate EJB, Web, and Enterprise Application Projects. Or you may have one project with different modules representing your partitions, for example, an Application Project with an EJB module, web module, and enterprise application module. So the Project drop-down menu lists all the open EJB Projects in the workspace. Once a project is selected, the modules in the project will be displayed in the Module Name drop-down menu. If the selected project does not contain a module, a warning message of "The source folder cannot be empty" will appear along the top of the dialog box. The folder must be the source folder of the EJB module. By default, it will contain the correct folder if the wizard is invoked from a Flexible project containing an EJB module. Unfortunately though, the field is not tied to the module name or project. So if either of them is changed, the folder is not automatically updated. Therefore, it is a good idea to use identifiable module names to make them easier to find.

Note The Generate an annotated bean class checkbox does not make a difference in the output of the wizard, since either way it uses the same template, and there is no conditional logic in the template to exclude annotations.

The next step in the EnterpriseJavaBean wizard (see Figure 9-4) prompts for information that initially will populate the annotations but eventually will describe the EJB in the standard EJB deployment descriptors.

Figure 9-4. *The third step in the EnterpriseJavaBean wizard gathers information for the deployment descriptors.*

The EJB name is used to uniquely identify an EJB within the context of the ejb-jar.xml deployment descriptor. It is primarily used for defining the relationships between the EJB and other elements in the deployment descriptors. The JNDI name is used to look up the local home interface from the JNDI context. The mechanism for mapping EJBs to JNDI names is not in the EJB Specification and is therefore not included in the standard EJB deployment descriptors. Most application servers include an application server–specific deployment descriptor that contains the application server–specific JNDI element. Some application servers, for example JBoss, use the EJB name by default as the JNDI name if the JNDI name is not explicitly defined. It is not uncommon to see JNDI names that match the EJB names as in Figure 9-4 where both the EJB name and JNDI name are Ticket. It is also not uncommon to see JNDI names that provide additional context like ejb/Ticket, ejb/entity/Ticket, or entity/Ticket.

Note Because the JNDI name is a vendor-specific setting and some application servers can work without a vendor-specific deployment descriptor, it is easy to create an EJB with a JNDI name other than the default and have it appear in the application server JNDI tree as the default. Or worse, try to look up the EJB and get a `javax.naming.NamingException` thrown even though you are looking up the JNDI name in the bean's annotations. To resolve this issue, make sure the vendor-specific deployment descriptor is being generated by going to Window ➤ Preferences ➤ J2EE Annotations ➤ XDoclet ➤ ejbdoclet and choosing the correct application server checkbox and the appropriate version from the drop-down menu. Before redeploying, you will need to regenerate the deployment descriptors by modifying and saving the bean class or explicitly rebuilding.

The display name and description are both optional elements of the EJB standard deployment descriptors. Some development tools and application servers may opt to display this additional information.

At this point, you also get to choose what type of state and transactions you want for your entity bean. The values in the drop-down list for state type are session bean specific. Later, we will change the generated annotation to CMP to make the bean container managed. For transaction type, you determine whether your entity bean transactions will be managed by the container (by choosing the Container option) or whether you will manage transactions yourself in code (by choosing the Bean option).

The final step in the EnterpriseJavaBean wizard, shown in Figure 9-5, is the standard Java Class page. It collects information about the class's modifiers, interfaces, and methods you want stubbed.

At this time, the last step in the process is more informational than useful. All the settings on this page are ignored. Therefore, changing the interfaces from `javax.ejb.SessionBean` to `javax.ejb.EntityBean` will not save any time in converting the resulting session bean to an entity bean.

Figure 9-5. *The fourth step in the EnterpriseJavaBean wizard is the Eclipse standard Class page.*

Upon completing the wizard, a session bean similar to the one shown in Listing 9-1 will be generated, complete with XDoclet annotations.

Listing 9-1. *Generated Session Bean*

```
/**
 *
 */
package com.projst.ticket.entity;

/**
 *
 * <!-- begin-user-doc -->
 * A generated session bean
 * <!-- end-user-doc -->
 * *
 * <!-- begin-xdoclet-definition -->
 * @ejb.bean name="Ticket"
 *           description="An entity bean for persisting Tickets"
 *           display-name="Ticket"
 *           jndi-name="Ticket"
```

```
 *              type="Stateless"
 *              transaction-type="Container"
 *
 * <!-- end-xdoclet-definition -->
 * @generated
 */

public abstract class TicketBean implements javax.ejb.SessionBean {

  /**
   *
   * <!-- begin-xdoclet-definition -->
   * @ejb.interface-method view-type="remote"
   * <!-- end-xdoclet-definition -->
   * @generated
   *
   * //TODO: Must provide implementation for bean method stub
   */
  public String foo(String param) {
    return null;
  }
}
```

Listing 9-1 is the session bean implementation you will need to modify to make an entity bean. The next section explains how to convert the session bean to an entity bean.

Converting a Session Bean to an Entity Bean

There are not a lot of changes required to convert the session bean to an entity bean. It requires changing some XDoclet annotations and the interface the bean implements, and removing the stubbed method. Listing 9-2 highlights the required changes.

Listing 9-2. *Hightlighted Changes Made to Session Bean to Make It an Entity Bean*

```
/**
 *
 */
package com.projst.ticket.entity;

/**
 *
 * <!-- begin-user-doc -->
 * A generated session bean
 * <!-- end-user-doc -->
 * *
 * <!-- begin-xdoclet-definition -->
 * @ejb.bean name="Ticket"
```

```
*            description="An entity bean for persisting Tickets"
*            display-name="Ticket"
*            jndi-name="Ticket"
*            type="CMP"
*            transaction-type="Container"
*            view-type="local"
*            cmp-version="2.x"
*            schema="ticket"
*
* @jboss.persistence table-name = "TICKET"
*                    datasource = "java:/jdbc/ticket"
*                    datasource-mapping = "Derby"
*                    create-table = "false"
*                    alter-table = "false"
*                    remove-table = "false"
* <!-- end-xdoclet-definition -->
* @generated
*/

public abstract class TicketBean implements javax.ejb.EntityBean {

}
```

In Listing 9-2, the first required modification is to change the type from the session bean–specific type of Stateless to the entity type of CMP in order to make the container do most of the work. The next step is to add three new attributes, view-type, schema, and cmp-version. The view-type attribute was added to specify which interfaces get generated. The default is to create both remote and local interfaces. But as the "Entity Beans Overview" section states, remotely accessing entity beans is a bad practice. Therefore, the view-type should be used to restrict remote access by only generating local interfaces. The cmp-version is used to specify the container-managed persistence version of the entity bean and can be either 1.x or 2.x. Entity beans with a CMP version of 2.x must also have an abstract schema name. The schema attribute specifies the abstract schema name used in EJB QL queries. The value is commonly the name of the bean.

Some application server–specific XDoclet annotations at the class level may be required as well depending on your application server. The annotations are used to complete the mappings in the generated application server–specific deployment descriptors. Listing 9-2 shows some of the JBoss CMP annotations. @jboss.persistence identifies the table the bean maps to, the datasource's JNDI name for looking up the connection, and the datasource mapping. The datasource mapping is the database name that the application server uses to map data types. There are also attributes that give instructions on what to do with the tables; create-table, alter-table, and remove-table. create-table will automatically create the table at deployment time if the table does not exist. alter-table automatically changes the table definition if it does not have columns that match. Finally, remove-table can be used to automatically remove the table and all of its data from the database when the application shuts down.

Tip Removing `<!--begin-user-doc-->` improves the readability of the hover-over Javadoc help. It does not have any effect on the HTML produced by Javadoc, because the browser treats it as an HTML comment.

After updating XDoclet annotations, you must change the bean to implement the `javax.ejb.EntityBean` interface rather than `javax.ejb.SessionBean`. In addition, you can remove the stubbed-out `foo` method and its XDoclet annotations. Now you are ready to add functionality to the entity bean.

Add Entity Bean Functionality

Now that you have an entity bean, you can add its attributes, create methods, and finder methods. You also need to add some container-specific XDoclet notations. Optionally, you can add convenience methods for converting the Data Transfer Object to the entity bean and back.

Typically, entity beans contain attributes that map to columns of a database. So, in order to know the attributes that must exist on an entity bean, it is helpful to know what columns exist in the database. See Listing 9-3 for the DDL used to create the `ticket` table the `TicketBean` maps to.

Listing 9-3. *Create Ticket Table DDL*

```
CREATE TABLE ticket (
  id BIGINT NOT NULL GENERATED ALWAYS AS IDENTITY primary key,
  summary VARCHAR(512) NOT NULL,
  detail VARCHAR(2000),
  submitted TIMESTAMP,
  lastModified TIMESTAMP,
)
```

In the create ticket table DDL in Listing 9-3, you can see that the `ticket` table has five columns. The first column is the `id` column, which is denoted as an auto-generated primary key. You will soon learn that these constraints have an impact on how you define the `id` attribute on the bean. The `ticket` table also has a `summary` column, which must not contain null values. To ensure a newly created `TicketBean` does not have a null summary value, you will provide an implementation of a create method that requires a summary. The remainder of the columns are not very interesting and only require getters and setters on the bean.

Declaring bean attributes is accomplished by creating `public abstract` getters and setters as well as some XDoclet annotations. Private fields or method implementations are not necessary because the application server will extend the entity bean and provide the implementation it sees fit. Listing 9-4 contains the attribute declarations of the `TicketBean`.

Listing 9-4. *TicketBean Attributes*

```
/**
 * @ejb.interface-method
 * @ejb.persistence
 *     column-name="ID"
 *     jdbc-type="BIGINT"
 */
```

```java
public abstract Integer getId();

/**
 * @ejb.interface-method
 * @ejb.persistence
 *     column-name="SUMMARY"
 *     jdbc-type="VARCHAR"
 */
public abstract String getSummary();

/**
 * @ejb.interface-method
 */
public abstract void setSummary(String summary);

/**
 * @ejb.interface-method
 * @ejb.persistence
 *     column-name="DETAIL"
 *     jdbc-type="VARCHAR"
 */
public abstract String getDetail();

/**
 * @ejb.interface-method
 */
public abstract void setDetail(String detail);

/**
 * @ejb.interface-method
 * @ejb.persistence
 *     column-name="SUBMITTED"
 *     jdbc-type="TIMESTAMP"
 */
public abstract Timestamp getSubmitted();

/**
 * @ejb.interface-method
 */
public abstract void setSubmitted(Date date);

/**
 * @ejb.interface-method
 * @ejb.persistence
 *     column-name="LASTMODIFIED"
 *     jdbc-type="TIMESTAMP"
 */
```

```
public abstract Timestamp getLastModified();

/**
 * @ejb.interface-method
 */
public abstract void setLastModified(Date date);
```

Notice in Listing 9-4 that all the getters and setters have a common @ejb.interface-method annotation. This annotation adds the method to the local interface. All the getter methods also have an @ejb.persistence, which is used to map the attribute to the column name and identify the JDBC data type. When XDoclet is run, this information will be used to map the fields and columns in the ejb-jar.xml and in most container-specific CMP deployment descriptors.

The first attribute declaration in Listing 9-4 is the primary key, id. Notice id only includes a getter. As you learned earlier, the ID is automatically generated by the database, and once it is initialized it cannot be changed. In addition to adding the getter method for the id column, an additional XDoclet attribute must be added to the @ejb.bean annotation to identify the primary key field (see Listing 9-5) and, depending on your application server, you may also require some other XDoclet annotations.

Listing 9-5. *@ejb.bean Identifying the Primary Key Field*

```
/**
 * <!-- begin-xdoclet-definition -->
 * @ejb.bean name="Ticket"
 *           description="An entity bean for persisting Tickets"
 *           display-name="Ticket"
 *           jndi-name="Ticket"
 *           type="CMP"
 *           transaction-type="Container"
 *           view-type="local"
 *           schema="ticket"
 *           cmp-version="2.x"
 *           primkey-field="id"
 *
 * @jboss.persistence table-name = "TICKET"
 *                    datasource = "java:/jdbc/ticket"
 *                    datasource-mapping = "Derby"
 *                    create-table = "false"
 *                    alter-table = "false"
 *                    remove-table = "false"
 *
 * @jboss.unknown-pk class="java.lang.Integer"
 *                   readonly="true"
 *                   column-name="ID"
 *                   auto-increment="true"
 * @jboss.entity-command name="get-generated-keys"
 *     class="org.jboss.ejb.plugins.cmp.jdbc.keygen.JDBC30GeneratedKeysCreateCommand"
 *
```

```
 * <!-- end-xdoclet-definition -->
 * @generated
 */
```

Listing 9-5 shows the JBoss-specific XDoclet attributes used to instruct JBoss how to handle the id field since it is auto-generated. @jboss.unknown-pk is necessary because at the time the create methods are called, it does not know the value of the primary key. It is not until the record is inserted does it get an ID. The class attribute defines the Java type of the primary key. The readonly attribute tells JBoss to treat it as a read-only field. The column-name identifies the column in the database that stores the primary key, and the auto-increment says the column will be auto-incremented.

The other thing JBoss needs to know is how to determine what the auto-generated key value is after the record is inserted. The @jboss.entity-command annotation is used for that. In the Listing 9-5 example, the org.jboss.ejb.plugins.cmp.jdbc.keygen.JDBC30GeneratedKeys➡ CreateCommand class is used. This class relies on the JDBC 3.0 getGeneratedKeys method to obtain the value from the identity column.

In order to initialize the bean and the database record, you can add an ejbCreate method. Listing 9-6 shows the ejbCreate method for the TicketBean that initializes the nonnull fields.

Listing 9-6. *TicketBean ejbCreate Method*

```
/**
 * @ejb.create-method
 */
public Integer ejbCreate(String summary) throws javax.ejb.CreateException {
  setSummary(summary);
  Date date = new Date();
  Timestamp now = new Timestamp(date.getTime());
  setSubmitted(now);
  setLastModified(now);
  return null;
}
```

Notice in Listing 9-6 that the ejbCreate method is annotated with an @ejb.create-method. This annotation instructs XDoclet to generate a corresponding create method in the local home interface. According to the EJB 2.1 Specification, an ejbCreate method must return a type equivalent to the primary key type and return the value of null if it is a CMP bean. This ejbCreate method takes a single parameter, which is used to set the only nonnull column, summary. It also uses the current date and time to initialize the submitted and last modified timestamps. This bean could have additional ejbCreate methods to initialize other attributes of the bean.

Adding a finder method to an entity bean is easy with XDoclet annotations. It does not even require any coding. By adding an @ejb.finder annotation to the bean class, a finder method is added to the local home interface (see Listing 9-7).

Listing 9-7. *Finder Method Annotation*

```
@ejb.finder
    signature="java.util.Collection findAll()"
    query="SELECT OBJECT(a) FROM ticket AS a"
```

Listing 9-7 demonstrates how to add a finder method that returns all instances of the tickets. The `signature` attribute defines the method signature of the finder method added to the local home interface. In this case, the `findAll` method will return a collection of local ticket entity bean interfaces. The query `attribute` contains EJB QL for selecting all the tickets from the `ticket` table.

The last things you may want to add to an entity bean are optional convenience methods for converting the entity bean to a Data Transfer Object and a Data Transfer Object back to an entity bean. XDoclet automatically generates a Data Transfer Object named after the bean with "Data" appended. XDoclet manages keeping the Data Transfer Object in sync with the entity bean. XDoclet can also generate `getData` and `setData` methods for copying the data to a transfer object and back to the entity bean. Listing 9-8 shows the necessary code.

Listing 9-8. *Data Transfer Object Convenience Methods*

```
/**
 * Provides access to the generated getData() method of the generated CMP class.
 * @ejb.interface-method
 */
public abstract TicketData getData();

/**
 * Provides access to the generated setData() method of the generated CMP class.
 * @ejb.interface-method
 */
public abstract void setData(TicketData data);
```

By adding the abstract `getData` and `setData` methods with an XDoclet annotation of `@ejb.interface-method` as shown in Listing 9-8, XDoclet will automatically generate the convenience methods and expose them as methods on the local interface.

Now that the entity bean is complete, you are ready for XDoclet to generate the glue. In the next section, we will review those classes, interfaces, and deployment descriptors.

Tip If you turned off the automatic builds based on the earlier tip, you should turn this feature back on now. To turn on automatic builds, select Project ➤ Build Automatically. If not, you should delete the session class that was generated when XDoclet thought you were building a session bean.

Generated Entity Files

Once a build occurs, the XDoclet Builder will launch and generate a bunch of new files. You will probably notice the XDoclet Builder running because the output is displayed in the console window. This process will produce a CMP class that extends the bean class, a local home interface, a local interface, a Data Transfer Object, and a utility class (all presented in Listing 9-9 through Listing 9-13, respectively, later in this chapter) in the EJB client module. It will also update the standard ejb-jar.xml deployment descriptor and possibly vendor-specific deployment descriptors (depending on your J2EE annotation configurations) if they exist or create them if they don't. The deployment descriptors are found in the EJB module's META-INF directory.

The class shown earlier in Listing 9-2 is not a true entity bean yet because it does not implement all the life cycle methods (ejbActivate, ejbPassivate, setEntityContext, unsetEnitiyContext, ejbRemove, ejbPostCreate) required by the javax.ejb.EnityBean interface. This is the reason the bean class is declared as abstract. In order to complete the entity bean, the XDoclet Builder generates a descendent of the bean class (see Figure 9-6 and Listing 9-9).

Figure 9-6. *Inherited relationship between the bean and generated session class*

Figure 9-6 shows the relationship of the bean class and the generated CMP class. The CMP class extends the bean class and implements life cycle methods as well as the getData and setData convenience methods. Looking at Listing 9-9, you can see the implementations of the life cycle methods are simply empty blocks.

As you can see from the UML class diagram in Figure 9-6, the separation of the bean and CMP classes makes for a clean separation of business attributes and what are typically just boilerplate life cycle methods. The business attributes like getSummary in this example belong in the bean class, and the life cycle methods belong in the CMP class.

Listing 9-9. *CMP Class That Extends the Bean Class*

```
/*
 * Generated by XDoclet - Do not edit!
 */
package com.projst.ticket.entity;

/**
 * CMP layer for Ticket.
 * @generated
 * @wtp generated
 */
public abstract class TicketCMP
    extends com.projst.ticket.entity.TicketBean
    implements javax.ejb.EntityBean
{

  public com.projst.ticket.entity.TicketData getData()
  {
    com.projst.ticket.entity.TicketData dataHolder = null;
    try
    {
      dataHolder = new com.projst.ticket.entity.TicketData();

      dataHolder.setId( getId() );
      dataHolder.setSummary( getSummary() );
      dataHolder.setDetail( getDetail() );
      dataHolder.setSubmitted( getSubmitted() );
      dataHolder.setLastModified( getLastModified() );

    }
    catch (RuntimeException e)
    {
        throw new javax.ejb.EJBException(e);
    }

    return dataHolder;
  }
```

```java
  public void setData( com.projst.ticket.entity.TicketData dataHolder )
  {
    try
    {
      setSummary( dataHolder.getSummary() );
      setDetail( dataHolder.getDetail() );
      setSubmitted( dataHolder.getSubmitted() );
      setLastModified( dataHolder.getLastModified() );
    }
    catch (Exception e)
    {
      throw new javax.ejb.EJBException(e);
    }
  }

/**
 * Generated ejbPostCreate for corresponding ejbCreate method.
 *
 * @see #ejbCreate(java.lang.String summary)
 */
public void ejbPostCreate(java.lang.String summary) {}

public void ejbLoad() {}

public void ejbStore() {}

public void ejbActivate() {}

public void ejbPassivate() {}

public void setEntityContext(javax.ejb.EntityContext ctx) {}

public void unsetEntityContext() {}

public void ejbRemove() throws javax.ejb.RemoveException {}

/* Value Objects BEGIN */

/* Value Objects END */

public abstract java.lang.Integer getId() ;
public abstract void setId( java.lang.Integer id ) ;

public abstract java.lang.String getSummary() ;
public abstract void setSummary( java.lang.String summary ) ;

public abstract java.lang.String getDetail() ;
public abstract void setDetail( java.lang.String detail ) ;
```

```
public abstract java.sql.Timestamp getSubmitted() ;
public abstract void setSubmitted( java.sql.Timestamp submitted ) ;

public abstract java.sql.Timestamp getLastModified() ;
public abstract void setLastModified( java.sql.Timestamp lastModified ) ;

}
```

Notice in Listing 9-9 that the file begins with a comment stating this file was generated by XDoclet and should not be edited. If you do decide to edit this file to provide functionality to the life cycle methods, your implementation will be overwritten the next time the XDoclet Builder runs. So, if you need to add functionality to the life cycle methods, implement the specific life cycle method in the bean class. When the CMP class gets regenerated, it will include a call to the superimplementation, which is the bean class.

Because the @ejb.bean view-type has a value of local, XDoclet generates a local interface (see Listing 9-10) and a local home interface (see Listing 9-11). These files are generated in the EJB client module because the client will need access to them at compile time and runtime. Just like the CMP class, these classes should not be modified because XDoclet will just overwrite them.

Listing 9-10. *Generated Local Home Interface*

```
/*
 * Generated by XDoclet - Do not edit!
 */
package com.projst.ticket.entity;

/**
 * Local home interface for Ticket.
 * @generated
 * @wtp generated
 */
public interface TicketLocalHome
   extends javax.ejb.EJBLocalHome
{
  public static final String COMP_NAME="java:comp/env/ejb/TicketLocal";
  public static final String JNDI_NAME="TicketLocal";

  public com.projst.ticket.entity.TicketLocal create(java.lang.String summary)
      throws javax.ejb.CreateException;

  public java.util.Collection findAll()
      throws javax.ejb.FinderException;

  public com.projst.ticket.entity.TicketLocal findByPrimaryKey(java.lang.Integer pk)
      throws javax.ejb.FinderException;

}
```

Listing 9-11. *Generated Local Interface*

```
/*
 * Generated by XDoclet - Do not edit!
 */
package com.projst.ticket.entity;

/**
 * Local interface for Ticket.
 * @generated
 * @wtp generated
 */
public interface TicketLocal
   extends javax.ejb.EJBLocalObject
{

  public java.lang.Integer getId( ) ;

  public java.lang.String getSummary( ) ;

  public void setSummary( java.lang.String summary ) ;

  public java.lang.String getDetail( ) ;

  public void setDetail( java.lang.String detail ) ;

  public java.sql.Timestamp getSubmitted( ) ;

  public void setSubmitted( java.sql.Timestamp date ) ;

  public java.sql.Timestamp getLastModified( ) ;

  public void setLastModified( java.sql.Timestamp date ) ;

  /**
   * Provides access to the generated getData() method of the generated CMP class.
   */
  public com.projst.ticket.entity.TicketData getData( ) ;

  /**
   * Provides access to the generated setData() method of the generated CMP class.
   */
  public void setData( com.projst.ticket.entity.TicketData data ) ;
}
```

The generated local home interface shown in Listing 9-10 is used by clients running inside the application server, typically a session bean, to get a reference to a local entity bean. This interface contains a create method that corresponds to the ejbCreate method in Listing 9-6.

When called, it creates a new record in the database and loads the new entity bean into memory. The local home interface also contains the required findByPrimaryKey method implemented by the container and the findAll method created by the annotation in Listing 9-7. In addition, it provides two convenience constants: the COMP_NAME constant is the bean's component name, and the JNDI_NAME constant is the bean's JNDI name. These constants should be used by the client when looking up the bean. This way, if the names ever change, the client code does not need to be updated because XDoclet will change the value of the constants. These constants are also used by the utility class discussed later.

Listing 9-11 shows the generated local interface. This interface is used by clients running inside of the application server, typically session beans. This interface exposes the methods declared as @interface-method in the bean. This includes the entity bean's attributes as well as the get and set data methods.

In order to support the Session Façade pattern, XDoclet generates a Data Transfer Object. Listing 9-12 shows the Data Transfer Object found in the TicketData.java file.

Listing 9-12. *Generated Data Transfer Object*

```
/*
 * Generated by XDoclet - Do not edit!
 */
package com.projst.ticket.entity;

/**
 * Data object for Ticket.
 * @generated
 * @wtp generated
 */
public class TicketData
   extends java.lang.Object
   implements java.io.Serializable
{
  private java.lang.Integer id;
  private java.lang.String summary;
  private java.lang.String detail;
  private java.sql.Timestamp submitted;
  private java.sql.Timestamp lastModified;

  /* begin value object */

  /* end value object */

  public TicketData() {}

   public TicketData(java.lang.Integer id,
       java.lang.String summary,java.lang.String detail,
       java.sql.Timestamp submitted,java.sql.Timestamp lastModified )
   {
```

```java
    this.id = id;
    setSummary(summary);
    setDetail(detail);
    setSubmitted(submitted);
    setLastModified(lastModified);
  }

  public TicketData( TicketData otherData )
  {
    this.id = otherData.id;
    setSummary(otherData.getSummary());
    setDetail(otherData.getDetail());
    setSubmitted(otherData.getSubmitted());
    setLastModified(otherData.getLastModified());
  }

  public java.lang.Integer getPrimaryKey() { return  getId(); }

  public java.lang.Integer getId() { return this.id; }
  public void setId( java.lang.Integer id ) { this.id = id; }

  public java.lang.String getSummary() { return this.summary; }
  public void setSummary( java.lang.String summary ) { this.summary = summary; }

  public java.lang.String getDetail() { return this.detail; }
  public void setDetail( java.lang.String detail ) { this.detail = detail; }

  public java.sql.Timestamp getSubmitted() { return this.submitted; }
  public void setSubmitted( java.sql.Timestamp submitted )
  {
    this.submitted = submitted;
  }

  public java.sql.Timestamp getLastModified() { return this.lastModified; }
  public void setLastModified( java.sql.Timestamp lastModified )
  {
    this.lastModified = lastModified;
  }

  public String toString()
  {
    StringBuffer str = new StringBuffer("{");

    str.append("id=" + getId() + " " + "summary=" + getSummary() + " " +
        "detail=" + getDetail() + " " + "submitted=" + getSubmitted() + " " +
        "lastModified=" + getLastModified());
    str.append('}');
```

```
      return(str.toString());
    }

    public boolean equals( Object pOther )
    {
      if( pOther instanceof TicketData )
      {
        TicketData lTest = (TicketData) pOther;
        boolean lEquals = true;

        if( this.id == null )
        {
          lEquals = lEquals && ( lTest.id == null );
        } else {
          lEquals = lEquals && this.id.equals( lTest.id );
        }
        if( this.summary == null )
        {
          lEquals = lEquals && ( lTest.summary == null );
        } else {
          lEquals = lEquals && this.summary.equals( lTest.summary );
        }
        if( this.detail == null )
        {
          lEquals = lEquals && ( lTest.detail == null );
        } else {
          lEquals = lEquals && this.detail.equals( lTest.detail );
        }
        if( this.submitted == null )
        {
          lEquals = lEquals && ( lTest.submitted == null );
        } else {
          lEquals = lEquals && this.submitted.equals( lTest.submitted );
        }
        if( this.lastModified == null )
        {
          lEquals = lEquals && ( lTest.lastModified == null );
        } else {
          lEquals = lEquals && this.lastModified.equals( lTest.lastModified );
        }

        return lEquals;
      }
      else
      {
          return false;
      }
    }
  }
```

```
public int hashCode()
{
  int result = 17;

  result = 37*result + ((this.id != null) ? this.id.hashCode() : 0);

  result = 37*result + ((this.summary != null) ? this.summary.hashCode() : 0);

  result = 37*result + ((this.detail != null) ? this.detail.hashCode() : 0);

  result = 37*result + ((this.submitted != null) ? this.submitted.hashCode(): 0);

  result = 37*result +
      ((this.lastModified != null) ? this.lastModified.hashCode() : 0);

  return result;
}

}
```

The Data Transfer Object shown in Listing 9-12 contains corresponding getters and setters for all the exposed entity bean attributes. XDoclet ensures that as attributes are added to or removed from the entity bean, they are added or removed from the Data Transfer Object. In addition to the getters and setters, the Data Transfer Object also contains three constructors as well as the overridden toString, equals, and hashCode.

XDoclet also generates a utility class (see Listing 9-13). The utility class contains methods for looking up both local home interfaces. In addition, it includes a utility method for generating globally unique identifiers (GUIDs).

Listing 9-13. *Generated Utility Class*

```
/*
 * Generated file - Do not edit!
 */
package com.projst.ticket.entity;

/**
 * Utility class for Ticket.
 * @generated
 * @wtp generated
 */
public class TicketUtil
{
  /**
   * Cached local home (EJBLocalHome). Uses lazy loading to obtain its
   * value (loaded by getLocalHome() methods).
   */
  private static com.projst.ticket.entity.TicketLocalHome cachedLocalHome = null;
```

```java
private static Object lookupHome(java.util.Hashtable environment,
    String jndiName, Class narrowTo) throws javax.naming.NamingException {
  // Obtain initial context
  javax.naming.InitialContext initialContext =
      new javax.naming.InitialContext(environment);
  try {
    Object objRef = initialContext.lookup(jndiName);
    // only narrow if necessary
    if (narrowTo.isInstance(java.rmi.Remote.class))
      return javax.rmi.PortableRemoteObject.narrow(objRef, narrowTo);
    else
      return objRef;
  } finally {
    initialContext.close();
  }
}


// Home interface lookup methods

/**
 * Obtain local home interface from default initial context
 * @return Local home interface for Ticket. Lookup using JNDI_NAME
 */
public static com.projst.ticket.entity.TicketLocalHome getLocalHome()
    throws javax.naming.NamingException
{
  if (cachedLocalHome == null) {
    cachedLocalHome = (com.projst.ticket.entity.TicketLocalHome) lookupHome(
        null, com.projst.ticket.entity.TicketLocalHome.JNDI_NAME,
        com.projst.ticket.entity.TicketLocalHome.class);
  }
  return cachedLocalHome;
}


/** Cached per JVM server IP. */
private static String hexServerIP = null;

// initialize the secure random instance
private static final java.security.SecureRandom seeder =
    new java.security.SecureRandom();

/**
 * A 32 byte GUID generator (Globally Unique ID). These artificial keys
 * SHOULD <strong>NOT </strong> be seen by the user, not even touched by the
 * DBA but with very rare exceptions, just manipulated by the database and
 * the programs.
 *
```

```java
 * Usage: Add an id field (type java.lang.String) to your EJB, and
 * add setId(XXXUtil.generateGUID(this)); to the ejbCreate method.
 */
public static final String generateGUID(Object o) {
  StringBuffer tmpBuffer = new StringBuffer(16);
  if (hexServerIP == null) {
    java.net.InetAddress localInetAddress = null;
    try {
      // get the inet address
      localInetAddress = java.net.InetAddress.getLocalHost();
    }
    catch (java.net.UnknownHostException uhe) {
      System.err.println("TicketUtil: Could not get the local IP address" +
          " using InetAddress.getLocalHost()!");
      // todo: find better way to get around this...
      uhe.printStackTrace();
      return null;
    }
    byte serverIP[] = localInetAddress.getAddress();
    hexServerIP = hexFormat(getInt(serverIP), 8);
  }

  String hashcode = hexFormat(System.identityHashCode(o), 8);
  tmpBuffer.append(hexServerIP);
  tmpBuffer.append(hashcode);

  long timeNow     = System.currentTimeMillis();
  int timeLow      = (int)timeNow & 0xFFFFFFFF;
  int node         = seeder.nextInt();

  StringBuffer guid = new StringBuffer(32);
  guid.append(hexFormat(timeLow, 8));
  guid.append(tmpBuffer.toString());
  guid.append(hexFormat(node, 8));
  return guid.toString();
}

private static int getInt(byte bytes[]) {
  int i = 0;
  int j = 24;
  for (int k = 0; j >= 0; k++) {
    int l = bytes[k] & 0xff;
    i += l << j;
    j -= 8;
  }
  return i;
}
```

```
private static String hexFormat(int i, int j) {
  String s = Integer.toHexString(i);
  return padHex(s, j) + s;
}

private static String padHex(String s, int i) {
  StringBuffer tmpBuffer = new StringBuffer();
  if (s.length() < i) {
    for (int j = 0; j < i - s.length(); j++) {
      tmpBuffer.append('0');
    }
  }
  return tmpBuffer.toString();
}

}
```

Notice in Listing 9-13 that the lookup method getLocalHome performs a basic JNDI lookup using the javax.naming.InitialContext. There is one caveat, though. This caches the interfaces to improve performance.

The generateGUID method on the utility class generates a 32-bit guaranteed unique identifier. This method can be helpful when the client, especially a remote client, creates instances of an object such as a DTO that must be uniquely identifiable before the instance is passed to the session façade.

XDoclet will also update or create the ejb-jar.xml deployment descriptor and possibly an application server–specific deployment descriptor based on the bean class's annotations. Listing 9-14 shows the entity bean newly added to the enterprise-beans element of ejb-jar.xml, Listing 9-15 shows the entity bean newly added to the enterprise-beans element of the jboss.xml, and Listing 9-16 shows the newly created JBoss CMP deployment descriptor, jbosscmp-jdbc.xml.

Tip There is a short cut to open the ejb-jar.xml file in the J2EE Perspective: right-click the EJB node in the J2EE Perspective and select Open.

Listing 9-14. *Generated Entity Deployment Descriptor in the ejb-jar.xml File*

```
<!-- Entity Beans -->
<entity>
  <description><![CDATA[An entity bean for persisting Tickets]]></description>
  <display-name>Ticket</display-name>

  <ejb-name>Ticket</ejb-name>

  <local-home>com.projst.ticket.entity.TicketLocalHome</local-home>
  <local>com.projst.ticket.entity.TicketLocal</local>
```

```xml
<ejb-class>com.projst.ticket.entity.TicketCMP</ejb-class>
<persistence-type>Container</persistence-type>
<prim-key-class>java.lang.Integer</prim-key-class>
<reentrant>False</reentrant>
<cmp-version>2.x</cmp-version>
<abstract-schema-name>ticket</abstract-schema-name>
<cmp-field >
  <description><![CDATA[]]></description>
  <field-name>id</field-name>
</cmp-field>
<cmp-field >
  <description><![CDATA[]]></description>
  <field-name>summary</field-name>
</cmp-field>
<cmp-field >
  <description><![CDATA[]]></description>
  <field-name>detail</field-name>
</cmp-field>
<cmp-field >
  <description><![CDATA[]]></description>
  <field-name>submitted</field-name>
</cmp-field>
<cmp-field >
  <description><![CDATA[]]></description>
  <field-name>lastModified</field-name>
</cmp-field>
<primkey-field>id</primkey-field>

<query>
  <query-method>
    <method-name>findAll</method-name>
    <method-params>
    </method-params>
  </query-method>
  <ejb-ql><![CDATA[SELECT OBJECT(a) FROM ticket as a]]></ejb-ql>
</query>
<!-- Write a file named ejb-finders-TicketBean.xml if you want to define
     extra finders. -->
</entity>
```

Listing 9-15. *Generated Entity Deployment Descriptor in the jboss.xml File*

```
<entity>
  <ejb-name>Ticket</ejb-name>
  <local-jndi-name>TicketLocal</local-jndi-name>

  <method-attributes>
  </method-attributes>

</entity>
```

Listing 9-16. *JBoss CMP Deployment Descriptor*

```
<?xml version="1.0" encoding="UTF-8"?>
<!DOCTYPE jbosscmp-jdbc PUBLIC "-//JBoss//DTD JBOSSCMP-JDBC 4.0//EN"
  "http://www.jboss.org/j2ee/dtd/jbosscmp-jdbc_4_0.dtd">

<jbosscmp-jdbc>

  <enterprise-beans>

  <!--
    To add beans that you have deployment descriptor info for, add
    a file to your XDoclet merge directory called jbosscmp-jdbc-beans.xml
    that contains the <entity></entity> markup for those beans.
  -->

  <entity>
    <ejb-name>Ticket</ejb-name>
      <datasource>java:/jdbc/ticket</datasource>
      <datasource-mapping>Derby</datasource-mapping>
      <create-table>false</create-table>
      <remove-table>false</remove-table>

      <table-name>TICKET</table-name>

      <cmp-field>
        <field-name>id</field-name>
        <column-name>ID</column-name>
      </cmp-field>
      <cmp-field>
        <field-name>summary</field-name>
        <column-name>SUMMARY</column-name>
      </cmp-field>
      <cmp-field>
        <field-name>detail</field-name>
        <column-name>DETAIL</column-name>
```

```
        </cmp-field>
        <cmp-field>
          <field-name>submitted</field-name>
          <column-name>SUBMITTED</column-name>
        </cmp-field>
        <cmp-field>
          <field-name>lastModified</field-name>
          <column-name>LASTMODIFIED</column-name>
        </cmp-field>

        <unknown-pk>
          <unknown-pk-class>java.lang.Integer</unknown-pk-class>
          <read-only>true</read-only>
          <column-name>ID</column-name>
          <auto-increment/>
        </unknown-pk>
      <entity-command name="get-generated-keys"
      class="org.jboss.ejb.plugins.cmp.jdbc.keygen.JDBC30GeneratedKeysCreateCommand">
      </entity-command>
<!-- jboss 3.2 features -->
<!-- optimistic locking does not express the exclusions needed -->
    </entity>

  </enterprise-beans>

</jbosscmp-jdbc>
```

Listing 9-14 shows the new Ticket entity bean configuration in the `ejb-jar.xml`. Notice `description`, `display-name`, `ejb-name`, `persistence-type`, `cmp-version`, `abstract-schema-name`, and `transaction-type` all match the values from the `TicketBean`'s annotations. Also notice the `local-home`, `local`, and `ejb-class` elements are the classes generated by XDoclet. The entity description also contains a list of all CMP fields corresponding to the exposed entity attributes and a `query` based on the finder annotation shown previously in Listing 9-7.

Depending on your configurations, you may also get a vendor-specific deployment descriptor. Listing 9-15 shows an example of a JBoss-specific deployment descriptor entry for the Ticket entity bean. `ejb-name` maps this configuration to the corresponding configuration in the `ejb-jar.xml` file. `local-jndi-name` is the JNDI name that can be used to look up the local home interface from JNDI.

Most application servers need an additional application server–specific deployment descriptor for CMP beans. Listing 9-16 shows JBoss's CMP deployment descriptor, `jbosscmp-jdbc.xml`. Notice it uses the `jboss` and `ejb` notations to map the entity bean to a table and JNDI datasource and then maps the entity fields to the table columns.

Once XDoclet has finished and all the files have been generated, the Entity Beans node in the J2EE Perspective will be updated to include the new entity bean (see Figure 9-7).

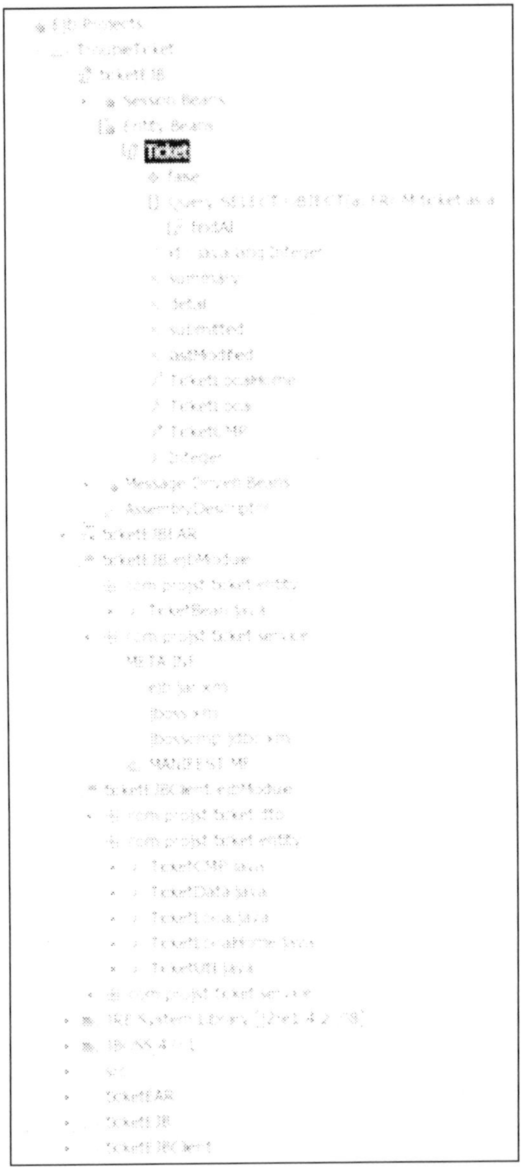

Figure 9-7. *J2EE Project Explorer after XDoclet completes*

Figure 9-7 shows an expanded view of the TroubleTicket project after the Ticket entity bean has been added. Notice the new Ticket bean is under the Entity Beans node. Underneath the Ticket bean are the related Ticket interfaces and the TicketCMP bean; in addition, all the attributes, primary keys, and finder methods are listed. Within the source folders, you can see generated files including `TicketBean.java`, `TicketCMP.java`, `ejb-jar.xml`, `jboss.xml`, `jbosscmp-jdbc.xml`, `TicketLocal.java`, and `TicketLocalHome.java`.

Note It is important to implement version control for your source code so you can guarantee repeatable builds at different points in time and consistent builds amongst a team of developers. Technically, you only need to control the version of the bean class because everything related to that class will be regenerated.

XDoclet Entity Bean Annotations

In order to generate the interfaces and deployment descriptors in JST, you must be familiar with your chosen annotation tool. Since XDoclet is the only option at this point, this section will introduce you to some of the entity bean–specific XDoclet annotations. This is not an exhaustive list. For a complete list, check out the XDoclet documentation at `http://xdoclet.sourceforge.net/`.

Tip The JST has XDoclet code assist. It can be invoked using Ctrl+space after @. Unfortunately, it does not include all XDoclet annotations.

Entity beans have many class-, method-, and field-level annotations. Because there are so many, we will limit ourselves to a couple of tables identifying the most common class-level tag, `@ejb.bean` (see Table 8-2), and the most common method-level tag, `@ejb.persistence` (see Table 8-3).

Table 8-2. *XDoclet Entity @ejb.bean Class Parameters*

Parameter	Type	Description	Required
name	Text	Enterprise bean name (ejb-name), which must be unique within an ejb-jar file	True
description	Text	Description of bean	False
display-name	Text	Short name	False
small-icon	Text	16×16 icon image	False
large-icon	Text	32×32 icon image	False
generate	Boolean	Generates bean deployment description	False
jndi-name	Text	Remote JNDI name	False
local-jndi-name	Text	Local JNDI name	False
view-type	Text	Whether bean is local, remote, Web Service, or all	False
type	Text	Whether bean is stateless or stateful	True
schema	Text	Abstract schema name	False
cmp-version	Text	CMP version, either 1.x or 2.x	False
primkey-field	Text	Primary key field	False
reentrant	Boolean	Whether multiple threads can access the same instance at the same time	False
use-soft-locking	Boolean	Uses version attribute to support optimistic locking	False
transaction-type	Text	Container or bean transaction	False

Table 8-3. XDoclet Entity @ejb.persistence Class Parameters

Parameter	Type	Description	Required
column-name	Text	Database column name	False
jdbc-type	Text	JDBC type	False
sql-type	Text	Field type in the database	False
read-only	Boolean	Indicates the field is read-only	False

Note Visit `http://xdoclet.sourceforge.net/` for application server–specific entity bean annotations.

Using the Entity Bean from a Session Bean

Now that the Ticket entity bean is complete and you have a Data Transfer Object, you can call the entity bean from your TicketService session bean and complete the implementation of a Session Façade pattern by creating service methods. These service method are examples of course-grain methods. Rather than have a remote client call the findAll method on a home interface of an entity bean and then call the getters and setters on their remote interfaces, a single call is made to the service method. The data is packaged up into a Data Transfer Object and sent back to the client. As an example, we will show you how to add a service method to retrieve all tickets. See Listing 9-17 for the implementation of this method.

Listing 9-17. *Retrieve All Tickets Service Method on TicketServiceBean.java*

```
/**
 * Returns all tickets.
 * @ejb.interface-method view-type="both"
 */
public Collection retrieveAllTickets() throws FinderException, NamingException {
  Collection ticketDTOs = new ArrayList();
  Collection tickets = TicketUtil.getLocalHome().findAll();
  for (Iterator iter = tickets.iterator(); iter.hasNext();) {
    TicketLocal ticket = (TicketLocal) iter.next();
    ticketDTOs.add(ticket.getData());
  }
  return ticketDTOs;
}
```

The retrieveAllTickets service method in Listing 9-17 begins with an annotation that instructs XDoclet to include this method in both the remote and local interfaces of the Ticket-Service session bean. The actual method implementation begins by creating an empty array list to hold the Data Transfer Objects. Then the utility class is used to get a reference to the Ticket bean's local home interface so its findAll method can be called. This returns a collection of local interfaces. Iterating through the collection of local interfaces, the getData method is called to create the Data Transfer Object. The Data Transfer Object is then put in the original collection and returned to the client.

> **Note** Chapter 11 discusses how to deploy the session bean to the application server. The application will need to be deployed for the client application to work.

Summary

In this chapter, you learned JST does not currently support creating entity beans. So we reviewed how to create entity beans by first using the EnterpriseJavaBean wizard to create a session bean. We then showed you which modifications needed to be made to convert the session bean to an entity bean. In the next chapter, you will learn how to create message-driven beans. Then in Chapter 11, you will see how to package, deploy, and debug EJBs in a J2EE application server. In Chapter 12, we will demonstrate how to use the Session Façade developed in this chapter to display tickets on a web page.

CHAPTER 10

Message-Driven Beans

Message-Oriented Middleware (MOM) is a major component of many enterprise applications. Java's implementation of MOM is the Java Message Service (JMS). JMS 1.1 is a required API in the J2EE 1.4 Specification and is therefore included with all certified J2EE application servers. MOM and JMS support three architecturally significant problems: asynchronous calls, integration, and decoupling.

For enterprise applications, being able to make asynchronous calls to complicated and time-consuming logic is critical. Without it, applications can seem unresponsive and even time out. For J2EE applications, JMS is especially critical since it is the only asynchronous alternative. Many non-J2EE applications use threads for asynchronous behavior, but according to the EJB 2.1 Specification section 25.1.2, "Programming Restrictions," "Enterprise beans must not attempt to manage threads." Why? Because managing threads is the responsibility of the container. Starting your own threads in the container can lead to many problems such as losing user identity, opening security holes, causing memory leaks, or preventing administrators from properly being able to manage thread pools.

JMS is often used to integrate with legacy systems. Many J2EE applications have one or more touch points with existing systems written in languages other than Java. These legacy systems typically do not support newer forms of interoperability such as Web Services, discussed in Chapter 15. JMS can provide the transport mechanism between the J2EE application and the legacy application. The additional value-add for legacy system integration is the asynchronous component. Legacy systems often take time to return results. Being asynchronous enables the J2EE application to perform additional logic until it is ready to pick up the response.

Finally, JMS solutions can decouple the callers from the receivers. This will be explained in more detail in the "JMS Overview" section. But imagine not having to recompile, reconfigure, or redeploy a J2EE application if it needs to change which back-end services it is integrating with.

The EJB Specification simplified consuming JMS messages by introducing message-driven beans (MDBs). This chapter shows how MDBs are developed using JST after providing an introduction to both JMS and MDBs.

JMS Overview

JMS is commonly used in distributed computing for sending and receiving messages to and from objects, components, or other systems. But unlike remote procedure calls, the objects do not send the messages directly to each other. Instead, they send the message to a destination (see Figure 10-1).

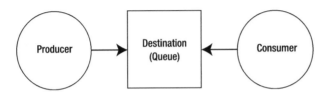

Figure 10-1. *JMS messaging model*

Rather than the producer and consumer communicating directly, Figure 10-1 shows how the producer delivers a message to a destination. The consumer then picks the message up from the destination and uses it accordingly. Depending on the purpose of the message, the producer may in turn expect a reply from the consumer. The producer of the message can specify in the message which destination the consumer should reply to. JMS refers to both the producer and consumer as a *JMS client*.

This model works extremely well for legacy integration. For example, a J2EE application may need to retrieve customer data from a legacy Customer Information Control System (CICS) application. The J2EE application can construct a find customer message and place it in a destination the CICS application watches. When the message arrives, the CICS application can pick up the message, look up the customer, and return the customer data in a new message to a destination of the producer's request. The producer can pick the reply message up and display it or use it as appropriate.

JMS defines two types of destinations, referred to as *message domains*: point-to-point (P2P) and publish/subscribe. A point-to-point message domain is implemented as a queue. This follows the model described in the previous paragraph. A single producer delivers a message to a destination, and a single consumer pulls the message off the queue. So the message is only processed one time. In addition, the consumer typically does not need to be listening to the queue at the time the message is delivered. The message will remain in the queue until it is picked up.

A publish/subscribe model is implemented as a topic. It follows the observable pattern. In other words, there is a one-to-many relationship between the producer and the consumer (see Figure 10-2).

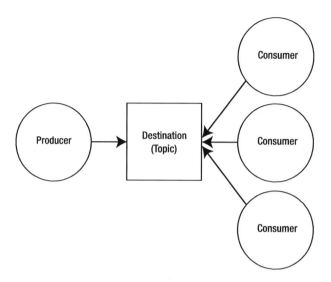

Figure 10-2. *Publish/Subscribe model*

Figure 10-2 shows that in a publish/subscribe model, the producer delivers the message to a destination, specifically a topic. Multiple consumers can subscribe to a topic. Each active subscriber will have an opportunity to process the message. If a subscriber is not active, that subscriber will miss out on the message unless the topic is made durable. A *durable topic* is a topic that will hold the message until all the subscribers retrieve the message.

Publish/Subscribe is often useful for handling event-based activities. This is especially true when those events require notifying multiple systems about the event. For example, when a new employee is added to a company, the human resource application should trigger a new employee event. This event should update central databases like LDAP, the accounting system, and of course the Trouble Ticket application we are developing throughout this book. By using a topic, the human resource application can be decoupled by the other systems requiring the notification and information about the new employee. In addition, other systems can be easily added to support the same event with no modifications to the human resource system.

Messages

Regardless of whether the destination is a queue or topic, JMS uses the same message structure. The message includes a header, properties, and a body. The header is made up of fields containing information about routing and identification. One example of routing information would be the reply mentioned earlier.

The properties contain application-defined values used for application-specific filtering. For example, a consumer may only care about picking up messages related to tickets being added. If a single ticket topic is used, a property of `EVENT` could be used with a value of `ADD TICKET` to indicate to the consumer that this is a new ticket. The consumer can use a message selector to exclude other messages placed on the same destination.

The final element of a message is the body itself. The body represents the content or data being sent. The body could be data representing an employee, trouble ticket, or anything else. The data can be stored in several formats depending on the message type. The message types include byte, map, object, stream, and text (see Figure 10-3).

Figure 10-3. *Message interfaces*

Figure 10-3 shows the UML class diagram of the message interfaces. All message types inherit from the Message interface. See Table 10-1 for a description of each of the message types.

Table 10-1. *JMS Message Types*

Type	Description
TextMessage	Contains a String object formatted as plain text or XML
MapMessage	Contains an unordered collection of name-value pairs in which the name is a String and the value is a primitive, String, or primitive wrapper
StreamMessage	Contains an ordered collection of primitives, Strings, or primitive wrappers
ObjectMessage	Contains a single Serializable object
BytesMessage	Contains a stream of uninterpreted bytes

JMS API

The JMS API is primarily a collection of interfaces contained within the javax.jms package. It follows the programming model depicted in Figure 10-4.

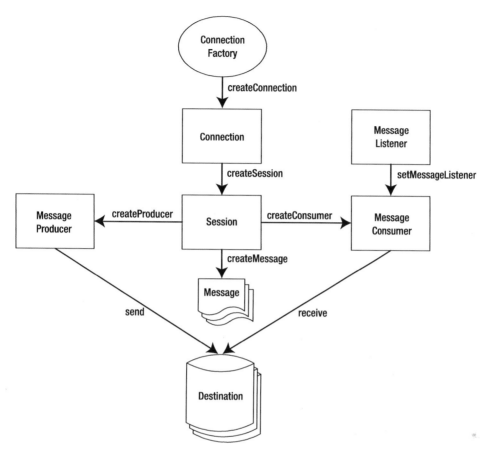

Figure 10-4. *JMS 1.1 API model*

Figure 10-4 shows that the JMS API relies heavily on the factory pattern. It begins with a ConnectionFactory interface and uses factory methods for creating the remaining instances of the interfaces. Bootstrapping the initial ConnectionFactory interfaces is done through a JNDI lookup. Once you have the ConnectionFactory, you can use the createConnection methods to get a Connection. Using the Connection, you can create a Session instance by calling createSession. With the Session reference, you can create Producers, Consumers, and Messages.

To create Messages, there are corresponding create message factory methods for each of the message types (see Figure 10-4 or Table 10-1).

For sending messages, you must create a MessageProducer by calling the createProducer method on the Session and passing it the Destination of where the message should be sent. The MessageProducer has several overloaded send methods that can be used to send the messages created from the Session.

For receiving messages, you can call the createConsumer, passing it a Destination from which you wish to pick up messages. Use the createConsumer on the Session to get an instance of a MessageConsumer. Once you have the MessageConsumer, you will need to register a listener with it. The listener will be responsible for processing the message. This is done by passing a class implementing the `MessageListener` interface into the `setMessageListener` method. The `MessageListener` interface will be discussed more in the "Message-Driven Beans Overview" section because it is critical to message-driven beans.

Both the `MessageProducer` and `MessageConsumer` were designed to be `Destination`-type agnostic. They can either send to or pick up from a topic or a queue. So how do you create a `Destination`? Which class contains the factory method? `Destination`s are not created using factory methods. Just like the `ConnectionFactory`, to get a reference to a `Destination`, you perform a JNDI lookup.

The JMS 1.1 API was designed to abstract the destination type from the API. However, you also have the options of using the `Topic` and `Queue` interfaces defined in JMS 1.0. The general concept of the programming model is the same. But instead of getting generic superinterfaces, you get destination-specific interfaces. For example, instead of retrieving a `ConnectionFactory`, you specifically request a `TopicConnectionFactory` or `QueueConnectionFactory`. Instead of a `createConnection` to get a `Connection`, you use `createTopicConnection` to get a `TopicConnection`. You get the idea.

JMS Implementations

JMS is a required service of a certified J2EE application server. So, if you have a J2EE application server, you already have a JMS server. Configuring topics and queues are application server–specific. The configuration process can vary from web page administration to XML configuration files. See your application server for specific configuration details.

Note   JBoss configuration details are covered in the "Configuring Topics and Queues in JBoss" sidebar later in this chapter.

JMS is an independent specification. So it is possible to use a JMS server independent of a J2EE application server. A commercial example is IBM's WebSphere MQ (`http://www.ibm.com/software/integration/wmq/`). An open source example is Codehaus's ActiveMQ (`http://activemq.codehaus.org/`).

Message-Driven Beans Overview

Now that you know the basics about JMS, understanding message-driven beans (MDB) is really easy. An MDB is simply an EJB that implements the `javax.jms.MessageListener` interface (see Listing 10-1) and therefore is a consumer of a topic or queue. OK, it is a little bit more complicated than that. It must also implement the `javax.ejb.MessageDrivenBean` interface (see Listing 10-2) and requires a couple of deployment descriptors. But compared to session and entity beans, MDBs are really quite easy. MDBs do not have any home, remote, or local interfaces and have much less complicated deployment descriptors (see Listing 10-3). Even compared to implementing a stand-alone JMS consumer, MDBs are much simpler because the container takes care of creating the connection, session, etc.

Listing 10-1. *javax.jms.MessageListener Interface*

```
package javax.jms;

public interface MessageListener {

    public void onMessage(javax.jms.Message message);

}
```

Listing 10-2. *javax.ejb.MessageDrivenBean Interface*

```
package javax.ejb;

public interface MessageDrivenBean extends EnterpriseBean {

    public void setMessageDrivenContext(MessageDrivenContext ctx)
        throws EJBException;

    public void ejbRemove()
        throws EJBException;

}
```

Listing 10-3. *Message-Driven Bean Deployment Descriptor*

```
<message-driven>
  <description>Emails trouble ticket confirmation.</description>
  <ejb-name>EmailTicket</ejb-name>
  <ejb-class>com.projst.EmailTicketBean</ejb-class>
  <transaction-type>Container</transaction-type>
  <message-selector>EVENT = 'ADD TICKET'</message-selector>
  <acknowledge-mode>Auto-acknowledge</acknowledge-mode>
  <message-driven-destination>
    <destination-type>javax.jms.Topic</destination-type>
    <subscription-durability>NonDurable</subscription-durability>
  </message-driven-destination>
</message-driven>
```

MDBs, like all JMS listeners, must implement the `javax.jms.MessageListener` interface shown in Listing 10-1. The interface consists of a single method, `onMessage`. That method accepts a single parameter of `javax.jms.Message`. Remember from Figure 10-3 that the `Message` interface is the superinterface of all the different types of messages. So the implementation of an `onMessage` method must check the message type using an `instanceOf` operator prior to doing anything with the message. The contents of an `onMessage` implementation can be any container-legal code. For example, an MDB might write the contents of the message to a database using a container-managed data source or send an e-mail.

The `javax.ejb.MessageDrivenBean` interface (shown in Listing 10-2) is also a simple interface and is typically implemented in a boilerplate manner. Its purpose is to notify the MDB of container-managed life cycle events. Just before the onMessage method is called by the container, the setMessageDrivenContext is invoked, passing a javax.ejb.MessageDrivenContext. This context provides access to container-managed security and transactions. The boilerplate implementation of the setMessageDrivenBeanContext is to store the context in a private variable. The ejbRemove method is called just before the container attempts to remove the bean. The boilerplate cleanup implementation is to set the private context variable to null.

Notice in Listing 10-3 that the MDB contains many of the same elements that session bean descriptors (discussed in Chapter 8) contain such as description, ejb-name, ejb-class, transaction-type, and many others not shown here. In addition to those, MDBs require some JMS-specific descriptors, primarily acknowledge-mode, message-selector, and message-driven-destination.

acknowledge-mode is used for bean-managed transactions as determined by the transaction-type deployment descriptor. Therefore, in Listing 10-3, acknowledge-mode will be ignored because this bean is using container-managed transactions. acknowledge-mode may contain either Auto-acknowledge to automatically notify the session when the onMessage has successfully completed or Dups-ok-acknowledge to asynchronously notify the JMS server of the message delivery.

Note If Dups-ok-acknowledge is used, the MDB must be written to ensure it can handle receiving a message more than once, because a JMS server may try to deliver the message again if it has not received the delivery acknowledgement.

The message-selector is used to filter which messages the MDB will consume by using an SQL-like syntax. For example, in Listing 10-3, the message selector indicates we don't want the MDB to consume every message placed on the Ticket topic, just messages that indicate a new ticket based on an add ticket event.

The message-driven-destination provides information about the destination it is consuming a message from. Its destination-type element is used to identify whether the MDB is consuming messages from a topic or queue. If the destination is a topic, the container also needs to know whether the topic is durable (Durable) or not (NonDurable).

At this point, you may be wondering to yourself, isn't a deployment descriptor missing? How does the MDB know which topic or queue to listen to? Well, this bit of information is container specific and can be found in the container-specific EJB deployment descriptors. You will have to consult your application server–specific documentation for more details, but typically application server–specific deployment descriptors contain an element identifying the JNDI name representing the topic or queue.

Tip If you want to learn more about JMS and message-driven beans, we suggest you read *Beginning J2EE 1.4: From Novice to Professional* by James L. Weaver, Kevin Mukhar, and Jim Crume (Apress, 2004) or *Pro J2EE 1.4: From Professional to Expert* by Meeraj Kunnumpurath and Sue Spielman (Apress, 2004).

Writing MDBs

Like session and entity beans in the previous chapters, JST supports writing MDBs by providing a MessageDrivenBean wizard, XDoclet annotations, and, of course, seamless deployment to the container (discussed in the next chapter).

Note In order to deploy an MDB in a J2EE application server, you will need to configure your topics and/or queues before deployment. This is application server specific, so consult your application server's documentation. If you are using JBoss, see the "Configuring Topics and Queues in JBoss" sidebar for instructions.

MessageDrivenBean Wizard

Assuming you are working in a Flexible project containing a J2EE EJB module and are using the J2EE Perspective, you can invoke the EnterpriseJavaBean wizard using the project's context menu and choosing New ➤ EnterpriseJavaBean. Alternatively, you can use File ➤ New ➤ Other ➤ EJB ➤ EnterpriseJavaBean.

Using the wizard to create a message-driven bean is a four-step process and almost identical to the session bean process. It begins by prompting for the type of EJB and the annotation provider (see Figure 10-5). The wizard includes support for creating session or message-driven beans by checking the appropriate radio button. Using the drop-down list, you may choose your preferred annotation provider. At this time, there is not a lot of choice. WTP only includes support for XDoclet annotations.

Figure 10-5. *The first step in the EnterpriseJavaBean wizard defines the type of bean and annotations to use.*

Underneath the covers, this first step identifies the code templates for generating the initial bean class. WTP uses the Java Emitter Templates (JET) from the Eclipse Modeling Framework (EMF) as the template engine. So a combination of message-driven bean and XDoclet will cause the templates in the `eclipse/plugins/org.eclipse.jst.j2ee.ejb.annotations.xdoclet_1.0.0/templates/ejb/message` directory to be used.

The second step in the EnterpriseJavaBean wizard, shown in Figure 10-6, involves collecting information about where the bean source code will be placed as well as standard class information including the package, class name, and class it inherits from.

Figure 10-6. *The second step in the EntpriseJavaBean wizard is used to identify where the output of the wizard goes.*

The first aspect of determining where to put the generated message-driven bean code is specifying the project. Depending on how your projects are organized, you may have multiple projects representing different partitions of your application. For example, you may have separate EJB, Web, and Enterprise Application Projects. Or you may have one project with different modules representing your partitions, for example, an Application Project with an EJB module, web module, and enterprise application module. So the Project drop-down menu lists all the open projects in the workspace. Once a project is selected, the modules in the project will be displayed in the Module Name drop-down menu. If the selected project does not contain a module, a warning message of "The source folder cannot be empty" will appear along the top of the dialog box. The folder must be the source folder of the EJB module. By default, it will contain the correct folder if the wizard is invoked from a Flexible project containing an EJB module. Unfortunately, though, the field is not tied to the module name or project. So if either of them is changed, the folder is not automatically updated. Therefore, it is a good idea to use identifiable module names to make them easier to find.

Note The Generate an annotated bean class checkbox does not make a difference in the output of the wizard, since either way it uses the same template, and there is no conditional logic in the template to exclude annotations.

The next step in the EnterpriseJavaBean wizard, shown in Figure 10-7, prompts for information that initially will populate the annotations. When XDoclet processes the annotations, the information will be used to update the standard EJB deployment descriptors to describe the message-driven bean.

Figure 10-7. *The third step in the EnterpriseJavaBean wizard gathers information for the deployment descriptors.*

The EJB name is used to uniquely identify the message-driven bean within the context of an ejb-jar file. It is primarily used for defining the relationships between the EJB and other elements in the deployment descriptors. The JNDI name is used to associate the message-driven bean with a topic or queue. The mechanism for mapping message-driven beans to a JNDI name is not described in the EJB Specification and is therefore not included in the standard EJB deployment descriptors. Most application servers include a vendor-specific deployment descriptor that contains the implementation-specific JNDI element. Please see your application server documentation for JNDI mappings.

The display name and description are both optional elements of the EJB standard deployment descriptors. Some development tools and application servers may optionally display this additional information.

The Destination field is the only field unique to the message-driven bean in the entire EnterpriseJavaBean wizard. It is used to indicate whether the destination the message-driven bean is listening to is a topic or queue.

As with session beans, transaction type determines whether the message-driven bean transactions will be managed by the container (Container option), or by you in code (Bean option).

The final step, shown in Figure 10-8, enables you to identify which class modifiers are applied to the new message-driven bean class, interfaces that must be implemented such as `javax.ejb.MessageDrivenBean` and `javax.jms.MessageListener`, and whether stub methods should be generated from superclass constructors or abstract methods. When using this wizard, keep in mind the EJB 2.1 Specification requires message-driven beans to be public and concrete. So, the public modifier must be checked and the abstract modifier must be unchecked.

Figure 10-8. *The fourth step in the EnterpriseJavaBean wizard is the Eclipse standard Class page.*

At this time, the last step in the process is more informational than useful. All the settings on this page are ignored. If you completely do the opposite by reversing the checkmarks and removing the interface, you will still get the same results because the templates do not do anything with this information.

Warning Early versions of the message-driven template `eclipse/plugins/org.eclipse.jst.j2ee.` `ejb.annotations.xdoclet_1.0.0/templates/ejb/message/typeStub.javajet` included the abstract modifier in the template. However, according to the EJB 2.1 Specification section 15.7.2, "Message-Driven Bean Class," message-driven beans must not be abstract. If you find yourself generating MDBs with an abstract modifier, remove the modifier and/or update the aforementioned template.

Upon completing the wizard, an MDB similar to the one in Listing 10-4 will be generated. In addition, a node representing the MDB will be added to the Message-Driven Beans section of the J2EE Project Explorer.

Listing 10-4. *Generated Message-Driven Bean*

```java
/**
 *
 */
package com.projst.ticket.service;

/**
 * <!-- begin-xdoclet-definition -->
 * @ejb.bean name="EmailTicket"
 *      acknowledge-mode="Auto-acknowledge"
 *      destination-type="javax.jms.Topic"
 *      subscription-durability="NonDurable"
 *      transaction-type="Container"
 *      destination-jndi-name="topic/ticket"
 * <!-- end-xdoclet-definition -->
 * @generated
 **/

public class EmailTicketBean implements javax.ejb.MessageDrivenBean,
            javax.jms.MessageListener {

  /**
   * <!-- begin-user-doc -->
   * <!-- end-user-doc -->
   * The context for the message-driven bean, set by the EJB container.
   * @generated
   */
  private javax.ejb.MessageDrivenContext messageContext = null;

  /**
   * Required method for container to set context.
   * @generated
   */
  public void setMessageDrivenContext(
            javax.ejb.MessageDrivenContext messageContext)
            throws javax.ejb.EJBException {
    this.messageContext = messageContext;
  }

  /**
   * Required creation method for message-driven beans.
   *
```

```
 * <!-- begin-user-doc -->
 * <!-- end-user-doc -->
 *
 * <!-- begin-xdoclet-definition -->
 * @ejb.create-method
 * <!-- end-xdoclet-definition -->
 * @generated
 */
public void ejbCreate() {
  //no specific action required for message-driven beans
}

/**
 * Required removal method for message-driven beans.
 * <!-- begin-user-doc -->
 * <!-- end-user-doc -->
 * @generated
 */
public void ejbRemove() {
  messageContext = null;
}

/**
 * This method implements the business logic for the EJB.
 *
 * <p>Make sure that the business logic accounts for asynchronous
 * message processing. For example, it cannot be assumed that the
 * EJB receives messages in the order they were sent by the client.
 * Instance pooling within the container means that messages are not
 * received or processed in a sequential order, although individual
 * onMessage() calls to a given message-driven bean instance are serialized.
 *
 * <p>The <code>onMessage()</code> method is required, and must take a
 * single parameter of type javax.jms.Message. The throws clause (if used)
 * must not include an application exception. Must not be declared as final
 * or static.
 *
 * <!-- begin-user-doc -->
 * <!-- end-user-doc -->
 * @generated
 */
public void onMessage(javax.jms.Message message) {
  // begin-user-code
  System.out.println("Message Driven Bean got message " + message);
  // TODO:  do business logic here
  // end-user-code
}
}
```

Notice in Listing 10-4 that the generated MDB includes the elements described in the "Message-Driven Bean Overview" section. The new MDB extends java.lang.Object and implements both the required javax.jms.MessageListener and javax.ejb.MessageDrivenBean interfaces. Just above this class declaration are class-level XDoclet annotations used for generating the deployment descriptor. The next section will address these MDB annotations.

Note MDBs do not need any method-level XDoclet annotations since there is only one method that will be called (onMessage).

The generated MDB also contains a setMessageDrivenContext method that sets the private messageContext and an ejbRemove method that sets the messageContext to null. Also, a required ejbCreate method was generated with an empty body. If you need to do any initialization, this is the place to do it. Because the setMessageDrivenContext method is called prior to the ejbCreate according to the MDB life cycle described in the EJB 2.1 Specification, you can assume you have a valid context during initialization.

A basic onMessage method is also generated. It really does not do much except write the Message to standard out. This is not likely to be the desired implementation, so the method also includes comments to begin-user-code and end-user-code as well as a TODO comment that will appear in the Tasks View. This is where you apply your application-specific implementation.

If Build Automatically is enabled, you will also have a utility class in the EJB client module generated by XDoclet. If Build Automatically is not enabled, the utility class will be generated the next time the project is built. The utility class has the same name as the EJB name plus a suffix of Util. Depending on whether the MDB is listening to a topic or queue, the utility class includes static utility methods to get references to the topic and topic connection or queue and queue connection, respectively. The utility class is already JNDI name aware, and changes to the JNDI name in the XDoclet annotations will automatically update this class. This enables producers wanting to put a message in a destination the MDB listens to not to have to worry about the JNDI name changing. In the "Writing a JMS Producer" section, we will show you how to use this utility class.

To create the EmailTicketBean that listens to a topic, complete the following steps:

1. In an EJB Project, choose File ➤ New ➤ Other ➤ EJB ➤ EnterpriseJavaBean and click Next.

2. Select MessageDrivenBean and XDoclet and click Next.

3. Enter the following and click Next:

    • *Java Package*: **com.projst.ticket.service**

    • *Class Name*: **EmailTicketBean**

4. Enter the following and click Next:

    • *EJB Name*: **EmailTicket**

    • *Destination JNDI Name*: **topic/ticket**

    • *Display Name*: **EmailTicket**

• *Description*: **Emails trouble ticket confirmation**

• *Destination*: **Topic**

• *Transaction Type*: **Container**

5. Click Finish.

The result should be an EmailTicketBean class that looks like Listing 10-4.

XDoclet MDB Annotations

Like with session and entity beans, JST uses XDoclet to manage keeping the bean in sync with the deployment descriptors by generating the deployment descriptor and utility classes from the code and XDoclet annotations. Similarly, it requires both generic EJB annotations and application server–specific annotations. Unlike the session and entity beans, message-driven beans have no method-specific annotations, since onMessage is the only method, and it is not exposed remotely and most likely would not be called directly by other EJBs within the application server.

Message-driven bean annotations use the @ejb.bean tag and a handful of its parameters. Table 10-2 shows the list of applicable @ejb.bean parameters.

Table 10-2. *XDoclet Message-Driven @ejb.bean Parameters*

Parameter	Type	Destination Type	Description	Required
name	Text	Topic and queue	Enterprise bean name (ejb-name), which must be unique within an ejb-jar file	True
description	Text	Topic and queue	Description of bean	False
display-name	Text	Topic and queue	Short name	False
small-icon	Text	Topic and queue	16×16 icon image	False
large-icon	Text	Topic and queue	32×32 icon image	False
generate	Boolean	Topic and queue	Generate bean deployment description	False
transaction-type	Text	Topic and queue	Container or bean transaction	False
message-selector	Text	Topic and queue	JMS message select or for filtering	False
acknowledge-mode	Text	Topic and queue	JMS acknowledgement semantics	False
destination-type	Text	Topic and queue	javax.jms.Topic or javax.jms.Queue destination	False
subscription-durability	Text	Topic	Durable or nondurable topic	False

Parameter	Type	Destination Type	Description	Required
destination-jndi-name	Text	Topic and queue	JNDI name of the topic or queue to listen to	False
connection-factory-jndi-name	Text	Topic and queue	Connection factory JNDI name used by utility class	False

XDoclet message-driven bean annotations also require at least one application server–specific tag that identifies the destination JNDI name. For JBoss, the tag is @jboss.destination-jndi-name and a parameter of name followed by the actual JNDI name.

Note Visit http://xdoclet.sourceforge.net/xdoclet/index.html for application server–specific message-driven bean annotations.

When fully configured, the EmailTicketBean XDoclet annotations look like Listing 10-5.

Listing 10-5. *EmailTicketBean XDoclet Annotations*

```
* @ejb.bean name="EmailTicket"
*      acknowledge-mode="Auto-acknowledge"
*      destination-type="javax.jms.Topic"
*      subscription-durability="NonDurable"
*      transaction-type="Container"
*      destination-jndi-name="topic/ticket"
*      connection-factory-jndi-name="ConnectionFactory"
*      message-selector="EVENT = 'ADD TICKET'"
*
* @jboss.destination-jndi-name
*      name="topic/ticket"
```

When the project is built and XDoclet is invoked, it will generate a message-driven bean element in both an ejb-jar.xml file (see Listing 10-6) and a jboss.xml file (see Listing 10-7).

Listing 10-6. *Message-Driven Bean Element in ejb-jar.xml*

```
<message-driven >
  <description><![CDATA[<!-- begin-xdoclet-definition -->]]></description>

  <ejb-name>EmailTicket</ejb-name>

  <ejb-class>com.projst.ticket.service.EmailTicketBean</ejb-class>

  <transaction-type>Container</transaction-type>
  <message-selector>EVENT = 'ADD TICKET'</message-selector>
```

```
<acknowledge-mode>Auto-acknowledge</acknowledge-mode>
<message-driven-destination>
  <destination-type>javax.jms.Topic</destination-type>
  <subscription-durability>NonDurable</subscription-durability>
</message-driven-destination>

</message-driven>
```

Listing 10-7. *Message-Driven Bean Element in jboss.xml*

```
<message-driven>
  <ejb-name>EmailTicket</ejb-name>
  <destination-jndi-name>topic/ticket</destination-jndi-name>
</message-driven>
```

Based on the message-driven bean description in Listing 10-6, the EmailTicket bean will allow the container to manage its transactions and automatically acknowledge receipt of messages. It will also listen to a nondurable topic for messages with a property of EVENT with a value of ADD TICKET.

Based on the JBoss-specific message-driven bean description in Listing 10-7, the EmailTicket bean will be listening to a topic with a JNDI name of topic/ticket.

Finishing the MDB Implementation

To complete the MDB, we still have to add the code to implement the building and sending of the trouble ticket confirmation e-mail. In order to make it easier to get fields from the Ticket object, the EmailTicket bean accepts an ObjectMessage containing an instance of the newly added Ticket (see Listing 10-8).

Listing 10-8. *EmailTicket onMessage Implementation*

```
public void onMessage(javax.jms.Message message) {
  // begin-user-code
  if (message instanceof ObjectMessage) {
    ObjectMessage objectMessage = (ObjectMessage) message;

    try {
      Ticket ticket = (Ticket)objectMessage.getObject();

      // build e-mail message using javax.mail API
      Context ctx = new InitialContext();
      Session session = (Session)ctx.lookup("java:/Mail");

      javax.mail.Message email = new MimeMessage(session);
      email.setRecipient(
          MimeMessage.RecipientType.TO,
          new InternetAddress(ticket.getEmail()));
```

```
        email.setSubject("Confirm receipt of ticket: " + ticket.getOid());
        email.setText(
            "This is an automated response that your trouble ticket was received.");

        Transport.send(email);

    } catch (Exception e) {
        e.printStackTrace();
    }
}
    // end-user-code catch
}
```

The onMessage implementation in Listing 10-8 begins by making sure the message is an ObjectMessage by using the instanceof operator. If it is not, the remainder of the message is skipped because it does not follow the proper protocol. Next, the Ticket object is retrieved and stored in a local variable. The next section uses the javax.mail API to build an e-mail message, connect to an SMTP server, and send the message. One interesting aspect of combining the JMS and JavaMail APIs is the fact they use common class names. For example, both APIs have a session and a message. In some cases, you have to fully qualify the classes to remove compiler ambiguity.

Rather than repeatedly set up the mail session each time this method is invoked or using a factory to return a cached instance, you can let the application server do the heavy work. Most application servers provide a means of configuring an SMTP server configuration. Once configured, a Session can be looked up using an InitialContext and a JNDI name. Next, the actual message can be created using an instance of MimeMessage. Recipients, subjects, body, parts, return addresses, and more can be added to the message to meet specific requirements. And finally, the message can be sent using the Transport's send method.

CONFIGURING TOPICS AND QUEUES IN JBOSS

The JBoss JMS implementation is sometimes referred to as *JBoss Messaging* or *JBossMQ*. It fully supports the JMS Specification including features like durable topics.

Assuming you are familiar with configuring some aspect of the JBoss application server or have read Appendix B, you will not be surprised that configuring topics and queues in JBoss simply requires a properly formatted XML document to be dropped in a JBoss application server deployment directory. The XML file can even be added while the server is running. The configuration files have a naming convention of *-service.xml and are located in JBoss configuration's deploy/jms directory. Listing 10-9 shows an example of the Trouble Ticket application's topics and queues configuration file.

Listing 10-9. *ticket-destination-service.xml*

```
<?xml version="1.0" encoding="UTF-8"?>
<server>

  <mbean code="org.jboss.mq.server.jmx.Topic"
      name="jboss.mq.destination:service=Topic,name=ticket">
```

```
  <depends
    optional-attribute-name="DestinationManager"
  >jboss.mq:service=DestinationManager</depends>
</mbean>

<mbean code="org.jboss.mq.server.jmx.Queue"
    name="jboss.mq.destination:service=Queue,name=ticket">
  <depends
    optional-attribute-name="DestinationManager"
  >jboss.mq:service=DestinationManager</depends>
</mbean>

</server>
```

Listing 10-9 shows the configuration for both a topic and a queue. Notice that both topics and queues are implemented as JMX beans like the rest of JBoss's architecture and configured using mbean elements. The specific JMX bean is noted using a code attribute, org.jboss.mq.server.jmx.Topic for topics and org.jboss.mq.server.jmx.Queue for queues. The mbean name attribute also includes the destination type as well as the JNDI name, which can be used to look up the destination. Based on the configuration in Listing 10-9, the topic JNDI name will be topic/ticket and the queue JNDI name will be queue/ticket.

Writing a JMS Producer

A JMS producer could be either a stand-alone client application or another EJB. In the case of the Trouble Ticket application, the JMS producer is the Ticket session bean created in Chapter 8. When the addTicket service is invoked, it creates a JMS object message containing the Ticket it was passed (see Listing 10-10).

Listing 10-10. *Send the JMS Add Ticket Message*

```
// code removed for brevity
Connection conn = EmailTicketDestinationUtil.getConnection();
Session session = conn.createSession(false, Session.AUTO_ACKNOWLEDGE);
MessageProducer producer = session.createProducer(EmailTicketUtil.getTopic());
ObjectMessage message = session.createObjectMessage();

message.setObject(ticket);
message.setStringProperty("EVENT","ADD TICKET");

producer.send(message);

// code removed for brevity
```

In Listing 10-10, we use the EmailTicketDestinationUtil, which is a copy of the EmailTicketUtil class generated by XDoclet. Unfortunately, XDoclet only generates a utility class specific to queues. So, we recommend making a copy of the generated utility class and replacing all the queue-specific references with destination references. You can then use the new class to get a JMS Connection. For this method to work, the @ejb.bean connection-factory-jndi-name parameter must be used on the bean so the class's CONNECTION_FACTORY_JNDI_NAME field is set. Once we have the connection, we can create a session, a message, and a producer. Creating the producer requires a Destination. We can use the getDestination method on the EmailTicketDestinationUtil to get a Destination. The advantage of using the getDestination method is that if the JNDI name of the topic the MDB listens to changes, the getDestination automatically changes to return the new topic.

Next, we can set the object on the message with the ticket passed to the session bean. We set the properties to the bean so it can use the message selector and finally send the message.

Note If your JMS producer is a stand-alone client running outside the application server and your application server is JBoss, your client will need a jndi.properties file and jbossall-client.jar file in its classpath.

Summary

In the previous two chapters, you learned how to write session and entity beans. In this chapter, we finished giving you the tour of EJBs by discussing message-driven beans and their underlying JMS dependency. In the next chapter, you will see how to package, deploy, and debug EJBs in a J2EE application server.

CHAPTER 11

EJB Packaging and Deployment

Deployment of an enterprise application is an important final step in making the executable contents and services provided by the enterprise application available to other application components or end users who might rely on it. In J2EE, applications to be deployed must be packaged into deployment structures specific to the target containers within which they would be deployed. We have discussed in Chapter 1 that these containers include the applet, application client, web, and EJB containers. In this chapter, we will concentrate only on the deployment of EJB modules into EJB containers. We will discuss Web-Tier deployments in Chapter 14.

As we have stated, prior to deployment, EJB source artifacts and the Java classes that they are dependent on, as well as additional resource files used by the application, are packaged into specific directory structures for deployment. An important file included within this deployment structure is the deployment descriptor for the deployment module. The deployment descriptor is an XML-formatted document that contains instructions to the target container on how to deploy the module, and we have discussed in preceding chapters the relevance of this document as well as some of the settings that can be found inside it.

Deployment modules are optionally archived using the Java Archive (JAR) file format, with the required directory structure and configuration files that exist within the archive differing based on the type of deployment unit being created. Though packaging of the deployment module into an archive file is not required by many application servers, it is often easier to move the multiple files and directories that make up a deployment module in this manner. The JAR file format is a platform-independent format for aggregating multiple files into a single one, and thus eliminating the inherent difficulties of transferring multiple files. It additionally provides the ability to compress these files to reduce their size and thereby transmission time over network connections.

There are three archival structures into which a server-side deployment can be packaged:

- **EJB JAR file**: Deployment package for EJB modules

- **Web Archive (WAR) file**: Deployment package for web modules

- **Enterprise Archive (EAR) file**: Deployment package for applications supporting multiple EJB and web modules

Although the three deployment modules carry different file extensions, they share the same underlying archive file format in the JAR file format as we have mentioned earlier.

Note The J2SE SDK provides a `jar` utility that can be used to manipulate files that use the JAR file format. Supported operations include creating JARs, viewing JAR file contents, extracting these contents, etc.

In this chapter, we will provide an in-depth introduction to the EJB JAR file, its structure and contents, and how this is used to package and deploy EJB code within Eclipse. We will also discuss the `ejb-jar.xml` deployment descriptor that is required to be packaged with every EJB JAR file. We will provide an example of how to invoke the methods of a deployed enterprise bean and introduce you to the EAR file as an alternative format of deploying multiple EJB modules.

Packaging EJBs

Enterprise beans are packaged and targeted for deployment in the EJB container of an application server. Although many application servers support the deployment of unarchived EJBs, for reasons we have stated earlier, namely ease of transmission and deployment, EJBs are often archived into a JAR file structure known as an *EJB JAR file*.

In JST, multiple EJB components can be created within an EJB module that exists in an EJB Project; after successful compilation, these components can then be collectively packaged into an EJB JAR file. When a Flexible Project structure is selected, multiple EJB modules can be created within a single EJB Project, and each of these modules produces a deployable EJB JAR file. An EAR file is an alternative packaging structure that can be used to package EJB components. EAR files are used to deploy enterprise applications and can include within them one or more EJB JAR files. JST supports the creation of both EJB JAR and EAR files and provides an Export wizard that can be used to easily export files from the projects in the workspace onto the file system. The choice of packaging structure is based on the users' needs and the project type being created. We will discuss the EAR file structure later in this chapter in the section "Enterprise Archive File." Figure 11-1 shows the EJB Project Creation dialog box and the advanced option available for packaging the EJB Project into an EAR file.

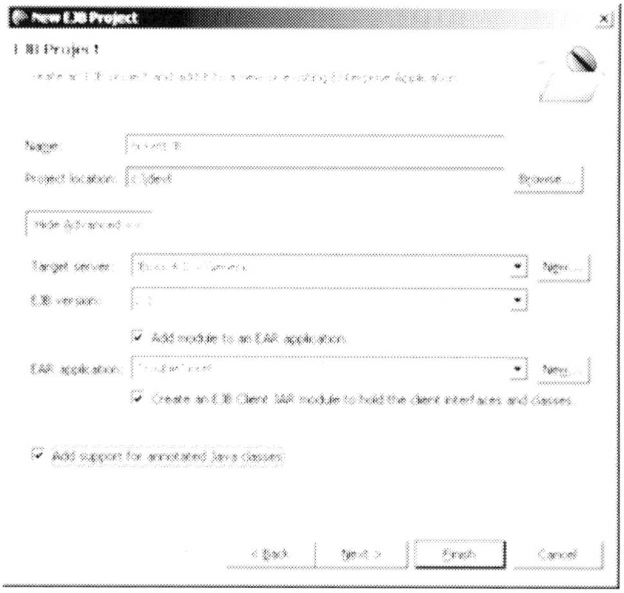

Figure 11-1. *Project Creation dialog box showing an EAR file as a packaging option*

You may notice in this figure that a choice of the target deployment server is required during the creation of an EJB module. This is essential because the target server configuration provides the libraries that this module will be compiled against. To create an application server–independent application, it is important not to use any classes provided by the application server that are not required by the J2EE specification. The module generated from this project can then be deployed easily on any application server. Also, keep in mind that most application servers require an application server–specific configuration document to be packaged with the deployment module being created. This configuration document is in addition to the required, server-independent deployment descriptor for EJB modules named `ejb-jar.xml`. Deployment descriptors are XML-based documents used to provide configuration information details to an application server about the contents of an EJB JAR file as well as how these contents of the EJB JAR file should be made available within the application server. The application server–specific deployment descriptors often provide users with the ability to configure features that are available within their related application server but that are beyond the base set of features required by any J2EE Specification. WebLogic, for instance, allows users to specify bean pool size and tuning information about each bean using the `weblogic-ejb.xml` deployment descriptor.

Packaging into the chosen format is triggered by running the application on the target server runtime instance. This can be done either by right-clicking the EJB Project from within the Package Explorer and then selecting Run As ➤ Run or by right-clicking the target server runtime within the Servers View and choosing Publish from the context menu. This initiates the compilation of the source artifacts within the project and the generation of the `ejb-jar.xml` and any server-specific deployment descriptor for the deployment module. The contents of the deployment descriptor can be managed by being directly edited or by using XDoclet annotations within the source files to specify values for elements within the descriptors.

The resulting EJB JAR file is created and deposited into the proper deployment directory of the target runtime server instance.

Exporting Files

Besides publishing your EJB JAR file to the deployment location on your application server, JST also provides you with the ability to deploy your packaged EJB deployment module to any location on the file system. This is done using the Export feature, which is provided by the base Eclipse platform and extended by JST to provide support for exporting J2EE deployment modules. Exporting your deployment module can be done by selecting File ➤ Export from the IDE menu. Choose the EJB JAR file or EAR file export option and indicate which project you wish to export from and what file system location you would like to store the resulting .jar or .ear file in.

EJB JAR File

As stated earlier, the EJB JAR file is an archival structure in the JAR file format containing the compiled source artifacts, libraries, and deployment descriptors that make up a complete EJB module. Though they simply carry the .jar file extension, packaged EJB deployment modules are referred to as EJB JAR files to highlight the fact that they are a specialized form of the JAR file. These specialized files contain a directory structure with a predefined format (shown in the code example that follows) and required content such as a deployment descriptor. Finally, EJB JAR files must be deployed within a J2EE-compliant EJB container for the contents to be useful.

The contents of an EJB JAR file includes compiled source artifacts such as the bean class and all the interfaces that are required by the EJB. Additional class files created as part of the project are also packaged within the EJB JAR file together with one or more deployment descriptors. These additional deployment descriptors are application server–specific, and we have listed some of them in Table 11-1. We have provided in the example that follows the contents of the EJB JAR file from the EJB module within our Trouble Ticket application. In our example, the EJB JAR file was generated from a project that contains a session bean named TicketService, an entity bean named Ticket, and a message-driven bean named EmailTicket. You may wish to refer to Chapters 8, 9, and 10 for the creation of these artifacts.

```
ticketEJBClient.jar
        META-INF\
            ejb-jar.xml
            jboss.xml
            manifest.mf
        com\
            projst\
                ticket\
                    entity\
                        TicketBean.class
                    service\
                        EmailTicketBean.class
                        TicketServiceBean.class
                        TicketServiceSession.class
```

You will notice from this listing that only the compiled artifacts are included within the EJB JAR file. The directory structure of these compiled source artifacts reflect the package statement defined within each of the source files. In this example, we have session beans and message-driven beans in the `com.projst.ticket.service` package and an entity bean in the `com.projst.ticket.entity` package. Included in this file is also the EJB client JAR file that contains the interfaces defined by the EJB and all auxiliary classes used by the EJBs. The contents of the included `ticketEJBClient.jar` client JAR file are displayed here:

```
META-INF\
        manifest.mf
com\
        projst\
                ticket\
                        dto\
                                Ticket.class
                        entity\
                                Ticket.class
                                TicketData.class
                                TicketPK.class
                                TicketHome.class
                                TicketLocal.class
                                TicketLocalHome.class
                                TicketUtil.class
                        service\
                                EmailTicketUtil.class
                                TicketService.class
                                TicketServiceHome.class
                                TicketServiceLocal.class
                                TicketServiceLocalHome.class
                                TicketServiceUtil.class
```

The other required directory structure within our EJB JAR file archive is the `META-INF` directory. As mandated by the J2EE Specification, application servers look within this directory for the `ejb-jar.xml` deployment descriptor. This file contains information about each of the EJBs to be deployed from the EJB JAR file and how to deploy them. Additional application server–specific deployment descriptors are also found within this folder. You may notice from the EJB JAR file contents shown previously that a `jboss.xml` file was packaged along with the `ejb-jar.xml` deployment descriptor. This is a JBoss-specific deployment descriptor. We have provided in Table 11-1 a list of some of these additional deployment descriptors that can be generated based on the target server choice you made.

Note The `manifest.mf` file created within the EJB JAR file is not required, but is often created by the `jar` utility as part of the packaging process.

Table 11-1. *Application Server Deployment Descriptors Generated by Eclipse*

Server	Deployment Descriptor	Description
Geronimo	openejb-jar.xml	Specifies different JNDI names and resource references for EJBs as well as manages CMP beans to database mapping
JBoss	jboss.xml	Specifies different JNDI names and resource references for an EJB
JBoss	jaws.xml	Manages details for CMP entity bean deployment
JBoss	jbosscmp-jdbc.xml	Manages details for CMP entity bean deployment
JOnAS	jonas-ejb-jar.xml	Specifies different JNDI names and resource references for an EJB
WebLogic	weblogic-cmp-jar.xml	Manages details for CMP entity bean deployment
WebLogic	weblogic-ejb-jar.xml	Specifies different JNDI names, JMS destinations, and resource references for an EJB

The generation of these optional files is an automated process managed by XDoclet and is based on the configuration of J2EE annotations within the workspace. You may view and alter the settings for generating these deployment descriptors by selecting Window ➤ Preferences ➤ J2EE Annotations ➤ XDoclet ➤ ejbdoclet. This setting provides you with the ability to select one or more target servers for which you want EJB module deployment descriptors to be generated. You are prompted for the specific version of each of the target servers you indicate, as XDoclet ensures that the tags being generated conform to the schema definition of those specific versions of the application servers.

The values placed in the generated deployment descriptors are based on the XDoclet tags that can be included within the source code. XDoclet supports the inclusion of server-specific tags to support settings that are unique to an application server. You may visit the XDoclet website at http://xdoclet.sourceforge.net/ for a list and description of these tags.

Because each of these files are XML-based text files, you have the ability to directly edit the content to suit your needs. You must exercise caution when updating this file, because XDoclet overwrites the content with values from the XDoclet tags within your source file. It is preferable to modify the XDoclet annotation tags within your source code.

ejb-jar.xml

The ejb-jar.xml deployment descriptor contains several details about the compiled EJBs within the EJB JAR archive file such as each EJB type and transaction types supported by each of these EJBs. These details are essential for the deployment of the file. Listing 11-1 shows the content of the ejb-jar.xml file for the EJB module of the Trouble Ticket project.

Listing 11-1. *The ejb-jar.xml Deployment Desciptor for the Trouble Ticket Project*

```
<?xml version="1.0" encoding="UTF-8"?>

<ejb-jar  xmlns="http://java.sun.com/xml/ns/j2ee"
          xmlns:xsi=http://www.w3.org/2001/XMLSchema-instance
          xsi:schemaLocation="http://java.sun.com/xml/ns/j2ee
          http://java.sun.com/xml/ns/j2ee/ejb-jar_2_1.xsd" version="2.1">
```

```
<description>
  <![CDATA[ticketEJB generated by eclipse wtp xdoclet extension.]]>
</description>
<display-name>ticketEJB</display-name>
```

\<enterprise-beans\>

```
<!-- Session Beans -->
<session >
    <description><![CDATA[A session bean named TicketService]]></description>
    <display-name>TicketService</display-name>
    <ejb-name>TicketService</ejb-name>
    <home>com.projst.ticket.service.TicketServiceHome</home>
    <remote>com.projst.ticket.service.TicketService</remote>
    <local-home>com.projst.ticket.service.TicketServiceLocalHome</local-home>
    <local>com.projst.ticket.service.TicketServiceLocal</local>
    <ejb-class>com.projst.ticket.service.TicketServiceSession</ejb-class>
    <session-type>Stateless</session-type>
    <transaction-type>Container</transaction-type>
</session>

<!-- Entity Beans -->
<entity>
    <description><![CDATA[An entity bean for persisting Tickets]]></description>
    <display-name>Ticket</display-name>

    <ejb-name>Ticket</ejb-name>
    <local-home>com.projst.ticket.entity.TicketLocalHome</local-home>
    <local>com.projst.ticket.entity.TicketLocal</local>

    <ejb-class>com.projst.ticket.entity.TicketCMP</ejb-class>
    <persistence-type>Container</persistence-type>
    <prim-key-class>java.lang.Integer</prim-key-class>
    <reentrant>False</reentrant>
    <cmp-version>2.x</cmp-version>
    <abstract-schema-name>ticket</abstract-schema-name>
    <cmp-field >
        <description><![CDATA[]]></description>
        <field-name>id</field-name>
    </cmp-field>
    <cmp-field >
        <description><![CDATA[]]></description>
        <field-name>summary</field-name>
    </cmp-field>
    <cmp-field >
        <description><![CDATA[]]></description>
        <field-name>detail</field-name>
    </cmp-field>
```

```xml
    <cmp-field >
       <description><![CDATA[]]></description>
       <field-name>submitted</field-name>
    </cmp-field>
    <cmp-field >
      <description><![CDATA[]]></description>
       <field-name>lastModified</field-name>
    </cmp-field>
    <primkey-field>id</primkey-field>

    <query>
       <query-method>
       <method-name>findAll</method-name>
       <method-params>
       </method-params>
       </query-method>
       <ejb-ql><![CDATA[SELECT OBJECT(a) FROM ticket as a]]></ejb-ql>
       </query>
       <!-- Write a file named ejb-finders-TicketBean.xml if you want to define
          extra finders. -->
</entity>


<!-- Message Driven Beans -->
<message-driven >
    <description><![CDATA[<!-- begin-xdoclet-definition -->]]></description>
    <ejb-name>EmailTicket</ejb-name>
    <ejb-class>com.projst.ticket.service.EmailTicketBean</ejb-class>
    <transaction-type>Container</transaction-type>
    <message-selector>EVENT = 'ADD TICKET'</message-selector>
    <acknowledge-mode>Auto-acknowledge</acknowledge-mode>
    <message-driven-destination>
       <destination-type>javax.jms.Topic</destination-type>
       <subscription-durability>NonDurable</subscription-durability>
    </message-driven-destination>
</message-driven>

</enterprise-beans>

<!-- Relationships -->

<!-- Assembly Descriptor -->
  <!--
    To specify your own assembly descriptor info here, add a file to your
    XDoclet merge directory called assembly-descriptor.xml that contains
    the <assembly-descriptor></assembly-descriptor> markup.
  -->
```

```
<assembly-descriptor >
</assembly-descriptor>
<ejb-client-jar>ticketEJBClient.jar</ejb-client-jar>

</ejb-jar>
```

Notice the two main tag sections (in bold) named `<enterprise-beans>` and `<assembly-descriptor>`. Within the `<enterprise-beans>` tag, each session, message-driven, and entity bean to be deployed is provided with a section about the file. Table 11-2 lists the tags that are often typically available within an `ejb-jar.xml` deployment descriptor as well as the contents of these tags.

Table 11-2. *Contents of ejb-jar.xml Deployment Descriptor*

Deployment Tag	Description
`<small-icon>`	An icon sized 16×16 pixels that represents the EJB module in a GUI tool.
`<large-icon>`	A larger icon sized 32×32 pixels that represents the EJB module in a GUI tool.
`<display-name>`	A short name to be displayed in a GUI tool.
`<description>`	A description of the EJB module.
`<enterprise-beans>`	Deployable enterprise beans contained within the enterprise application file. A separate `<session>`, `<entity>`, or `<message-driven>` tag is used for each of the beans that is being deployed, matching the type of the bean.
`<assembly-descriptor>`	Additional information about the deployment of the packaged EJB including transaction and security information for the beans.

Although the `<session>`, `<entity>`, and `<message-driven>` tags contain different subtags based on the information specific to that type of bean, the three EJB types share a few tags in common:

- `<description>`: A description of the EJB

- `<ejb-name>`: A name with which the EJB would be referenced within the deployment descriptor

- `<ejb-class>`: The fully qualified class name of the compiled class that contains the EJB code

It should be noted that since EJB 1.1, 2.0, and 2.1 Specifications support different features, the tags available within the deployment descriptors for a project would feature only those tags that are meaningful to the EJB Project version being created.

Deploying EJBs

As we have stated, before EJBs can be used, they must be packaged and deployed into an EJB container of an application server. In JST, the deployment of EJBs is a two-step process. These two steps include the building of the source artifacts and the publishing of the artifacts to an application server.

Building EJBs

The build process involves the conversion of the source files into compiled classes and the generation (or regeneration) of any necessary files. This process is handled by the various builders that exist within the EJB Project. These builders can be viewed by selecting Project ➤ Properties ➤ Builders in the IDE. The builders in this list are dynamic and are based on choices made in the project. Configuring XDoclet, for instance, and specifying that you would use J2EE annotations within your project during the EJB Project creation step will cause an XDoclet Builder to be inserted in the correct step within your project.

The build process can be set to commence automatically or configured to wait for a user-requested build. If automatic build is enabled for the project (using the Project ➤ Build Automatically menu option), the builders are automatically run whenever a file is edited. If automatic build is disabled, you will have to initiate a build through the Project menu or by using the context menu of the project. The build process compiles the complete set of EJB source files and any other source files included within the project into a .deployables folder within the project folder on the file system. The XDoclet-generated files are also created and placed into this folder.

Tip You can find the location of your project folder on the file system by selecting the project within the Project Explorer View and choosing Properties ➤ Info from the context menu.

Publishing EJBs

The promotion of a packaged EJB JAR file into the appropriate location within your application server for deployment is known as *publishing*. Before you can publish a file, you must have a server configuration defined for the EJB module to be hosted in. Once this is done, the publishing process packages the generated source files within the .deployables directory into an archival structure and places them into the appropriate deployment location within your chosen deployment server configuration. JST provides multiple options for publishing, such as the ability to publish the latest compiled files before starting a server or to auto-publish files to the server after a specific time interval. These options are available by selecting Window ➤ Preferences ➤ Server.

EJBs must be hosted within an application server that contains an EJB container because EJBs can only be properly deployed within an EJB container. In JST, each instance of an application server to which modules can be deployed is represented by a server configuration. Care should be taken not to confuse a server runtime environment with a server configuration. The two items, however, do have a relationship. A server configuration represents a single executable instance of an installed server runtime environment containing such information as host and port address for the server to receive requests on.

Note For EJB projects that require a complicated build-and-deployment process, you may choose to use Ant, the popular Java-based build tool, to manage the packaging and deployment of the application. Both the build and deployment processes we have discussed internally use Ant scripts for their tasks; if you are new to the creation of Ant scripts, you may choose to export the Ant scripts used by JST into your project and make the necessary edits to this file. Alternatively, you could create your Ant scripts from scratch and use those instead. Eclipse provides extensive support for Ant, and we discuss this tool at length in Chapter 14.

Creating Server Configurations

JST expectedly supports the creation of servers for the hosting of your deployed EJBs. Each server can have multiple J2EE modules deployed to the server, and JST provides you with the facility to easily manage these. On the first deployment of a project, if no previous server configuration exists, JST requires you to create a server configuration within which you will deploy your module. Subsequent deployments can then skip this step and publish directly to this same target server. Defining a new server is done using the Server Creation wizard, and this can be launched by selecting File ➤ New ➤ Other ➤ Server ➤ Server. Alternatively, the wizard can be launched from the Servers View by selecting New ➤ Server from the context menu of the view.

The Server Creation wizard is a four-step process to assist you in creating a target server within which your enterprise modules will be deployed. The initial page of this wizard prompts for the host on which the server exists and the type of server that you intend to define. Figure 11-2 shows this page containing a list of available servers. We will select the JBoss 4.0.1 server as our deployment environment for this example.

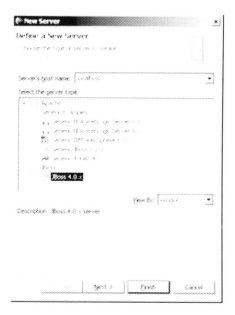

Figure 11-2. *The first step of the Server Creation wizard*

If the selected server type does not have a server runtime environment defined, you will be prompted to create one. The version of this page that you will be prompted with is based on the choice of server type made in the previous step. In all instances, this page will at a minimum prompt for the Java Runtime Environment (JRE) to use for executing the server as well as information about the installation directory of the server. This step is skipped if you are deploying on the same server type as the target server chosen for your project, because Eclipse would already have the configuration details. You may wish to refer to Chapter 7 for further details about defining multiple Java Runtime Environments and also creating multiple server runtime definitions.

The next step of the wizard is also based on the server type being created. For JBoss 4.0.1, this prompts for the server address and the port on which the server will be listening. Additionally, it prompts for the server configuration within the JBoss installation to host the deployed artifacts in. You may refer to Appendix A for information about the installation of JBoss and management of JBoss server configurations. Figure 11-3 shows the server configuration step in the wizard.

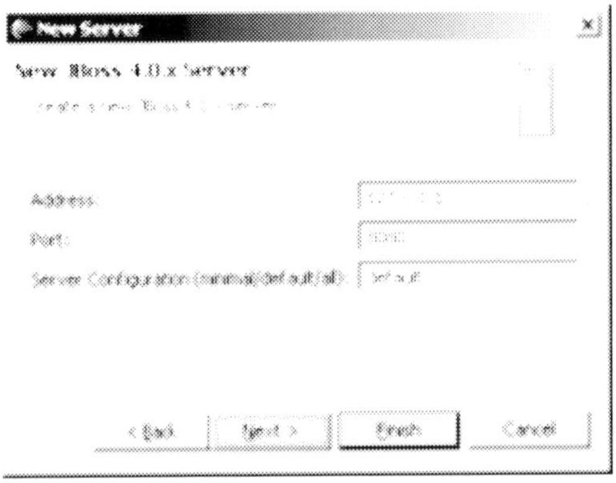

Figure 11-3. *The server configuration step*

The final step of the Server Creation wizard lists all the projects existing in the current workspace and allows you to select which project you want to deploy to the server being created using the available Add and Remove buttons. Selections made during this step can later be edited by choosing the server in the Servers View and selecting the Add and remove projects option from the available context menu. Figure 11-4 shows this wizard page containing a list of the projects in our workspace.

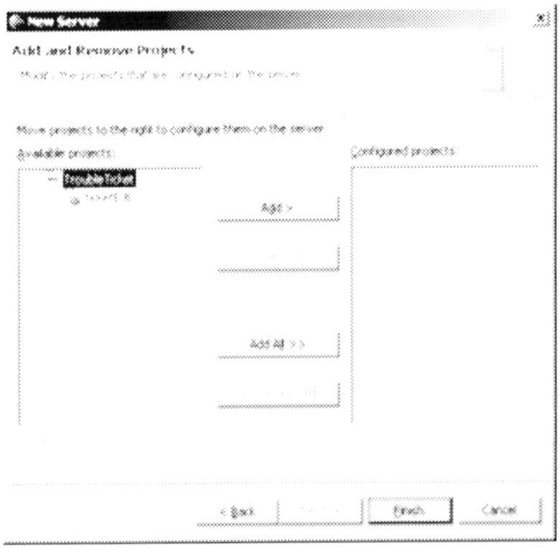

Figure 11-4. *Selecting projects to deploy to the server*

The defined server is immediately available in the Servers View as shown in Figure 11-5. Management of this server is possible through the server context menu and also the toolbar attached to the view. JST supports the deployment of many projects to a single server and additionally supports the deployment of a single project to multiple servers. When multiple servers are being used, care should be taken to either use a separate port for each of the servers or start only one server instance when multiple servers are attached to a single port.

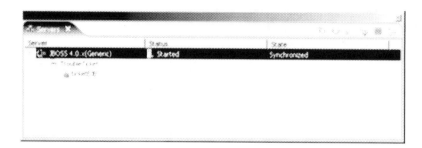

Figure 11-5. *The Servers View showing the configured JBoss server*

As shown in Figure 11-5, we have created only a single server instance to host the EJBs from our Trouble Ticket application.

Tip Editing the server can be accomplished by selecting the server within the Servers View and choosing Open from the context menu. A server overview page is provided to edit the server settings. Any changes made to this document must be saved before they will be reflected on the server.

To conclude the deployment process, we simply need to start the application server from the Servers View and view the output contents of this process in the Console View. Included in Listing 11-2 is an abbreviation of the output from the JBoss startup process. We have provided in bold font the section showing the deployment of our EJBs to the server. Once the server startup is completed, the new state of the server is reflected in the Servers View, and we can then access the EJB from any client application.

Listing 11-2. *Sample JBoss Server Starting Output*

```
13:05:39,109 INFO  [Server] Starting JBoss (MX MicroKernel)...
13:05:39,109 INFO  [Server] Release ID: JBoss [Zion] 4.0.1sp1 (build:
CVSTag=JBoss_4_0_1_SP1 date=200502160314)
13:05:39,119 INFO  [Server] Home Dir: C:\Java\Jboss\jboss-4.0.1
13:05:39,119 INFO  [Server] Home URL: file:/C:/Java/Jboss/jboss-4.0.1/
...
13:05:39,179 INFO  [Server] Starting General Purpose Architecture (GPA)...
13:05:41,212 INFO  [ServerInfo] Java version: 1.4.2_02,Sun Microsystems Inc.
```

```
13:05:41,212 INFO  [ServerInfo] Java VM: Java HotSpot(TM) Client VM
1.4.2_02-b03,Sun Microsystems Inc.
13:05:41,212 INFO  [ServerInfo] OS-System: Windows XP 5.1,x86
13:05:42,704 INFO  [Server] Core system initialized
...
13:06:37,393 INFO  [EjbModule] Deploying Ticket
13:06:37,723 INFO  [EjbModule] Deploying TicketService
13:06:37,763 INFO  [EjbModule] Deploying EmailTicket
14:35:34,167 INFO  [EJBDeployer] Deployed:
file:/C:/Java/Jboss/jboss-4.0.1/server/default/deploy/ticketEJB.jar

...
13:06:42,991 INFO  [Http11Protocol] Starting Coyote HTTP/1.1 on http-0.0.0.0-8080
13:06:43,552 INFO  [ChannelSocket] JK2: ajp13 listening on /0.0.0.0:8009
13:06:43,592 INFO  [JkMain] Jk running ID=0 time=0/201  config=null
13:06:43,672 INFO  [Server] JBoss (MX MicroKernel) [4.0.1sp1
(build: CVSTag=JBoss_4_0_1_SP1 date=200502160314)] Started in 1m:3s:591ms
```

Note Application servers may have memory leaks, so starting and stopping them within Eclipse can cause memory problems. One thing that may help is setting the -vmargs -Xmx arguments on the Eclipse command line.

Accessing the Deployed EJB

Objects that need to request services from the deployed EJB are known as *clients* of the EJB and require the interface types of each of the EJBs they intend to invoke from the application server to be made available to them. These interface types consist of the home and remote interfaces of each EJB that would be accessed as well as the primary key class for entity beans. These classes are often packaged into EJB client JAR files and are provided to every potential client of the deployed EJB.

During the creation of an EJB Project, JST creates a supporting EJB client module that will contain the interfaces for the project. For every enterprise bean created within your EJB Project, the necessary interfaces are created and stored within the corresponding client project. Additional classes exposed by the EJB such as return types and exception classes need to be made available to the client as well.

Eclipse eases the process of making these interfaces available to the EJB application clients by providing a mechanism to export classes out of both the EJB and EJB client project. You access this feature by choosing the project in use and selecting Export from the context menu. The exported file would need to be made available in the classpath of any application that intends to invoke a method from the deployed EJB.

Creating EJB Clients

We have provided in Chapter 8 an example of a client application that would access the Tick-etService EJB created within our application. This client would require the TicketService EJB interface types for the compilation of the EJB and also for connecting to it. Figure 11-6 shows how these interface types mediate access to the deployed EJB.

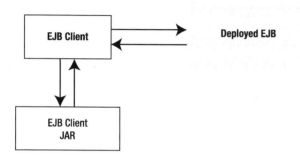

Figure 11-6. *Accessing a deployed EJB using an EJB client JAR*

By having the interface classes available locally, you can create an object of the same type as the EJB and only connect to the EJB when needed. We have shown how JST provides the EJB client JAR file that is required to access the deployed EJB. Listing 11-3 shows the EJB client we included in Chapter 8 to connect to our session bean.

Listing 11-3. *An EJB Client Class*

```
package com.projst.client;

import java.rmi.RemoteException;

import javax.ejb.CreateException;
import javax.naming.NamingException;

import com.projst.ticket.service.TicketService;
import com.projst.ticket.service.TicketServiceHome;
import com.projst.ticket.service.TicketServiceUtil;

/**
 * Remote TicketService (Session Bean) client.
 * @author cjudd
 */
public class Main {
```

```
/**
 * Application main entry point.
 * @param args command-line arguments
 */
public static void main(String[] args) {
    try {

        TicketServiceHome home = TicketServiceUtil.getHome();
        TicketService service = home.create();
        String result = service.ping("ping");
        System.out.println(result);

    } catch (NamingException e) {
        e.printStackTrace();
    } catch (RemoteException e) {
        e.printStackTrace();
    } catch (CreateException e) {
        e.printStackTrace();
    }
    System.out.println("\nDone");
  }
}
```

This class allows you to invoke methods that exist within the deployed TicketService bean. Compiling and running this code results in output being written to the Console View by the client application. Figure 11-7 shows a sample output from the client application.

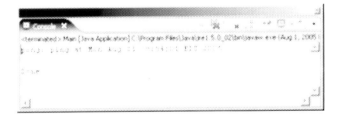

Figure 11-7. *Client accessing a deployed EJB*

Enterprise Archive File

It is important to remember that a deployed EJB module may not necessarily encapsulate an entire enterprise application. In fact, since many enterprise applications contain both Web Tier and EJB Tier contents, and an EJB JAR can only be composed of EJB-related content, it is reasonable to expect that an enterprise application would require additional deployment artifacts to support the entire application.

Within the EJB Tier, a common design concept to leverage reuse is to create compact EJB modules that are tasked with the provision of solutions to a specific set of problems. Enterprise applications can therefore be built through a composition of these EJB modules, web modules, and any other necessary artifacts that suit the need of that specific application. Figure 11-8 shows the possible composition of enterprise applications from a collection of available EJB and web modules as well as third-party client JARs.

Tip When Flexible projects are employed as we have described in Chapter 7, many of these compact EJB modules can be created within a single project.

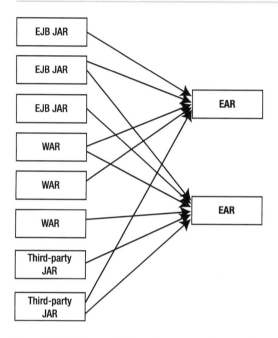

Figure 11-8. *Composition of an enterprise application*

As shown in Figure 11-8, J2EE deployment modules can be combined in various ways to create different enterprise applications. Each enterprise application is composed of multiple deployment modules packaged together within a single archive file. This archive file is known as the Enterprise Archive file, usually referred to as an EAR file. The EAR file uses the JAR file format, and this enables it to aggregate the multiple EJB JAR, WAR, and auxiliary files that together compose a complete enterprise application in a single file structure.

You can specify that deployable artifacts from your project be packaged into EAR files by creating an Enterprise Application Project and adding all the modules you want to combine together into a single EAR file to this project. The export feature, which is accessible by selecting File ➤ Export, can then be used to generate an EAR file from your Enterprise Application Project and export this file to the file system. An EAR file typically contains the following:

- `application.xml` deployment descriptor

- Enterprise beans in EJB JAR files

- Web applications in WAR files

- Application clients in JAR files

- JCA connectors in RAR files

- Dependent classes and third-party JAR files

A good way to look at an EAR file, therefore, is as a package of J2EE deployment artifacts and dependent libraries slated for deployment together within the same server environment. The target server for an EAR file must be one that contains both a web and an EJB container in order to guarantee that the EAR file will deploy properly. You therefore cannot use an application server like Tomcat or Jetty, both of which contain only a web container, as a target server for the deployment of an EAR file. We have shown in Figure 11-9 the possible contents of an EAR file.

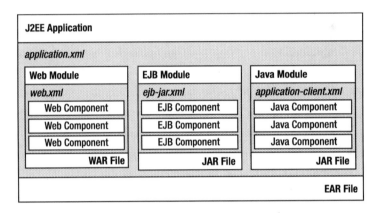

Figure 11-9. *Contents of an EAR file*

The web application and EJB modules within the EAR file each contain their own deployment descriptor appropriately packaged within the deployment module. For the EAR file, the `application.xml` deployment descriptor within the file must be located in the META-INF folder of the EAR file. This descriptor provides information about the deployable contents of the EAR file to any application server into which the file would be deployed. Table 11-3 shows the general contents of the `application.xml` file.

Table 11-3. *Contents of the application.xml Deployment Descriptor*

Deployment Tag	Description
`<icon>`	A 16×16 `<small-icon>` and a 32×32 `<large-icon>` that represent the J2EE application in a GUI tool.
`<display-name>`	A short name to be displayed in a GUI tool.
`<description>`	A description of the application.
`<module>`	Deployable modules contained within the enterprise application file. A separate `<module>` tag is used to describe each module and within this, a `<web>`, `<ejb>`, or `<java>` tag is included specifying a WAR, EJB JAR, or application client JAR file, respectively.
`<security-role>`	Security roles for the application.

Summary

In this chapter, we introduced the forms in which enterprise applications are packaged for deployment into an application server. Concentrating on the packaging of EJB Tier code, we described how this code is often packaged into EJB JAR files to aid the transfer of the multiple files required by the deployment module. We also described the contents of an EJB deployment module including the location for EJB code content and the required deployment descriptor named `ejb-jar.xml`. Furthermore, we discussed the use of application server–specific deployment descriptors that are required by many application servers to provide them with additional information about the components being deployed.

Deployed EJBs need to be accessed by a client that often exists within a different environment. In such instances, the client needs to have a copy of the interface types for each of the EJBs they intend to invoke. We described how Eclipse simplifies the provision of this EJB client library, and we created a client to invoke methods from the TroubleTicket project, which we have presented in preceding chapters.

Finally, we examined the creation of EAR files as deployable modules that often contain the Web-Tier and EJB-Tier elements that make up an enterprise application. We examined the packaging of such a file as well as the `application.xml` deployment descriptor that it requires.

CHAPTER 12

JavaServer Pages

Java's popularity began with applets providing client-side functionality on web pages. However, Java's strengths shined when it began being used on the server side to generate dynamic web content. Initially, content was generated using servlet technology, the topic of Chapter 13. Due to the complexities of the development cycle and having to maintain HTML in Java code (including escaping characters), servlets have become more of an infrastructure or framework technology and less of a dynamic web content technology. Developers quickly adopted JavaServer Pages (JSP) in order to avoid some of the servlet complexities. Like servlets, JSP pages enable server-side dynamic content generation. However, unlike servlets, JSP pages are a template-based technology that makes the maintenance of the HTML easier. In some cases, JSP pages can even be modified and maintained by web designers rather than Java developers. Both JSP pages and servlets are included in J2EE 1.4.

Beginning with J2EE 5.0, a new server-side web technology joins JSP pages and servlets: JavaServer Faces (JSF). JSF is also a server-side web technology. But rather than being template based like JSP pages or a course-grained class like servlets, JSF is a user interface (UI) component framework. The goal of JSF is to provide reusable UI components with different renders depending on the client device making the request.

Note Because at this time JST is intended to support J2EE 1.4 development, JSF is not covered in this book or in JST.

In this chapter, we will explore developing JSP pages with JST, beginning with a brief overview of JSP pages. Then we will outline some JSP-related and supporting technologies, JSP Standard Tag Library (JSTL) and the open source Apache Struts framework. We will also explain how to configure and use them within JST. Finally, we will conclude by showing you how to use JSP pages, HTML, JSTL, and Struts to interact with stateless session beans in your Business Tier.

JavaServer Pages Overview

JavaServer Pages are a template-based Java technology for developing dynamic web applications. JSP pages are similar to other template-based technologies such as Microsoft Active Server Pages (ASP) and PHP. Most people think of JSP pages as HTML with Java sprinkled in, while they think of servlets as Java with HTML sprinkled in. Listing 12-1 shows the most basic JSP example that displays a "Hello World" message followed by the date.

Listing 12-1. *Basic JSP Example*

```
<%@page import="java.util.*" %>
<html>
 <head>
  <title>Hello World</title>
 </head>
 <body>
  <h1>Hello World</h1>
  <p>
   Today's date is <%= new Date().toString() %>
  </p>
 </body>
</html>
```

Notice that the majority of the example in Listing 12-1 looks like HTML. It is only the first page directive and the printing of the new date that are not HTML. The page directive gives instructions to the application server on how to handle the page. In this case, it is only instructing the application server to import the classes in the java.util package. But other attributes can be used to give additional instructions about handling the session, threads, buffer size, errors, and more.

The <%= **expression** %> notation used to print out the date is called an *expression*. It can evaluate any expression that evaluates to a String. The resulting String is then inlined into the response at the location the expression is declared. JSP pages also have a notation that can contain any valid Java code called a *scriptlet*. The notation is similar to the expression <% **code** %>. The scriptlet is typically considered an antipattern because using scriptlets makes it too tempting to introduce business logic where it does not belong.

JSP pages have many other kinds of notations, features, and expression languages that are outside the scope of this chapter.

Tip A wonderful tool for learning JSP pages is Sun's free JavaServer Pages Syntax Card available at http://java.sun.com/products/jsp/syntax/2.0/card20.pdf.

One of the aspects developers and architects did not like about earlier template-based technologies was that each time the template was accessed it would be reinterpreted. So, JSP pages were architected to only be interpreted on the first request. On that first request, JSP pages are therefore compiled to a servlet. This is just one example of servlets being more of an infrastructure technology. All subsequent requests will use the compiled and loaded servlet in memory. If a JSP page changes, though, it is recompiled and the request uses the new version.

This is the primary reason an application server must use a Java Developer Kit (JDK) rather than the Java Runtime Environment (JRE). The application server needs the compiling tool available in the JDK to compile the JSP page to a servlet.

JSP pages are not typically used in a vacuum. JSP pages, of course, are used in conjunction with other web technologies like Cascading Style Sheets (CSS) and JavaScript. But they are also often used in conjunction with servlets in an MVC pattern (see the "Model-View-Controller Pattern" sidebar) and tag libraries.

MODEL-VIEW-CONTROLLER PATTERN

To reduce the problems of reuse and separation of concerns when developing and designing web applications with JSP pages and servlets, developers commonly use the model-view-controller (MVC) or Model 2 pattern. This design pattern separates the data (model) from the presentation (view) and the workflow (controller), as the following diagram shows. Typically, the model is implemented as a JavaBean, the view as JSP pages, and the controller as a servlet. Unfortunately, without a careful design, this practice can also turn into a difficult-to-manage design as well. Servlets can become large nested if/else statements that are difficult to read and maintain. Many open source MVC frameworks have been developed to minimize bad practices and increase development velocity. One example is Struts.

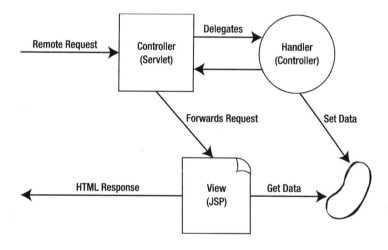

Typically, a controller is implemented as a servlet that initially receives an HTTP request and delegates the request to a controller handler based on the URL using a mapping from a configuration file. The handler is responsible for application-specific functionality based on the request. The handler may look up information from datasources such as relational databases through JDBC, data-access objects, and EJB services, or through legacy systems. The results are then placed into a model, which is implemented as a JavaBean or Plain Old Java Object (POJO). The model is passed to the view layer as an attribute of the request object. When the handler is complete, it returns a status that the controller can then use to forward the request.

When the request gets forwarded to the view (JSP), the view gets the model out of the request attribute and displays it appropriately. The view should never contain any business logic. To ensure business logic is not introduced in the view layer, it is a common practice to use tag libraries such as JSTL to display data and iterate through collections.

Like servlets and other web-related files, JSP pages are packaged in a web archive or WAR file. A WAR file has its own deployment descriptor named `web.xml` and is located in the web applica- tion's `WEB-INF` directory. Depending on whether the web components have dependencies on EJBs, the web archive can be deployed on its own or as part of an Enterprise Archive, or EAR.

JSP Standard Tag Library Overview

Shortly after JSP pages were released, it was obvious that JSP pages suffered from a reuse problem. The only ways to share common functionality was to have common JSP pages and include them or to use a POJO. Writing libraries based on included JSP pages just never felt right and made it difficult to maintain JSP pages. POJOs, on the other hand, caused a lot of duplicate code in JSP scriptlets. Every time a POJO was used, it would have to be instantiated, and the common web objects like the request, response, and session would have to be passed to it. This too made the JSP pages difficult to maintain.

Fortunately, custom tag libraries were introduced and became a standard means of reuse in JSP pages. Custom tag libraries use a simple XML tag format and hide all the ugly details of creating and initializing the object. In a lot of ways, they employ a pattern similar to that of dependency injections. Custom tag libraries are easy to write, use, and debug. So, unfortunately, everybody started creating their own tag libraries. Each vendor, open source web framework team, and development team had their own. Of course, each library had a lot of overlap, like iterating and conditionals, but each did such things slightly differently. Using a vendor's tag library often led to vendor lock-in. So, the JSP Standard Tag Library was created to consolidate and standardize the most common tags.

JSTL includes many of the common constructs you would probably expect from a reusable JSP library. They are categorized into five different libraries. Table 12-1 contains a list of the libraries and their descriptions.

Table 12-1. *JSTL Tag Libraries*

Library	Description
Core	Contains iterator, conditional, exception, and out tags
Formatting	Contains date and time formatters as well as messages from resource bundles
SQL	Contains JDBC tags for querying, updating, getting connections, and transaction management
XML	Similar to the core library except it uses XML rather than JavaBeans as the datasource
Functions	Contains `String`-related functions—for example, contains `indexOf` and `replace`

It is highly recommended that when using tag libraries you opt for using the JSTL tags over vendor- or framework-specific tags for the same functionality. Many vendors and frameworks such as Struts have announced they are deprecating tags that overlap with the JSTL tags. For example, the Struts documentation recommends using the JSTL `fmt:message` tag over its own `bean:message`.

The most commonly used JSTL implementation is the reference implementation from the Apache Jakarta Taglibs project, hosted at `http://jakarta.apache.org/taglibs/`. They offer versions 1.0 for the JSP 1.2 Specification and 1.1 for the JSP 2.0 Specification. JSTL 1.1 is the appropriate version for J2EE 1.4 containers. The implementation can be downloaded at `http://jakarta.apache.org/site/downloads/downloads_taglibs-standard.cgi`.

We will be using the JSTL core library in the example at the end of this chapter. Before that, we will show you how to install it and other tag libraries shortly.

Struts Overview

Struts has become the de facto standard MVC framework for Java web development (see the "Model-View-Controller Pattern" sidebar). It is an open source Apache project found at `http://struts.apache.org`. Combined with JSP pages, it contains everything needed for an MVC framework: controller, model, and view. But it includes a lot more as well: a validation framework, simplified file uploading, and some internationalization functionality. It is also flexible enough to use a wide variety of view technologies including JSF, Velocity, XSLT, and rich clients like Flex and Lasslo.

Struts resembles the description of MVC frameworks in the "Model-View-Controller Pattern" sidebar. The controller for Struts is the `ActionServlet`. It starts up at deployment time and loads the `struts-config.xml` file to determine its mappings. It delegates application-specific logic to `Action` classes. For the model, it can use JavaBeans or a specialized JavaBean called an `ActionForm`. The advantage of using an `ActionForm` over a standard JavaBean is that Struts can automatically populate the `ActionForm` on your behalf with values from an HTML form. As mentioned before, Struts applications typically use JSP pages as the view technology. For this reason, Struts also provides several tag libraries for simplifying JSP development. Table 12-2 lists and describes the Struts tag libraries. To further simplify the view layer, Struts includes the Tiles framework for assembling pages by creating reusable view components called *tiles*. These tiles can be aggregated together using a screen definition, which is much more flexible than using standard JSP page includes for headers, footers, and menus.

Table 12-2. *Struts Tag Libraries*

Library	Description
Bean	Contains tags for using cookies and header and request parameters, as well as interacting with JavaBeans
HTML	Contains Struts-style tags for common HTML tags like those for generating forms, buttons, and hyperlinks
Logic	Contains tags for iteration and conditional logic
Nested	Same as tags in the bean, HTML, and logic libraries, with the added ability to relate tags by nesting them
Tiles	Tags for using the Tiles framework for assembling view components

As mentioned in Chapter 4, open source frameworks like Struts that don't implement a JCP-based standard are out of scope for JST, even though Struts has become the de facto standard web application MVC framework. That said, most of the basic Java tools and XML tools built into JDT and WTP provide enough functionality to successfully use Struts. Unfortunately, you don't get any fancy wizards, dialog boxes, or action mapping graphs, but those aren't really necessary. If you need that kind of support, there are multiple commercial and open source Struts plug-ins that could be used alongside JST.

Tip If you want to learn more about JavaServer Pages or JSTL, we suggest you read *Beginning J2EE 1.4: From Novice to Professional* by James L. Weaver, Kevin Mukhar, and Jim Crume (Apress, 2004) or *Pro J2EE 1.4: From Professional to Expert* by Meeraj Kunnumpurath and Sue Spielman (Apress, 2004). If you want to learn more about Struts, we suggest you read *Pro Jakarta Struts, Second Edition* by John Carnell and Rob Harrop (Apress, 2004).

Configuring Web Applications

For a Dynamic Web Project, the root of the web application is the WebContent directory. Within this directory, you will find externally addressable web elements such as HTML and JSP files. You may also find other externally addressable subdirectories such as images and styles for holding JPEGs, GIFs, and CSS. There is also a required WEB-INF directory, which is not externally addressable and therefore usually stores configuration files.

A web application's primary configuration is done in the web application's deployment descriptor, the web.xml file. The deployment descriptor is required to be in the WEB-INF directory. This directory is traditionally where all other web framework and tag library definitions are stored as well. For example, the Struts configuration file and JSTL's tag library definition files are commonly stored in the WEB-INF directory. These three configuration files are discussed in the next three sections.

Web Application Deployment Descriptor

The web application deployment descriptor, web.xml, is an XML file that contains configurations for servlets, tag libraries, filters, MIME type mapping, and security. This file really does not contain any configurations specific to JSP pages. However, frameworks like Struts and tag libraries like JSTL require configurations to be made here.

Caution When a Dynamic Web Project is initially created, it comes with a simple web.xml. If a servlet is added to the project using the Servlet wizard, an XDoclet Builder is also added to the project and begins running. When XDoclet runs the xdocletweb.xml script, it overwrites the existing web.xml file. This happens any time a servlet with XDoclet annotations is modified and saved or a build is explicitly invoked. To prevent this surprise from happening, you may want to create a servlet immediately after creating a Dynamic Web Project (see Chapter 13). The downside is any time you make changes to the merge files like servlets.xml, servlet-mappings.xml, or taglibs.xml, you will have to run an explicit build to regenerate the web.xml file. In addition, there must be at least one XDoclet-annotated servlet in the project or XDoclet Builder won't run the xdocletweb.xml script and regenerate the web.xml file even if the build is explicitly invoked.

Just as EJB deployment descriptors are generated from annotations in the EJB beans, the web application deployment descriptor can be generated from annotations in servlets. Chapter 13 explains the servlet-specific XDoclet annotations. While JSP pages cannot contain XDoclet annotations, the fact that the web.xml file is generated affects how you configure JSP-related frameworks. If you have experience developing web applications, you may have made modifications to the web.xml directly. With XDoclet generating this file, you will not want to modify it directly or your changes will get overwritten. Instead, XDoclet provides smaller files that represent subsets of the web.xml file that are merged together. These files and their descriptions are contained in Table 12-3.

Table 12-3. *XDoclet Merge Files*

File	Description
filters.xml	Filter declaration
filter-mappings.xml	Filter to URL or servlet mappings
listeners.xml	Listener declarations
servlets.xml	Servlet declarations
servlet-mappings.xml	Servlet to URL mapping
mime-mappings.xml	MIME type to extension mapping
error-pages.xml	Error code or exception mapping to URL
taglibs.xml	Tag library declaration
web-security.xml	Security settings
web-settings.xml	Web application display name, description, and context parameters
welcomefiles.xml	List of file names to use if a specific file is not specified in the URL

The merge files listed in Table 12-3 must be placed in the XDoclet merge directory. For Dynamic Web Projects, the web merge directory is the WEB-INF directory. When the XDoclet Builder runs, it will merge these files and any annotations defined in servlets to generate the web.xml file in the WEB-INF directory.

Note The XDoclet Builder runs the \plugins\org.eclipse.jst.j2ee.ejb.annotations.xdoclet_
1.0.0\templates\builder\xdocletweb.xml Ant script.

In the next sections, we will demonstrate adding a Struts servlet and servlet mapping as well as a tag library declaration to the merge files.

Struts

Configuring a Dynamic Web Project to use Struts requires a couple of steps. First, you must include Struts and its dependent libraries in the web application's classpath. Second, you must configure the Struts ActionServlet in the web.xml file. Finally, you must create the primary Struts configuration file struts-config.xml. If you also choose to use the Struts tag libraries, you must configure those as well. Configuring tag libraries is discussed in the next section.

The Struts JAR and its dependent libraries can be extracted from the lib directory of the Struts tar or zip file. Depending on the version of Struts, these may include struts.jar, antlr. jar, commons-beanutils.jar, commons-digester.jar, commons-fileupload.jar, commons-logging. jar, commons-validator.jar, and jakarta-oro.jar. In order to add the files to the web application classpath, copy them to the WEB-INF/lib directory. This is a special directory that, according to the servlet specification, includes all *.jar files to that web application's classpath. Likewise, there is a special WEB-INF/classes directory that is also included in the classpath.

To add a servlet such as the Struts ActionServlet in a JST Web Project with an XDoclet Builder, you must create a servlets.xml and servlet-mappings.xml file in the WEB-INF directory. To do this, you can use the Eclipse File wizard. Listing 12-2 shows the minimal Struts ActionServlet configuration necessary, and Listing 12-3 shows the conventional ActionServlet mapping.

Listing 12-2. *Struts ActionServlet Declaration in servlets.xml*

```
<servlet>
  <servlet-name>action</servlet-name>
  <servlet-class>org.apache.struts.action.ActionServlet</servlet-class>
  <init-param>
    <param-name>config</param-name>
    <param-value>/WEB-INF/struts-config.xml</param-value>
  </init-param>
  <load-on-startup>1</load-on-startup>
</servlet>
```

In Listing 12-2, you can see that the Struts ActionServlet is being declared with a servlet name of action. The action name is used in Listing 12-3 to map the ActionServlet to a URL pattern. The ActionServlet must be told where its configuration file, traditionally called struts-config.xml, is located within the web context. This is done using an initialization parameter named config. Lastly, this configuration shows a load-on-startup element. It is used to instruct the application server of the order in which servlets should be loaded. If this element is not included, the servlet is loaded the first time a web browser makes a request for it. In order to improve performance on the first request, it is common to load the ActionServlet as the first servlet.

Listing 12-3. *Struts ActionServlet Mapping in servlet-mappings.xml*

```
<servlet-mapping>
  <servlet-name>action</servlet-name>
  <url-pattern>*.do</url-pattern>
</servlet-mapping>
```

By convention, the Struts application usually uses a *.do URL pattern to direct requests to the ActionServlet. The ActionServlet then uses the request to determine the appropriate action configured in the struts-config.xml file to fulfill the request. While *.do is the most common URL pattern used, it is by no means the only URL pattern that could be used. Listing 12-3 shows how the standard *.do is mapped to the ActionServlet.

In the Listing 12-2, you saw how to configure the ActionServlet to point to the struts-config. xml file. This file contains many types of configurations including form beans, exception handlers, resource bundles, forwards, and action mappings. In the "Writing a Struts Action" section, you will learn how to configure an action. At this point, all we want to do is demonstrate creating the base struts-config.xml file so we can add to it later. The basic struts-config.xml file is listed in Listing 12-4.

Listing 12-4. *Basic Starting struts-config.xml File*

```
<?xml version="1.0" encoding="UTF-8"?>
<!DOCTYPE struts-config
    PUBLIC "-//Apache Software Foundation//DTD Struts Configuration 1.1//EN"
    "http://jakarta.apache.org/struts/dtds/struts-config_1_1.dtd">
<struts-config>
  <form-beans>
  </form-beans>
  <action-mappings>
  </action-mappings>
  <message-resources
      parameter="com.projst.ticket.web.ApplicationResources" />
</struts-config>
```

Listing 12-4 sets up the common sections of a struts-config.xml file. The form-beans section contains named JavaBeans that extend org.apache.struts.action.ActionForm. Struts uses the values from HTML forms to automatically populate these form beans. These beans are then passed as parameters to an Action class's execute method.

As you will see later, the action mapping maps a URL to a class that handles the request. The class handling the request must extend org.apache.struts.action.Action. Actions typically override the execute method to perform some logic, interacting with a database, legacy system, or service in this case. Once they handle the request, they usually put information to be displayed by the view, JSP, in the request attribute list or on a form bean.

> **Note** XDoclet can be used to generate the struts-config.xml file from annotations in the action and form bean classes. However, by default, the xdocletweb.xml script included with JST is not configured to generate the XDoclet mappings. It could, however, be modified to do so.

The message-resources are the last configuration in the struts-config.xml found in Listing 12-4. They reference a properties file that can contain labels and text that are displayed on JSP pages. These values can be displayed using the Struts bean message tag or as a part of the validation process. One of the primary reasons for using message-resources is to support multiple languages.

Tag Libraries

Configuring a tag library is a three-step process. First, put the tag library files in the classpath. Second, copy the tag library definition (tld) files to the WEB-INF directory. Finally, configure the tag library in the web.xml file. In this section, we will show you how to configure the JSTL core, Struts bean, and Struts HTML tag libraries.

> **Note** Explicit configuring of tag libraries in the web.xml file is not necessary for JSP 1.2 and beyond due to automatic tld discovery.

Just like you need to include Struts in the web application's classpath, you must copy tag library JARs to the `WEB-INF/lib` directory. If you have configured your application for Struts, then you already have the necessary classes for the Struts bean and HTML tag libraries. To include the JSTL classes, extract the `jstl.jar` and `standard.jar` files from the `lib` directory of the `jakarta-taglibs-standard` tar or zip file and put them in the `WEB-INF/lib` directory.

Commonly, tld files are stored in the `WEB-INF` directory like other configuration files. To use the Struts bean and HTML tag libraries, copy `struts-bean.tld` and `struts-html.tld` from the `lib` directory of the Struts tar or zip file to the `WEB-INF` directory. To use the JSTL core tag library, copy `c.tld` from the `tld` directory of the `jakarta-taglibs-standard` tar or zip file to the web application's `WEB-INF` directory.

You will also need to configure the libraries in the `web.xml` file. For Dynamic Web Projects that include an XDoclet Builder, a `taglibs.xml` file must be created in the `WEB-INF` directory using Eclipse's New File wizard to contain the configuration. When the XDoclet Builder runs, the contents of the file will be merged into the `web.xml` file. Listing 12-5 shows an example of the `taglibs.xml` file with JSTL core, Struts bean, and Struts HTML libraries declared.

Listing 12-5. *Some Tag Libraries Configured in the taglibs.xml File*

```
<taglib>
  <taglib-uri>struts-bean</taglib-uri>
  <taglib-location>/WEB-INF/struts-bean.tld</taglib-location>
</taglib>
<taglib>
  <taglib-uri>struts-html</taglib-uri>
  <taglib-location>/WEB-INF/struts-html.tld</taglib-location>
</taglib>
<taglib>
  <taglib-uri>jstl-core</taglib-uri>
  <taglib-location>/WEB-INF/c.tld</taglib-location>
</taglib>
```

Listing 12-5 shows the JSTL core, Struts bean, and Struts HTML tags configured in the `taglibs.xml` file. The `taglib-uri` value is used by a JSP `taglib` directive to locate the tld file referenced in the `taglib-location`.

Writing a Struts Action

In this section, you are going to see how to create and configure a Struts action that uses the session bean and service methods from Chapters 8 and 9 to retrieve a list of all the trouble tickets in the system. There are no special wizards or utilities included with JST to support building Struts actions. However, the standard Eclipse Class wizard can easily be used to create a class that extends the `org.apache.struts.action.Action` class. Then you can use the standard Eclipse Override/Implement Methods utility to override the `execute` method and implement the service lookup and calls.

Create Action Class

To invoke the New Java Class wizard while in the Java Perspective, choose File ➤ New ➤ Class from the main menu. On the Java Class page (see Figure 12-1), make sure you select the source folder of your web project. If this class is placed in the EJB or other source folder, the web application will not be able to find it, and you will get a ClassNotFoundException at runtime. It is a common practice to put all actions in an action or actions package. For a large web application, you will probably have many actions. So, make sure the action name is descriptive. Also, make sure to change the superclass to org.apache.struts.action.Action.

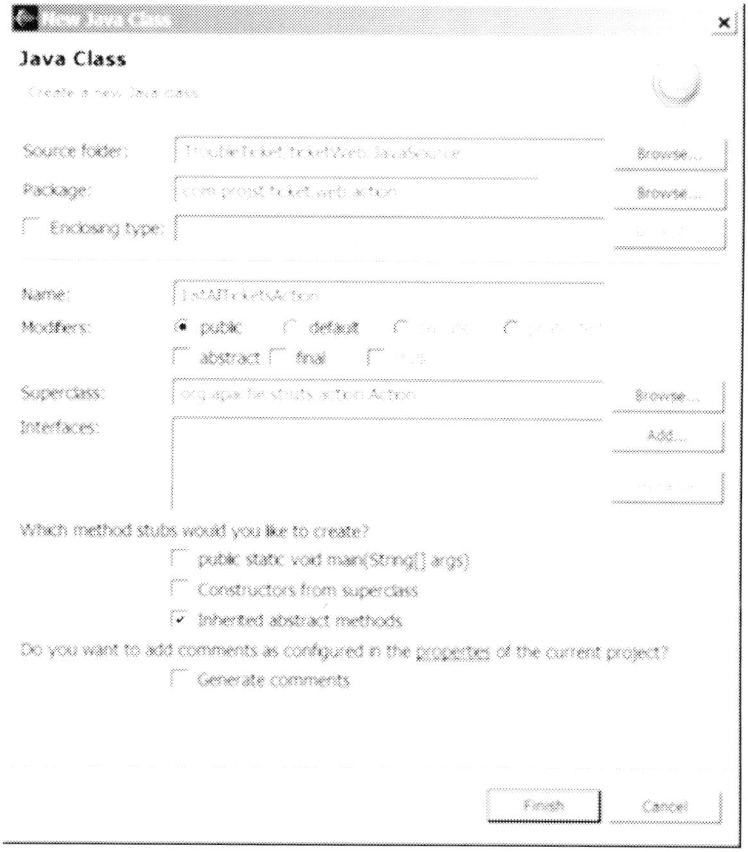

Figure 12-1. *Creating a Struts action with the New Java Class wizard*

When complete, the wizard will generate the action shown in Listing 12-6.

Listing 12-6. *Initial ListAllTicketAction*

```
package com.projst.ticket.web.action;

import org.apache.struts.action.Action;

public class ListAllTicketsAction extends Action {

}
```

To override the execute method of org.apache.struts.action.Action, choose Source ➤ Override/Implement Methods from the main menu. In the Override/Implement Methods dialog box, select the execute method that accepts the HttpServletRequest and HttpServletResponse parameters as shown in Figure 12-2.

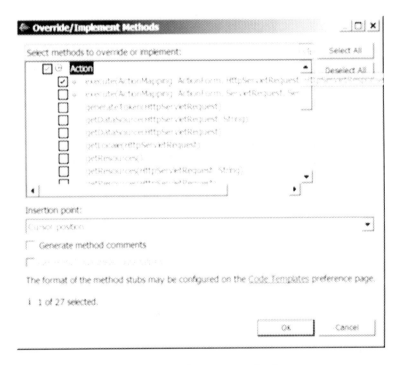

Figure 12-2. *Overriding the Action's execute method*

After using the Override/Implement Method utility, you should get an execute method like the one in Listing 12-7.

Listing 12-7. *ListAllTicketAction After Overriding the execute Method*

```
package com.projst.ticket.web.action;

import javax.servlet.http.HttpServletRequest;
import javax.servlet.http.HttpServletResponse;
```

```
import org.apache.struts.action.Action;
import org.apache.struts.action.ActionForm;
import org.apache.struts.action.ActionForward;
import org.apache.struts.action.ActionMapping;

public class ListAllTicketsAction extends Action {

  public ActionForward execute(ActionMapping arg0, ActionForm arg1,
      HttpServletRequest arg2, HttpServletResponse arg3)
      throws Exception
  {
    // TODO Auto-generated method stub
    return super.execute(arg0, arg1, arg2, arg3);
  }

}
```

As you can see in Listing 12-7, the Override/Implement Method utility generates an execute method stub. The parameter names are not very friendly, and the implementation does not do much. So you want to finish the action by changing it to look like Listing 12-8.

Listing 12-8. *Finished ListAllTicketsAction*

```
package com.projst.ticket.web.action;

import java.util.Collection;

import javax.servlet.http.HttpServletRequest;
import javax.servlet.http.HttpServletResponse;

import org.apache.struts.action.Action;
import org.apache.struts.action.ActionForm;
import org.apache.struts.action.ActionForward;
import org.apache.struts.action.ActionMapping;

import com.projst.ticket.service.TicketServiceLocal;
import com.projst.ticket.service.TicketServiceUtil;

public class ListAllTicketsAction extends Action {

  private static final String SUCCESS_FORWARD = "success";

  public ActionForward execute(ActionMapping mapping, ActionForm form,
      HttpServletRequest request, HttpServletResponse response) throws Exception
  {
    TicketServiceLocal service = TicketServiceUtil.getLocalHome().create();
    Collection tickets = service.retrieveAllTickets();
    request.setAttribute("tickets",tickets);
```

```
        return mapping.findForward(SUCCESS_FORWARD);
    }

}
```

First, notice in Listing 12-8 that the parameters are much more readable. Next, notice the actual implementation of the execute method. First, the TicketServiceUtil class is used to create a TicketServiceLocal. You can and should use the local interfaces from a web application because they will be deployed in the same JVM as the EJBs. Using the local interface will provide the best performance. Next, the retrieveAllTickets service method is called. This returns a collection of TicketData Data Transfer Objects. This collection is then placed in the request attribute map with the name of tickets. In the JSP, you will iterate over this collection to print out the details of each of the tickets. Finally, you use an ActionMapping object (see Listing 12-9 in the next section) representing the XML mapping in the struts-config.xml file to look up a forward called success. This forward can either be to another action or a view technology like JSP, a Struts tiles definition, or a third-party view technology like Apache Velocity or even JavaServer Faces.

Mapping Action Class

Once the action is complete, it needs to be mapped in the struts-config.xml to a URL so the ActionServlet knows when to invoke it. Since this is the first page of the Trouble Ticket application, it will be mapped to the index.do URL. See Listing 12-9 for the mapping.

Listing 12-9. *ListAllTicketsAction struts-config.xml Mapping*

```
<?xml version="1.0" encoding="UTF-8"?>
<!DOCTYPE struts-config
    PUBLIC "-//Apache Software Foundation//DTD Struts Configuration 1.1//EN"
    "http://jakarta.apache.org/struts/dtds/struts-config_1_1.dtd">

<struts-config>
  <form-beans>
  </form-beans>
  <global-exceptions>
  </global-exceptions>
  <global-forwards>
  </global-forwards>
  <action-mappings>
    <action
        type="com.projst.ticket.web.action.ListAllTicketsAction"
        scope="request" path="/index">
      <forward name="success" path="/WEB-INF/jsp/listtickets.jsp" />
    </action>
  </action-mappings>
  <message-resources parameter="com.projst.ticket.web.ApplicationResources" />
</struts-config>
```

In Listing 12-9, the highlighted action is the mapping added to the original struts-config.xml file from Listing 12-4. Based on the path attribute of /index, the ActionServlet is instructed to execute the action when /index.do is requested according to the *.do mapping in Listing 12-3. This invokes the execute method on the com.projst.ticket.web.action.ListAllTicketsAction base on the type attribute.

The action mapping in Listing 12-9 contains a forward with the name of success. This is the success forward the ListAllTicketsAction looked up using the mapping instance in Listing 12-8. The forward instructs the ActionServlet to forward the request on to the listtickets.jsp you will learn how to create in the next section.

Writing JavaServer Pages

In this section, you will learn to use the JSP wizard and JSP editor to create the web page shown in Figure 12-3 to display trouble tickets retrieved from ListAllTicketsAction. In order to do this, we will demonstrate the use of both JSP and JSTL features.

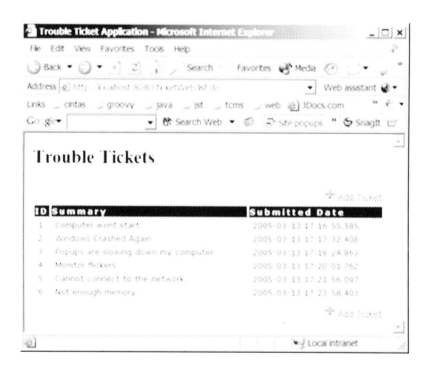

Figure 12-3. *Trouble tickets page*

JSP Wizard

Creating a JSP using the wizard is a two-step process. The first step is selecting the directory and file name (see Figure 12-4). The second step is choosing a JSP template (see Figure 12-5).

In the J2EE Perspective, the JSP wizard can be invoked by right-clicking the project and choosing New ➤ JSP. Otherwise, you can always get to it by choosing File ➤ New ➤ Other ➤ Web ➤ JSP.

Best Practice It is a good practice to put JSP pages related to Struts applications in a directory under the WEB-INF directory such as WEB-INF/jsp. This is because the WEB-INF directory contents are not externally addressable. This prevents them from being invoked directly by a user and bypassing the actions needed for setup.

Figure 12-4. *The first step in the JSP wizard*

As the preceding best practice states, JSP pages should be placed in a subdirectory of the WEB-INF directory. These files typically have a .jsp, .jsv, .jtpl, or .jspx extension. This page is named listtickets.jsp because it will iterate through all the tickets in the system and display them in an HTML table.

The second page enables you to choose from one of three JSP templates included in JST. You can also opt to create your own JSP template. This is a good idea, since it is likely you will commonly use the same tag libraries and you can put all your tag library directives in the template and save some typing. This page makes that easy by providing a hyperlink styled JSP Templates at the top of the page. Clicking that link will immediately take you to the template editor. You can also get to the JSP template editor by choosing Windows ➤ Preferences ➤ Web and XML ➤ JSP Files ➤ JSP Templates. Not only can you configure new file templates, you can also define JSP tags, attributes, and attribute values. So if you find yourself constantly typing a JSTL <forEach> tag, make it a template and save some typing. The results of the wizard for the New JSP File (html) option are shown in Listing 12-10.

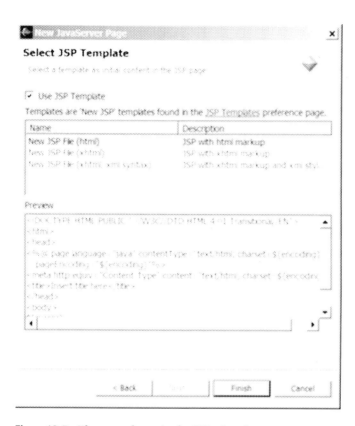

Figure 12-5. *The second step in the JSP wizard*

Listing 12-10. *Result of the New JSP Wizard*

```
<!DOCTYPE HTML PUBLIC "-//W3C//DTD HTML 4.01 Transitional//EN">
<html>
<head>
<%@ page language="java" contentType="text/html; charset=ISO-8859-1"
    pageEncoding="ISO-8859-1"%>
<meta http-equiv="Content-Type" content="text/html; charset=ISO-8859-1">
<title>Insert title here</title>
</head>
<body>

</body>
</html>
```

As you can see in Listing 12-10, the wizard generates a very simple HTML file with the
only JSP element being the page directive.

The JSP editor is a very complicated Structured Source Editor (SSE) because it must support
not only the JSP syntax, but also HTML, JavaScript, XML, and Java. It contains many helpful
features such as automatically finishing tags when </ is typed, hover help for HTML tags, and

code assist (Ctrl+space) for HTML, JSP tags, and any custom tag libraries declared in a taglib directive on that page. It also provides access to the JSP and HTML templates using code assist.

To iterate through the ticket collection the ListAllTicketsAction put in the request, you will want to use the JSTL core library's <forEach> tag and print the values of the TicketData attribute's <out> tag. See Listing 12-11 for the final JSP page.

Listing 12-11. *Final listtickets.jsp*

```
<!DOCTYPE HTML PUBLIC "-//W3C//DTD HTML 4.01 Transitional//EN">
<html>
<head>
  <link rel="stylesheet" type="text/css" href="styles/default.css"/>
<%@ page language="java" contentType="text/html; charset=ISO-8859-1"
    pageEncoding="ISO-8859-1"%>
<%@ taglib uri="jstl-core" prefix="c" %>
<meta http-equiv="Content-Type" content="text/html; charset=ISO-8859-1">
<title>Trouble Ticket Application</title>
</head>
<body>
<h2>Trouble Tickets</h2>
<table width="100%" border="0">
  <tr class="add">
    <td>
      <a href="/newTicket.do">
        <img src="images/add.gif" border="0" /> Add Ticket
      </a>
    </td>
  </tr>
</table>
<table width="100%">
  <tr class="heading">
    <th>ID</th>
    <th>Summary</th>
    <th>Submitted Date</th>
  </tr>
<c:forEach items="${tickets}" var="ticket">
  <tr class="row">
    <td> <c:out value="${ticket.id}"/></td>
    <td> <c:out value="${ticket.summary}"/></td>
    <td> <c:out value="${ticket.submitted}"/></td>
  </tr>
</c:forEach>
</table>
<table width="100%" border="0">
  <tr class="add">
    <td>
      <a href="/newTicket.do">
```

```
        <img src="images/add.gif" border="0" /> Add Ticket
      </a>
    </td>
  </tr>
</table>

</body>
</html>
```

Listing 12-11 highlights the changes to the originally generated JSP. It includes the addition of the JSTL core `taglib` directive so the `<c:out>` and `<c:forEach>` tags could be used. It also contains a more appropriate Trouble Ticket application title and a level-2 header in the body of the trouble ticket. After the header is the first of two small tables used for formatting the add ticket functionality. One is above the main table and the other is below.

The main table contains a row for the headers. The header includes the hard-coded labels of ID, Summary, and Submitted Date. These labels could have been stored in a resource bundle and read at runtime using the JSTL formatting library. For the body of the table, the `<c:forEach>` tag is used to iterate over the collection of `TicketData`s stored in the request attributes. The property notation `${tickets}` is used to look for an attribute named `ticket` in the page, request, session, and application scopes. During each iteration, the current `TicketData` object is stored in a variable called `ticket` according to the `var` attribute. In each cell, a `<c:out>` tag is used to get the value of a ticket attribute. A property notation is used rather than having to explicitly call the getter method.

After you learn how to deploy the application in Chapter 14, you can use the URL `http://localhost:8080/ticketWeb/index.do` to view the page running in the application server.

Summary

In this chapter, you learned that JSP, Struts, and JSTL are technologies that can be used together to create complex and maintainable web applications. You also learned how to configure and use each of them in the context of JST. In the next chapter, we will review the other web technology, servlets, followed by how to package and deploy web applications in Chapter 14.

CHAPTER 13

Servlets

Servlets, an integral part of many web applications, provide a web container with the ability to dynamically process requests sent over HTTP. Users of a web application can submit their data entered from within a web page to a servlet for processing or alternatively craft an HTTP request in such a manner that it contains additional information that is useful to the servlet for its processing needs.

In this regard, servlets are very similar to JavaServer Pages, but while JavaServer Pages use templated HTML pages to provide dynamic responses, servlets rely completely on Java code and the vast Java object library available to the servlet class to process input and create responses. For this reason, servlets are clearly not limited to usage in clients that render HTML documents alone; they can also be used to generate responses in a wide variety of formats. This is why servlets, in addition to heavy usage in web applications, can sometimes be seen in implementations of Java-based Service Oriented Architectures (SOAs) to process Web Services requests and generate appropriate SOAP responses. We provide an extended discussion of Web Services in Chapter 15.

In this chapter, we will focus on servlets and their usage within web applications. We begin with an overview of the servlet technology and discuss the important doGet and doPost methods that provide HTTP-based servlets with the functionality to handle web processing requests. Furthermore, we will discuss the creation of servlets and the configuration of these web components in the web.xml deployment descriptor of a web application. Finally, we will discuss the tools provided by JST to ease the creation and configuration of servlets as part of our Trouble Ticket application.

Servlet Overview

Servlets can be described as small Java-based programs that exist within web containers and provide a request/response interface to users for the processing of requests and the dynamic generation of responses. These requests are often web requests made over HTTP. The current servlet specification, the Java Servlet 2.4 Specification, is defined by JSR 154 and is a required API of the J2EE 1.4 Specification. Together with JavaServer Pages, which we discussed in the previous chapter, servlets make up the two major components that exist within the web container of an application server.

> **Note** Other Web Tier components include filters and web event listeners, but a discussion of these is beyond the scope of this text. If you want to learn more about them, we suggest you read *Pro J2EE 1.4: From Professional to Expert* by Meeraj Kunnumpurath and Sue Spielman (Apress, 2004).

A common description of servlets is that they are a Java-based implementation of Common Gateway Interface (CGI) technology providing web containers with the ability to accept input data sent using the HTTP request, process this data, generate a response page, and display it to the user in a browser. This is a very simplified description of servlets, but a forgivable one. Servlets were indeed originally proposed by Sun as a replacement to CGI and can actually replace the functionality of any CGI script, however they can do significantly more than this. Their extended capacity includes support for request/response mechanisms beyond that provided by HTTP, built-in session management facilities, inheritance of the Write Once, Run Anywhere (WORA) platform-independent capability of the Java language, as well as complete access to the large collection of APIs available within the Java Platform.

The request/response messaging model for which, as we have stated, servlets provide support is a messaging model whereby a client makes a request to a server by referencing a specific resource on the server. The client often passes useful data to the server as part of this request. The resource available on the server to respond to this request processes this information passed by the client and generates a response back to the client. We have shown in Figure 13-1 a servlet being invoked from an HTML page.

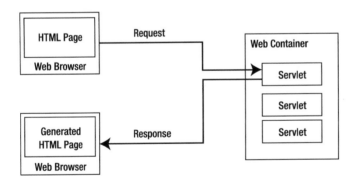

Figure 13-1. *Web servers handling HTTP requests*

The information sent from the HTML page to the servlet is known as the *request,* and within the servlet this information is encapsulated in the javax.servlet.http.HttpServletRequest object. The HttpServletRequest object provides useful methods to the servlet to easily retrieve information that was passed as part of the request. The servlet performs some internal processing on this information and provides a response through the javax.servlet.http.HttpServletResponse object. These two objects are very essential to much of a servlet's processing capabilities. The HttpServletRequest and HttpServletResponse classes are HTTP-specific implementations of the javax.servlet.ServletRequest and javax.servlet.ServletResponse interfaces. For the rest of this chapter, our reference to servlets will imply reference specifically to an HTTP servlet, i.e., a servlet extending from the HttpServletRequest class.

Servlet Structure

Servlets are Java classes that directly or indirectly implement the `javax.servlet.Servlet` interface. The HTTP servlets that we are concerned with indirectly implement the `Servlet` interface by extending from the `javax.servlet.http.HttpServletRequest` class. We have shown in Figure 13-2 the relationship between `javax.servlet.http.HttpServlet` and the `Servlet` interface as seen from the Hierarchy View in Eclipse.

Figure 13-2. *Relationship between the HttpServlet class and the Servlet interface*

In Figure 13-2, the `HttpServlet` class is seen inheriting from the `GenericServlet` class, which implements the `Servlet` interface. From this figure, you can also see the `ChartTickets` servlet class, which we will be using to respond to web requests. `ChartTickets` extends from `HttpServlet` exactly as we stated previously, making it a `Servlet` implementation. In Listing 13-1, we have provided the skeletal structure of a servlet class.

Listing 13-1. *A Sample Servlet Source File*

```java
package com.projst.ticket.web;

import java.io.IOException;
import javax.servlet.ServletException;
import javax.servlet.http.HttpServletRequest;
import javax.servlet.http.HttpServletResponse;

/**
 * Servlet implementation class for Servlet: ChartTickets
 */
 public class ChartTickets extends javax.servlet.http.HttpServlet {

    public ChartTickets() {
        super();
    }

    public void init() throws ServletException {
        super.init();
```

```
        // provide additional initialization statements here
    }

    public void destroy() {
        super.destroy();
        // provide additional destruction statements here
    }

    protected void doGet(HttpServletRequest arg0, HttpServletResponse arg1)
            throws ServletException, IOException {
        // provide method implementation here
    }

    protected void doPost(HttpServletRequest arg0, HttpServletResponse arg1)
            throws ServletException, IOException {
        // provide method implementation here
    }

    public String foo() {
        // provide method implementation here
        return null;
    }

    private int bar() {
        // provide method implementation here
        return -1;
    }

}
```

The init and destroy methods shown in Listing 13-1 are life cycle methods and are invoked on the creation and destruction of the servlet, respectively. These methods are declared within the Servlet interface and implemented by the GenericServlet class (see Figure 13-2). We will further discuss the servlet life cycle later in this chapter in the section "Servlet Life Cycle."

The doGet and doPost methods defined in the listing are part of the list of methods known as the doXXX methods. This is because a specific doXXX method is provided for each request type supported by the servlet. On invocation of the servlet, only one of these methods is directly invoked. The method invoked is the one that corresponds to the request type made of the servlet. If a GET request was made to our servlet, any code we have written in the doGet method will be executed. If a PUT request type was made, however, it will be serviced by the HttpServlet superclass which implements all the doXXX methods since we did not directly override the doPut method. We will discuss the different request types and their usage later in the section "Handling Requests."

Also from Listing 13-1, note the existence of the two methods foo and bar. These are ordinary Java methods that are used to perform any necessary processing activities that are supported by the servlet. Servlets do not impose any additional limitations on the type of methods that can be included within a servlet class. The distinction between these methods and the doXXX and life cycle methods is that these standard methods have to be invoked from within other methods and are not automatically invoked by the servlet engine.

Handling Requests

Requests to a servlet are made through HTTP and use any of the request types supported by this protocol. Seven of the HTTP request types are supported by the HttpServlet class and they include GET, POST, HEAD, PUT, DELETE, OPTIONS, and TRACE. Each one of these request types has a specific function as defined by the HTTP 1.1 Specification (available at http://www.w3.org/Protocols/rfc2616/rfc2616.html) and the HttpServlet class provides a corresponding doXXX method to handle each of the request types in the servlet. The GET and POST methods, however, are the two request types that are most frequently in use due to the HTML <form> tag making it easy for individuals to generate requests of these two types. We have provided in Table 13-1 a list of all the request types supported by servlets as well as the conditions under which each type is suitable for use.

Table 13-1. *Request Types Supported by Servlets*

Request Type	Usage
GET	Retrieves a resource from a server using the Request URI to identify the resource. GET requests are often used in situations where it is safe to make multiple GET requests from the server without causing any permanent action on the server.
POST	Sends information to a server-based resource and additionally performs an action. Multiple requests of this type should not be made of the server without having the user reconfirm it, as POST requests often make permanent changes on the server.
HEAD	Retrieves header information about a resource from a server but not the actual resource. This is what distinguishes the HEAD request from the GET request. HEAD requests are useful to retrieve the characteristics of a resource on the server (such as the file modification time) without actually downloading the result and thus saving bandwidth.
PUT	Publishes information enclosed within the request to the URI identified by the request. PUT requests were originally created to allow uploading of files to a server similar to what is available using FTP.
DELETE	Deletes a resource, identified by a Request URI from a server.
OPTIONS	Requests information about the types of requests that are available from the server.
TRACE	Debugs client/server HTTP communications. A TRACE request returns the header information sent to the server in the Request URI back to the client.

Information being sent to a servlet is often sent from an HTML page. The <form> tag within the page is the most important part of this process, as it serves as a container for HTML form elements that hold values that would be sent to the servlet. We have provided Listing 13-2, which shows the HTML source for invoking a servlet. You may remember from Chapter 5 that WST provides tools for the creation and editing of HTML documents.

Listing 13-2. *HTML Page to Invoke the ChartTickets Servlet*

```
<!DOCTYPE HTML PUBLIC "-//W3C//DTD HTML 4.01 Transitional//EN">
<html>
  <head>
  <meta http-equiv="Content-Type" content="text/html; charset=ISO-8859-1">
  <title>Retrieve Trouble Tickets</title>
</head>
<body>
  <center>
    <h2>
      <u>Chart Trouble Tickets</u>
    </h2>
  </center>
  <br/><br/>
  <form action="/ChartTickets" method="get">
  <table>
    <tr>
      <td>Include Items:</td>
      <td><select name="status">
          <option value="all">Both Open and Closed Tickets</option>
          <option value="open" selected="selected">Open Tickets</option>
          <option value="closed">Closed Tickets</option>
        </select>
      </td>
      <td> </td>
    </tr>
    <tr>
      <td>Submitted person email:</td>
      <td><input name="email" type="text" /></td>
      <td><i>Leave blank to include all<i></td>
    </tr>
    <tr>
      <td> </td>
      <td><br/><input type="submit" value="Generate Chart" /></td>
      <td> </td>
    </tr>
  </table>
  </form>
</body>
</html>
```

In Listing 13-2, you may notice that we have provided several items in bold. This section contains the <form> tag that holds the data being passed to the servlet. We have highlighted in bold the <form> and the <input> tags (which render into HTML elements) found within the <form> tag. The rest of the HTML code on this page exists merely to ensure that we render a properly formatted document. You will notice that the <form> tag has the following definition:

```
<form action="/ChartTickets" method="get">
```

- `action`: Refers to a relative path to the servlet within the server. The form data will be submitted to this servlet for processing. This can also be a virtual path to the servlet based on the existence of a `<servlet-mapping>` tag within the `web.xml` deployment descriptor.

- `method`: The type of request being sent. This is either a GET or a POST request.

Note The `<form>` tag supports additional attributes that are not included here. These attributes can easily be viewed and modified by clicking the tag and opening the Properties View.

Enclosed within the `<form>` tag are `<input>` tags for fields in which we want the user to supply data. These fields make up the form data that will be submitted to the servlet for processing. Each input type has a name attribute that is passed on to the servlet as a request parameter together with the value provided to this object by the user. The button available on the page is used to generate a request from the `<form>` tag's attribute and content and then submit this request to the servlet. Figure 13-3 provides a rendering of the HTML code from Listing 13-2 shown within a browser.

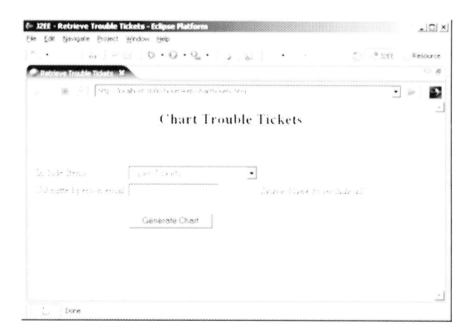

Figure 13-3. *Rendering of HTML page to access a servlet*

An alternative method of making a servlet request is by directly accessing the servlet URL. This method of access can easily be done through the address bar of most browsers. It should be noted that only GET requests can be made through this mechanism. This means that the doGet method within the servlet will be invoked. To make a servlet request using a URL, the request must be crafted as follows:

```
protocol://host:port/Servlet
```

The parts of the preceding URL will be replaced with the following values:

- protocol: Protocol used to access the servlet. This is usually http or https.

- host: The DNS name of the host or the IP address. When the server is started locally, the name localhost or the IP address 127.0.0.1 can be used.

- port: The port address on which the web server is listening. For Apache Tomcat, the default port is 8080.

- Servlet: The relative path to the servlet you wish to invoke. This can contain either the fully qualified package name of the servlet or a shortcut mapped in the deployment descriptor for the servlet.

Often, additional information is needed to be passed to the servlet. This is done by appending information using the following syntax to the request:

```
?paramater1=value&parameter2=value&parameter2=value
```

The parts of the data appended to the URL serve the following purposes:

- ?: Denotes the end of the request URL and the start of the appended data segment

- parameter: Specifies the name of a parameter that maps to the name attribute of an <input> tag contained within a <form> tag

- value: Specifies the value of the parameter taken from the appropriate <input> tag

- &: Separates each parameter/value pair

An example of a URL to invoke our servlet is as follows:

```
http://localhost:8080/ticketWeb/ChartTickets?email=user@projst.com&status=open
```

The parameter names and their assigned values can then be retrieved within the servlet using the getParameter method from the HttpServletRequest class. The code snippet in Listing 13-3 will retrieve a value from the form fields in the HTML code from Listing 13-2.

Listing 13-3. *Retrieving Form Fields in a Servlet*

```
protected void doGet(HttpServletRequest arg0, HttpServletResponse arg1)
            throws ServletException, IOException {

    String strEmail = arg0.getParameter("email");
    String strStatus = arg0.getParameter("status");

}
```

The code snippet from Listing 13-3 stores the value from the email text field and the value from the status select object in the web page into local variables named strEmail and strStatus, respectively.

Caution By default, a servlet handles GET and POST requests with different methods, and thus you could end up with a servlet that provides different functionality based on the method used. We have provided a strategy in the sidebar "Using GET and POST" later in this chapter to prevent the inadvertent occurrence of this situation.

Providing Responses

Response from a servlet is handled through the HttpServletResponse class. This object provides a servlet with the ability to generate output that will be sent back to the origin of the request. Servlets servicing web requests often have to construct a complete HTML document as part of the response to be sent back to the originating source.

Two types of responses can be created within a response: textual data and binary data. There are two objects available within the HttpServletResponse object to handle each type:

- **Textual data**: Use the PrintWriter object returned by the getWriter() method.

- **Binary data**: Use the ServletOuputStream object returned by the getOutputStream() method. The resulting ServletOuputStream object can also be used to send text data.

We have provided in Listing 13-4 an implementation of the doGet method where fields passed to the servlet from the HTML <form> tag are inserted into the output generated by the servlet. This process is often used to allow users to confirm input they have entered. In our example, we have chosen to generate output using the PrintWriter object. Remember that the usage of the ServletOutputStream is another valid option for textual data.

Listing 13-4. *A doGet Method Implementation to Respond to a Servlet Request*

```
protected void doGet(HttpServletRequest arg0, HttpServletResponse arg1)
            throws ServletException, IOException {

    String strEmail = arg0.getParameter("email");
    String strStatus = arg0.getParameter("status");

    // set the MIME type
    arg1.setContentType("text/html");

    // retrieve object for writing response
    PrintWriter out = arg1.getWriter();

    // write the response
    out.println("<html>");
    out.println("<head>");
    out.println("<title>Chart Servlet</title>");
    out.println("</head>");
```

```
    out.println("<body>");
    out.println("<h3 align=\"center\">Chart Servlet</h3>");
    out.println("<br /><br />");
    out.println("Email: " + strEmail);
    out.println("<br />");
    out.println("Status: " + strStatus);
    out.println("</body>");
    out.println("</html>");
}
```

Invocation of the ChartTickets servlet using the URL

```
http://localhost:8080/ticketWeb/ChartTickets?status=open&email=user@projst.com
```

generates a valid HTML document, the content of which we have shown in Listing 13-5. In Figure 13-4 we have provided a rendering of this generated HTML page as shown in the internal Eclipse browser.

Listing 13-5. *HTML Code Generated by the doGet Method in Listing 13-4*

```
<html>
<head>
<title>Chart Servlet</title>
</head>
<body>
<h3 align="center">Chart Servlet</h3>
<br /><br />
Email: user@projst.com
<br />
Status: open
</body>
</html>
```

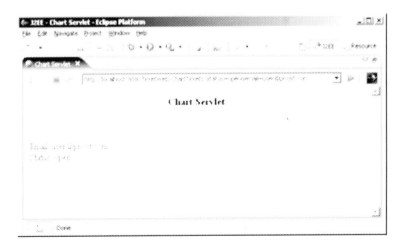

Figure 13-4. *Rendering of HTML code in Listing 13-5*

Servlet Life Cycle

There are three methods that make up a servlet life cycle, and these are the init, service, and destroy methods. All three methods are defined within the HttpServlet class, and so they are always in existence within every servlet. You may override these methods whenever you intend to provide a specific implementation within your application. The default function and usage of these methods are described here:

- init: This method is called when the servlet is invoked for the first time and is called only once during the entire lifetime of the servlet. Only code that should be executed once during the entire lifetime of the servlet should be included in this method.

- service: This method is invoked whenever a request is made of the servlet. It then dispatches the request to the appropriate doXXX method for processing. It is unnecessary to override this method.

- destroy: This method is called just before the servlet is taken out of service and is thus also called only once during the lifetime of the servlet.

USING GET AND POST

The HTTP GET and POST request types are very often interposed and misused. We have discussed the usage of each of these request types in Table 13-1. However, since the method attribute in a <form> tag accepts either a GET or POST, developers often supply the first value that occurs to them. To prevent your servlet from inadvertently ignoring either a GET or a POST request because of this, you may want to implement the common strategy shown in Listing 13-6.

Listing 13-6. *Strategy to Ensure the doGet and doPost Methods Perform the Same Processing*

```
protected void doGet(HttpServletRequest arg0, HttpServletResponse arg1)
        throws ServletException, IOException {
    doProcess(arg0, arg1);
}

protected void doPost(HttpServletRequest arg0, HttpServletResponse arg1)
        throws ServletException, IOException {
    doProcess(arg0, arg1);
}

protected void doProcess(HttpServletRequest arg0, HttpServletResponse arg1)
        throws ServletException, IOException {
    // provide implementation here
}
```

In this case, both the GET and POST requests will be eventually routed to the doProcess method. This is possible because the doGet and doPost service methods both accept the same types of parameters.

Writing Servlets

To ease the creation and configuration of servlets, JST provides the Servlet wizard for the automated generation of servlets. This tool provides you with the ability to generate a servlet and also include annotations in the servlet that will automatically be converted into appropriate tags within the web.xml deployment descriptor. The included annotation tags utilize the XDoclet tool. You may wish to review our discussion about annotations and XDoclet in Chapter 8.

Servlet Wizard

Servlets are created within a J2EE web module and can be accessed by choosing the web module into which you want to generate the servlet and bringing up the context menu. From this context menu, you should select New ➤ Servlet to bring up the Servlet wizard. Alternatively, you could select File ➤ New ➤ Other ➤ Servlet to launch the wizard. This action opens the first step of the Servlet wizard as shown in Figure 13-5.

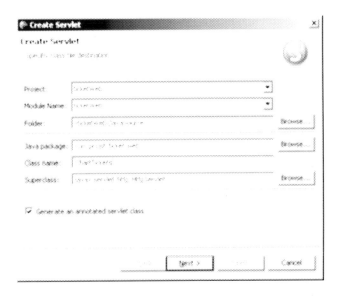

Figure 13-5. *The first step of the Servlet wizard*

The servlet creation process is a three-step process starting with the initial page shown in Figure 13-5. This page prompts the user for the project into which the servlet will be generated as well as the module within the project. The folder within which to generate the servlet is also prompted for. Additional details gathered in this step include the package structure for the servlet and also the servlet class name. The superclass of the servlet defaults to javax.servlet.http. HttpServlet. We have discussed that servlets must inherit directly, or indirectly, from this class. In certain cases, a custom class is created for a project that inherits from the HttpServlet class, and all servlet classes in the project then inherit from the custom class.

The final item prompted for on this page is the usage of annotations. Before choosing this option, you must ensure that you have set up the XDoclet tool by selecting Window ➤ Preferences ➤ J2EE Annotations ➤ XDoclet.

Clicking the Next button takes you to the second step of the wizard. This screen prompts for information that would be stored in the deployment descriptor of the web module. If the use of annotations was specified, doclet tags would be generated within the servlet class to easily manage the modification of the deployment descriptor contents.

As shown in Figure 13-6, the page prompts for a description of the servlet as well as a virtual name that can be used to refer to the servlet with the application. Initialization parameters are also prompted for on this page, providing the servlet with the ability to manage application-wide default values that can be used by the servlet within web.xml. Values specified here can be retrieved within the applet by using the following code snippet:

```
getServletConfig.getInitParameter(param)
```

Figure 13-6. *The second step of the Servlet wizard*

The value passed to the getInitParameter method would be the name of an initialization parameter such as the one shown in Figure 13-6. The last item prompted for in this step is a list of URL mappings for the servlet. URL mappings provide a virtual path to access a servlet. The values provided in this list are converted to <servlet-mapping> tags in the deployment descriptor.

The third and final step of the wizard can be accessed by clicking the Next button. This provides the page shown in Figure 13-7, which prompts for structural information about the servlet class.

Figure 13-7. *The final step of the Servlet wizard*

The information prompted for by this page includes the choice of modifier for the class definition and also a selection of additional interfaces that should be implemented by the class. Information about the methods to create are also prompted for. After making the necessary selection, you click the Finish button to initiate the code generation process.

Note It is possible to click the Finish button at any point during the creation of the servlet. This allows the wizard to use default values for all the prompts provided. Code generated by the servlet can later be edited to match the actual needs of the servlet.

Listing 13-7 shows the code generated from the choices made in the Servlet wizard.

Listing 13-7. *Code Generated by the Servlet Wizard*

```
package com.projst.ticket.web;

import java.io.IOException;
import javax.servlet.ServletException;
import javax.servlet.http.HttpServletRequest;
import javax.servlet.http.HttpServletResponse;

/**
```

```
 * Servlet implementation class for Servlet: ChartTickets
 *
 * @web.servlet
 *   name="ChartTickets"
 *   display-name="ChartTickets"
 *   description="Servlet to create a chart of existing trouble tickets"
 *
 * @web.servlet-mapping
 *   url-pattern="/ChartTickets"
 *
 * @web.servlet-init-param
 *     name="status"
 *     value="open"
 *     description="Ticket type to include in chart"
 *
 */
public class ChartTickets
          extends javax.servlet.http.HttpServlet
          implements javax.servlet.Servlet {
   /**
    *
    */

   /* (non-Java-doc)
    * @see javax.servlet.http.HttpServlet#HttpServlet()
    */
   public ChartTickets() {
       super();
   }

   /* (non-Java-doc)
    * @see javax.servlet.http.HttpServlet#doGet(HttpServletRequest arg0,
    *                                             HttpServletResponse arg1)
    */
   protected void doGet(HttpServletRequest arg0, HttpServletResponse arg1)
               throws ServletException, IOException   {
      // TODO Auto-generated method stub
   }

   /* (non-Java-doc)
    * @see javax.servlet.http.HttpServlet#doPost(HttpServletRequest arg0,
    *                                             HttpServletResponse arg1)
    */
   protected void doPost(HttpServletRequest arg0, HttpServletResponse arg1)
               throws ServletException, IOException   {
      // TODO Auto-generated method stub
   }
}
```

Tip It is possible to see a warning in your Problem View about the servlet that has just been created stating that a serialVersionUID had not been declared for the serializable class. To fix this, simply click the line in the editor containing the servlet class definition. Press Ctrl+1 to bring up the Quick Fix tool and choose any of the provided options to add the serial version ID.

The highlighted section within Listing 13-7 is the XDoclet annotations at the class level. The information from these doclet tags are automatically converted by the XDoclet builder into appropriate values and included inside the web.xml deployment descriptor. The doclet tags from Listing 13-7 resolve into the <servlet>, <init-param>, and <servlet-mapping> tags shown in Listing 13-8.

Listing 13-8. *Deployment Descriptor Snippet Generated by the Servlet Wizard*

```
<servlet>
    <servlet-name>ChartTickets</servlet-name>
    <display-name>ChartTickets</display-name>
    <description>
        <![CDATA[Servlet to create a chart of existing trouble tickets]]>
    </description>
    <servlet-class>com.projst.ticket.web.ChartTickets</servlet-class>

    <init-param>
        <param-name>status</param-name>
        <param-value>open</param-value>
        <description><![CDATA[Ticket type to include in chart]]></description>
    </init-param>
</servlet>

    <servlet-mapping>
    <servlet-name>ChartTickets</servlet-name>
    <url-pattern>/ChartTickets</url-pattern>
</servlet-mapping>
```

XDoclet Servlet Annotations

We have shown some of the tags that are supported by XDoclet for the use of providing configuration information about our servlet to the web.xml deployment descriptor. There are many more tags supported by XDoclet than those included in Listing 13-7, so we have provided in this section a list of additional tags useful during the creation of servlets. For a complete list of all XDoclet tags, check out the XDoclet documentation at http://xdoclet.sourceforge.net/xdoclet/index.html.

The following tables list the most common class-level tags used for configuring servlets. These include @web.servlet (see Table 13-2), which is used to provide general information such as display name and description about the servlet; @web.servlet-mapping (see Table 13-3), which is used to make the servlet available at specified URLs; and @web.servlet-init-param (see Table 13-4), which is used to provide initialization values to the servlet.

Table 13-2. *XDoclet Session @web.servlet Class Parameters*

Parameter	Type	Description	Required
name	Text	Servlet name, must be unique within the application	True
display-name	Text	Short name	False
icon	Text	Icon image	False
description	Text	Description of bean	False

Table 13-3. *XDoclet Session @web.servlet-mapping Class Parameters*

Parameter	Type	Description	Required
url-pattern	Text	URL to invoke the servlet from	False

Table 13-4. *XDoclet Session @web.servlet-init-param Class Parameters*

Parameter	Type	Description	Required
name	Text	Name of the initialization parameter	True
value	Text	Value of the parameter	False
description	Text	Description of the parameter	False

Tip XDoclet code assist can be invoked during the creation of a servlet using Ctrl+space after @.

Completing the Servlet Implementation

While the servlet generated by the Servlet wizard provides the correct structure for a servlet, it does not contain any implementation, as you would expect. In order to become a useful part of our project, we must now complete the implementation of our ChartTicket class. As this class involves the use of creating a chart to show the count of trouble tickets within the system, we will be using an image-generation package. We have chosen the chart-generation library called JFreeChart, which is available at http://www.jfree.org/jfreechart, to generate the chart. This popular, open source chart generation library provides extensive features for charting data and generating images from them. Extended discussion about this package is beyond the scope of this book, but you can find usage information and download relevant files about the project from the URL previously supplied.

We have created a Java class file named TicketDBData to access our database and retrieve the data from within our Ticket table. You may remember from the previous chapters that this table holds the data entered for each trouble ticket. In Listing 13-9, we have provided the contents of the Java class that will be used to access and retrieve information about our trouble tickets from the database table.

Listing 13-9. *The TicketDBData Class*

```java
package com.projst.ticket.dto;


import java.sql.*;
import org.jfree.data.category.DefaultCategoryDataset;

public class TicketDBData {

    private Connection configureConnection() throws Exception {
        String dbUrl = System.getProperty("ticketdb.url",
                                    "jdbc:derby:net://localhost:1527/ticket");
        String dbDriver = System.getProperty("ticketdb.driver",
                                        "org.apache.derby.jdbc.EmbeddedDriver");
        String dbUser = System.getProperty("ticketdb.user", "sa");
        String dbPassword = System.getProperty("ticketdb.password", "sa");
        Connection conn = null;

        try {
            Class.forName(dbDriver);
            conn = DriverManager.getConnection(dbUrl, dbUser, dbPassword);
        } catch (Exception e) {
            throw new Exception("Failed to load database driver.");
        }
        return conn;
    }

    public DefaultCategoryDataset getDataset(String status, String email)
            throws Exception {
        DefaultCategoryDataset dataset = new DefaultCategoryDataset();
        if (email == null || email.equals("")) {
            email = "%";
        }

        int open = retrieveDataCount("open", email);
        int closed = retrieveDataCount("closed", email);

        if (status.equals("all")) {
            dataset.addValue(new Integer(open + closed), "Total", "");
            dataset.addValue(new Integer(open), "Open", "");
            dataset.addValue(new Integer(closed), "Closed", "");
        } else if (status.equals("open")) {
            dataset.addValue(new Integer(open), "Open", "");
        } else if (status.equals("closed")) {
            dataset.addValue(new Integer(closed), "Closed", "");
        }
```

```
            return dataset;
    }

    private int retrieveDataCount(String status, String email) throws Exception {
        int count = 0;
        String sql = "SELECT * FROM TICKET WHERE STATUS LIKE ? AND EMAIL LIKE ?";

        Connection conn = configureConnection();
        PreparedStatement stmt = conn.prepareStatement(sql);
        stmt.setString(1, status);
        stmt.setString(2, email);

        ResultSet result = stmt.executeQuery();
        if (result.next())
            count = result.getInt(1);

        conn.close();
        return count;
    }


}
```

Configuration information can be provided to this listing through the use of environment variables. On instancing the class and invoking getDataset, the database is accessed, and a DefaultCategoryDataset object is generated that contains the data found within the database in a manner that is meaningful to the chart library that we are using. Listing 13-10 concludes the implementation by making a call to the Java class in Listing 13-9 and generating HTML output.

Listing 13-10. *An Implementation of the ChartTicket Class*

```
package com.projst.ticket.web;


import java.io.*;
import javax.servlet.ServletException;
import javax.servlet.http.*;

import org.jfree.chart.*;
import org.jfree.chart.plot.PlotOrientation;
import org.jfree.data.category.CategoryDataset;

import com.projst.ticket.dto.TicketDBData;

/**
 * Servlet implementation class for Servlet: ChartTickets
 *
```

```
 * @web.servlet name="ChartTickets"
 * display-name="ChartTickets"
 * description="Servlet to create a chart of existing trouble tickets"
 *
 * @web.servlet-mapping url-pattern="/ChartTickets"
 *
 * @web.servlet-init-param name="status" value="open"
 * description="Ticket type to include in chart"
 *
 */
public class ChartTickets
        extends javax.servlet.http.HttpServlet
        implements javax.servlet.Servlet {

    // Variable to hold the location of the temporary directory
    private String tempDir = "";

    /**
     * Initialization method called once during the servlet life cycle
     */
    public void init() throws ServletException {
        super.init();
        tempDir = this.getServletContext().getRealPath(".");
    }

    /**
     * Respond to HTTP GET requests
     */
    protected void doGet(HttpServletRequest arg0, HttpServletResponse arg1)
            throws ServletException, IOException {
        doProcess(arg0, arg1);
    }

    /**
     * Respond to HTTP POST requests
     */
    protected void doPost(HttpServletRequest arg0, HttpServletResponse arg1)
            throws ServletException, IOException {
        doProcess(arg0, arg1);
    }

    /**
     * Process HTTP requests
     */
    protected void doProcess(HttpServletRequest arg0, HttpServletResponse arg1)
            throws ServletException, IOException {
```

```java
        String strEmail = arg0.getParameter("email");
        String strStatus = arg0.getParameter("status");
        if (strStatus==null) {
            strStatus = this.getServletConfig().getInitParameter("status");

        }

        // set the MIME type
        arg1.setContentType("text/html");

        // retrieve object for writing response
        PrintWriter out = arg1.getWriter();

        // write the response
        out.println("<html>");
        out.println("<head>");
        out.println("<title>Chart Servlet</title>");
        out.println("</head>");
        out.println("<body>");
        out.println("<h3 align=\"center\">Chart Servlet</h3>");
        out.println("<br /><br />");
        out.println("Email: " + strEmail);
        out.println("<br />");
        out.println("Status: " + strStatus);
        out.write("<br/>");

        createChart(out, arg0.getSession().getId(), strStatus, strEmail);

        out.println("</body>");
        out.println("</html>");
    }

    private void createChart(PrintWriter out, String sid,
                                        String status, String email) {
        try {
            TicketDBData data = new TicketDBData();
            CategoryDataset dataset = data.getDataset(status, email);

            // Create the chart object
            JFreeChart chart = ChartFactory.createBarChart3D(
                    "", "Ticket Status", "", dataset,
                    PlotOrientation.VERTICAL, true, true, false);
            chart.setBackgroundPaint(java.awt.Color.white);

            // Create a temporary image file
            String filePath = tempDir + "/images/";
            File outfile = new File(filePath + sid + ".jpg");
```

```
                outfile.deleteOnExit();
                FileOutputStream fos = new FileOutputStream(outfile);
                ChartUtilities.writeChartAsJPEG(fos, 1.0f, chart, 300, 200);
                fos.flush();
                fos.close();

                //Reference the temporary file in the generated HTML
                out.println("<br/><img src=\"" + outfile.getAbsolutePath() + "\">");

        } catch (Exception e) {
            out.println("Error: Unable to create chart");
            e.printStackTrace(System.out);
        }
    }
}
```

■ **Note** Don't forget to remove the TODO comment after you add your own implementation.

This concludes the servlet and makes it available for use after build and deployment. We will discuss the process of building and deploying web modules in Chapter 14. You may notice that this servlet generates HTML output. The generated HTML code is embedded with a reference to the image file generated by our chart library. Compiling and executing this code generates the HTML page rendered in Figure 13-8.

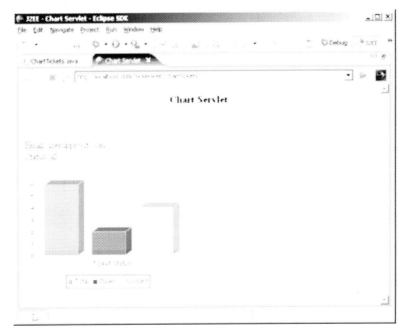

Figure 13-8. *Result of executing the ChartTickets servlet*

We will provide in the next chapter detailed information on how to compile, deploy, and execute servlet classes that are a part of a web module.

Summary

We have provided a description of Java servlets in this chapter and described the general structure of servlets as well as their usage in generating dynamic responses to web requests. We discussed the different types of HTTP requests available and how a servlet could respond differently to each request.

We also provided information on accessing a servlet. This can be done through either using a form submission or by directly accessing the servlet URL for HTTP GET requests. The processing of responses was also discussed, as well as the configuration of servlets within the web.xml deployment descriptor. In Chapter 15, we will describe how to package, deploy, and debug servlets in a J2EE application server.

CHAPTER 14

Web Packaging and Deployment

In Chapter 12 and Chapter 13, we walked you through the process of creating JavaServer Pages and servlets using tools provided by JST. However, before the web components you create can be made available to users, you must build and package the artifacts and then deploy them into a *runtime environment* capable of hosting web applications. This runtime environment, also known as a *web container*, is available within many commercial and open source J2EE application server implementations. The process of packaging and deploying a web module is functionally similar to what we demonstrated in Chapter 11, where you saw how to package, deploy, and access EJB Tier components contained within an EJB module. The major difference here is that while EJBs are deployed in the EJB Tier of an application server, web components are deployed in the Web Tier.

In JST, source artifacts targeted for deployment into a web container are managed within a web module as part of either a Dynamic Web Project or an Enterprise Application Project. You may remember this from our discussion in Chapter 7 about the different types of projects that are supported by JST. A web module supports the creation of dynamic web content in the form of JSPs and servlets and also supports the inclusion of other Java classes, such as bean and helper classes, that the JSPs and servlets depend on. All these files can then be packaged into the proper format and deployed into the web container of any J2EE-compliant application server such as Tomcat.

Web applications to be deployed are often packaged into an archive file known as a WAR file. You may remember from our discussion in Chapter 11 about packaging EJB modules that we described the WAR file as being an archive file in the JAR file format that contains an aggregated collection of files and directories. We will discuss the specific structure of a WAR file later in this chapter as well as explain how to package WAR files within EAR files.

When packaged as a WAR file, the web application is a stand-alone deployment unit with the resources and auxiliary files that the web application relies on included with the WAR file. This file represents a deployable web module and, similar to an EJB module, it contains a deployment descriptor that instructs the web container on how to configure services within the module and additionally make them accessible to external users.

In this chapter, we will discuss the structure of a web module and describe the contents typically found within that structure. We will focus primarily on the deployment descriptor that is a required file for web applications and the type of configuration parameters available within the file. Next, we will discuss the deployment process of web applications, and we will cover alternative tools that can be used in the packaging and deployment of enterprise applications. Finally, we will describe how web applications can be accessed and the process provided by JST for debugging web applications.

Packaging Web Applications

We have shown that web applications are composed of JSP pages, servlets, Java classes, third-party code libraries, and additional static documents that are important for the presentation and configuration of the web application. These static documents often include image files, configuration files, JavaScript source files, style sheets, and, importantly, a deployment descriptor. Based on the intended use of each of these file types, there is a specific location within the web application file structure where the application server expects to find each file.

Once the appropriate directory structure is created and the necessary configuration files are added, the web application is ready for deployment. Many web applications are packaged into a WAR file for deployment, but it should be noted that this is not a requirement for every application server; a WAR file simply provides a convenient mechanism to transfer the myriad files that could potentially make up a web application. In either an archived or unarchived state, the directory structure of a deployable web module generally contains the following:

- A public folder for JSP pages, HTML files, and other publicly accessible documents

- A `/WEB-INF/web.xml` deployment descriptor file

- A `/WEB-INF/classes` directory to hold compiled classes

- A `/WEB-INF/lib` directory to hold classes packaged into JAR format

Contents of the root folder structure are publicly accessible when the enterprise application is deployed; these artifacts can be retrieved when the correct URL that references them is requested through such tools as a web browser. Additional directories can be created within the root directory to hold different artifacts that make up the web application. These subdirectories are also publicly available, and the decision to create them is often made to group the huge number of items that exist within the web application in the most logical way. Provided here is the directory structure found in the Trouble Ticket web application:

```
ticketWeb/
        index.jsp
        charttickets.html
        jsp/
                listtickets.jsp
        styles/
                default.css
        images/
                add.gif
                calendar.gif
                delete.gif
                editgif
                warn.gif
        wsdl/
```

```
                    TicketWebService.wsdl
        WEB-INF/
                web.xml
                struts-config.xml
                c.tld
                struts-bean.tld
                struts-html.tld
                classes/
                        com/
                                projst/
                                        ticket/
                                                action/
                                                    ListAllTicketsAction.class
                                                web/
                                                        ChartTickets.class
                                                ws/
                                                    TicketWebService.class
        lib/
                antlr.jar
                axis.jar
                commons-beanutils.jar
                commons-digester.jar
                commons-fileupload.jar
                commons-logging.jar
                commons-validator.jar
                wsdl4j.jar
                ticketEJBClient.jar
```

The only required content of a web application is actually the WEB-INF directory and the web.xml deployment descriptor contained within this directory. This deployment descriptor, as you shall see later in this chapter, holds initialization values and configuration settings for the web application. The WEB-INF directory is not accessible to users of the deployed application, and therefore it is the perfect location for the deployment descriptor. This has significant security implications because the deployment descriptor will often contain details about your application that you may not want to share with the public. This inaccessibility of the WEB-INF directory is another reason why many Web Tier frameworks such as Struts and Tiles store configuration information within this directory. Tag Library Definitions for JSP tags constitute another type of configuration file that is typically found within this directory.

The classes directory contains compiled Java classes that are of use to the web application. The servlets and JavaBeans that compose the logic of the web application are compiled and stored within this directory together with other classes they rely on. These could include JavaBeans and JSP customs tags. Directories are created starting from WEB-INF/classes to match the package structure of the compiled class. This means that a file named ChartTickets.java that has the following package statement:

```
package com.projst.ticket.web
```

will be compiled and stored in the following directory structure within the deployed web module:

```
WEB-INF/classes/com/projst/ticket/web/ChartTickets.class
```

When compiled classes are packaged into JAR files, they must be stored in the lib directory, which is found under the WEB-INF directory. Though JST compiles and packages source artifacts within the active Dynamic Web Project into the WEB-INF/classes directory, other packaging tools like Ant, which we will discuss later in this chapter, can be used to modify this default behavior and package the items in a manner that suits the needs of the developer. The choice of placing compiled files in either the lib or classes directory, though, is of little concern to the end user of the application. In both instances, the compiled classes that exist within either of the two directories are accessible to all other code artifacts within the application.

Caution Though many directories can be created and packaged within the WEB-INF directory, these directories are not directly accessible to the end user during the program execution. Therefore, they should not be used to hold files that are meant to be viewable by the application users.

The WEB-INF/lib directory is mostly used to hold third-party libraries that are employed within the web application. The hosting web container automatically adds the contents of this directory to the classpath for the web application. You should remember that both the classes and lib directories are optional and only have to be included when you have content to store within them.

Note Although not required by the J2EE 1.4 Specification, if a META-INF directory is provided at the root level inside a deployed web application, the contents of the folder are also made inaccessible to users of the application.

In addition to the web.xml deployment descriptor, different application servers also require the generation of additional deployment descriptors to be placed inside the WEB-INF directory. These deployment descriptors are application server–specific and contain supplemental information about the web application that is not required by the J2EE Specification. Table 14-1 provides a list of the deployment descriptors that can be included with a web application for some JST-supported application servers.

Table 14-1. *Server-specific Web Application Deployment Descriptors*

Server	Deployment Descriptor	Description
Geronimo	geronimo-jetty.xml	Configures the context root and JNDI names of external references used within the web application
JBoss	jboss-web.xml	Configures the context root, virtual hosts, and JNDI names of external references used within the web application
JOnAS	jonas-web.xml	Contains JNDI names of referenced resources, context root, and virtual hosts for servlets
WebLogic	weblogic.xml	Specifies the context root, security settings, additional servlet configuration, as well as a series of other information to fully utilize the feature-rich WebLogic application server

These deployment descriptors can be generated using the XDoclet annotation tool, or they can be created within an appropriate editor and added to the project. It is also possible to include multiple application server–specific deployment descriptors within the web application if the server being used in the development environment will differ from the actual application server type in which the application will be deployed.

web.xml

A web application deployment descriptor manages configuration information for the different web components of an enterprise application such as servlets and tag libraries and it guides how these artifacts can be used within an HTML or a JSP page. Additionally, it manages such details as the default welcome page that is presented to users of the web application and can also be used to configure details regarding the user's interaction with the application. The web.xml deployment descriptor is therefore extremely important to the smooth functioning of a web application.

As we have previously mentioned, this file is an XML-formatted document that resides in the WEB-INF directory and must be named web.xml. The deployment descriptor contains multiple configuration options for the web application, though all of these configurations are optional. In Table 14-2, we have included some of the different types of configuration information that are included within the file. This list, by no means exhaustive, provides a cross-section of configuration parameters that are typically seen in the web.xml file.

Table 14-2. *Contents of web.xml Deployment Descriptor*

Deployment Tag	Description
\<description\>	A general description of the web application.
\<display-name\>	A short name to be displayed in a GUI tool.
\<distributable\>	Specifies that the web application can be deployed in a clustered server environment.
\<icon\>	An icon that represents the J2EE application in a GUI tool.
\<error-page\>	A listing of pages that automatically is shown when an HTTP error or an exception is thrown within the web container.
\<context-param\>	This provides a mechanism for the creation of initialization parameters that can be retrieved by all servlets and JSPs that exist within a web application.
\<servlet\>	Each servlet is configured within its own servlet tag, and this tag provides a mechanism to create an alias for the servlet that differs from the actual servlet class name. Additionally, initialization parameters unique to the servlet can be included here. Note that initialization parameters in the \<context-param\> tag are accessible to every servlet in the web application.
\<session-config\>	A mechanism to specify a maximum period of inactivity before the inactive HttpSession object is invalidated and marked for garbage collection.
\<taglib\>	The location and URI of a JSP tag library for use within the web application.
\<welcome-file-list\>	An ordered list of files that would be iterated through to determine what page a user will see if the URI path of a web application is accessed without a file being specified, e.g., http://localhost:8080/ticketWeb/.

For the web.xml deployment descriptor generated for the Trouble Ticket application, you may notice that many of these configuration elements are missing. This is quite common, as all the elements within a web.xml file are optional. Listing 14-1 shows the web.xml file generated for the Trouble Ticket application.

Listing 14-1. *Trouble Ticket Web Application web.xml*

```xml
<?xml version="1.0" encoding="UTF-8"?>
<web-app xmlns="http://java.sun.com/xml/ns/j2ee"
                xmlns:xsi=http://www.w3.org/2001/XMLSchema-instance
                xsi:schemaLocation="http://java.sun.com/xml/ns/j2ee
                http://java.sun.com/xml/ns/j2ee/web-app_2_4.xsd" version="2.4">

    <distributable/>

    <servlet>
        <servlet-name>ChartTickets</servlet-name>
        <display-name>ChartTickets</display-name>
        <description>
            <![CDATA[Servlet to create a chart of existing trouble tickets]]>
        </description>
        <servlet-class>com.projst.ticket.web.ChartTickets</servlet-class>

        <init-param>
            <param-name>status</param-name>
            <param-value>open</param-value>
            <description><![CDATA[Ticket type to include in chart]]></description>
        </init-param>
    </servlet>

    <servlet-mapping>
        <servlet-name>ChartTickets</servlet-name>
        <url-pattern>/ChartTickets</url-pattern>
    </servlet-mapping>

    <welcome-file-list>
        <welcome-file>index.jsp</welcome-file>
        <welcome-file>view.html</welcome-file>
    </welcome-file-list>

    <taglib>
        <taglib-uri>http://jakarta.apache.org/taglibs/application-1.0</taglib-uri>
        <taglib-location>/WEB-INF/taglibs-application.tld</taglib-location>
    </taglib>
</web-app>
```

Each top-level tag shown (and described in Table 14-2) contains one or more tags that are used to provide information necessary to the server. You will need to consult the appropriate schema document for the J2EE web application version you are using to find out detailed information about the useful subtags. Some of the configuration information provided to the example application by the deployment descriptor include the following:

- The ChartTickets servlet class (which is packaged inside our WEB-INF/classes directory) is accessible through the root context at ChartTickets.

- The session is configured to expire after 30 minutes of inactivity.

- A default file is provided to the user when the URI of the web application is entered without a file name specified.

We also created a jboss-web.xml file to provide some supplemental configuration information to the web container that is not required by the web.xml deployment descriptor. Listing 14-2 shows the content of this file and the single element it contains. This element, the context name, which is not a J2EE required element, is provided by jboss-web.xml.

Listing 14-2. *jboss-web.xml Deployment Descriptor*

```
<?xml version="1.0" encoding="UTF-8"?>
<!DOCTYPE jboss-web PUBLIC "-//JBoss//DTD Web Application 2.3V2//EN"
                    "http://www.jboss.org/j2ee/dtd/jboss-web_3_2.dtd">
<jboss-web>
   <context-root>ticket</context-root>
</jboss-web>
```

Without the inclusion of the jboss-web.xml file from Listing 14-2, the context name of the web application will be matched to the name of the deployed WAR file. This means that for an application server running on port 8080 on the local machine with a web application packaged into a file named ticketWeb.war, access to the web application is available only at the following URL:

http://localhost:8080/ticketWeb

However, if you deploy this same web application using a JBoss application server that includes the jboss-web.xml file in Listing 14-2, JBoss uses the new context information from jboss-web.xml and makes the application available to the user at

http://localhost:8080/ticket

It should be noted that this change in context only occurs when JBoss is being used as the deployment server. Tomcat, JOnAS, and other application servers will ignore the jboss-web.xml file. The difference in this scenario is subtle, but it underscores the importance of application server–specific deployment descriptors as a vehicle for providing developers with a means of including useful supplemental configuration that is not required by the J2EE Specification.

Note Though the web.xml deployment descriptor does not support specifying a context for deployed web applications, this configuration detail is required in the application.xml deployment descriptor when WAR files are packages as part of an EAR file.

EAR Files

An alternative form of packaging web applications that is described by the J2EE 1.4 Specification and duly supported by JST is the packaging of web applications into EAR files. In Chapter 11, we described EAR files as archival structures in the JAR file format that can be composed of multiple EJB JAR and WAR files that represent EJB-Tier and Web-Tier deployment modules. As we have shown in Figure 14-1, an EAR file can also hold other files such as JAR files containing classes that are used by the EJB JAR and WAR files.

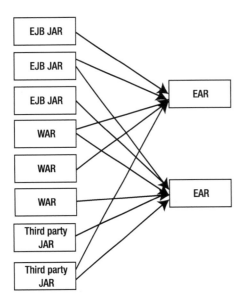

Figure 14-1. *Composition of an EAR file*

Using this method of composition, the multiple web and EJB deployment modules that together provide functionality for an enterprise application are packaged together inside a single archive. The choice to package as either a WAR file or an EAR file depends on the type of project you choose to create. If a Dynamic Web Project is selected, you will only be able to package your deployment module as a WAR file; however, you can choose to create an Enterprise Application Project also and add any module within your Dynamic Web Project to this Enterprise Application Project. This allows you to generate an EAR file that holds all the WAR files that have been included as modules in the Enterprise Application Project. The internal structure of each WAR file still matches the structure we described earlier in this chapter, and the application.xml deployment descriptor of the EAR file is updated to include a reference to the WAR file such as in Listing 14-3.

Listing 14-3. *Web Module Element in application.xml*

```
<module>
    <web>
        <web-uri>ticketWeb.war</web-uri>
        <context-root>ticket/</context-root>
    </web>
</module>
```

Note As we described in Chapter 7, EAR files can also hold Application Client JAR files and RAR files that are deployment units for Application Clients and J2EE Connectors, respectively.

Exporting Artifacts

Eclipse provides the ability to easily export the deployable artifact from a project to the file system. This is done using the Export wizard and for web applications can generate WAR files or EAR files. As we have previously discussed, to generate an EAR file that holds a WAR file, you must add a module that exists within your Dynamic Web Project to your Enterprise Application Project. This can be done by selecting the Enterprise Application Project in the Project Explorer and choosing Project ➤ Properties ➤ EAR modules. From this dialog box, you will be able to specify the modules from projects that exist within your workspace that will be contained within the EAR file. If you don't have an existing Enterprise Application Project, you will need to create one before performing these steps.

Once you are ready to export your deployment artifact, you will need to launch the Export wizard. This can be done by selecting File ➤ Export from the IDE menu. Choosing the WAR file or EAR file export option will present you with a dialog box through which you can select the project to export from and the location to export the files to on the file system. You will also have the choice to include your source files within your project.

The resulting WAR or EAR file from this process can be deployed within any suitable J2EE application server.

Caution Make sure you know the audience for your WAR or EAR file before selecting Export source file from the Export menu.

Deploying Web Modules

Similar to what we did to our EJBs in Chapter 11, web modules also need to be built and deployed before the application logic that is contained within them can be made available to end users of the application. The steps involved in this process are as follows:

- **Building**: This involves the compilation of source files within the web module using builders associated with the project. On completion of this step, a deployable instance of the web application is available in a `.deployables` directory found within the project location on the file system.

- **Publishing**: This makes the content of the `.deployables` directory available to a defined server instance within which the web module will be hosted. Multiple options are available to control how frequent deployable content is automatically published to a server. These settings can be managed by selecting Window ➤ Preferences ➤ Server.

Before the web application can be published, an instance of the server that you are publishing to must be created. The server is the target for the publishing process, and for web applications the target server being defined must contain a web container.

This server definition occurs only the first time a web application is being deployed. Subsequent publishing can then be targeted to the same application server. See Chapter 11 for the steps involved in creating a server environment configuration into which your J2EE modules can be deployed. Multiple server instances can also be created with the web application deployed on many of these instances at the same time. Care has to be taken to assign the different server instances distinct port numbers because only a single active server instance can listen on a port. Other server instances that try to use the port will generate exceptions and fail to start. The generated exceptions can be viewed in the Console View. The Servers View provides a very useful mechanism for viewing each of the server definitions and controlling the execution of these servers. Figure 14-2 shows the project selection page in the Server Creation wizard that is being used to create a Tomcat server instance to host the Trouble Ticket web application.

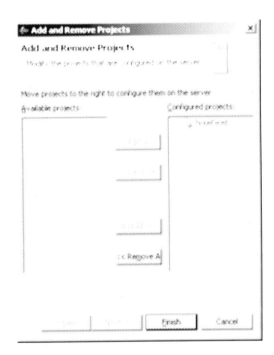

Figure 14-2. *Deployment of a web module*

Publishing a web application to an application server does not always generate a WAR file. When using Geronimo, JBoss, JOnAS, or WebLogic as deployment server targets, a WAR file is created containing the packaged web application. However, for deployments into Tomcat, a WAR file is not generated. JST simply links the .deployables directory created as part of the build process into Tomcat as a deployment directory for a web application. Figure 14-3 shows the server configuration page that is accessible by selecting the Tomcat server instance within the Servers View and then choosing Open from the context menu. The Modules tab that lists all the web modules deployed on this instance of the Tomcat server is displayed in Figure 14-3.

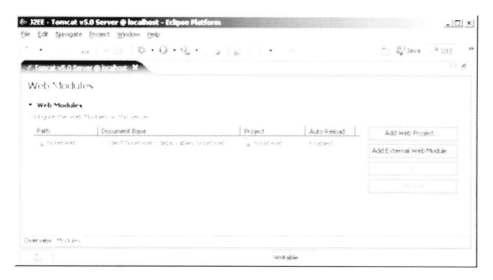

Figure 14-3. *Tomcat configuration showing deployed web modules*

The directory provided in this picture is very useful in determining where to locate the deployable instance of the application server. JST provides an export facility that can be used to package the contents of this .deployables directory into a WAR file.

Tip Selecting a server instance from the Servers View and choosing Open from the context menu loads a configuration page for the defined server instance. This page is very useful in modifying the settings of the server instance.

Managing Deployment with Ant

In certain cases, the project being deployed requires a complicated enough build process that it might become necessary for the developer to take over from Eclipse the process of packaging and deploying the enterprise application. It is not unusual for the packaging and deployment of a J2EE deployment module to require the involvement of many processes, thus becoming quite complicated. One tool that is made available for such a situation as this is Ant, the popular Java-based build tool created by The Apache Software Foundation. Ant extends Eclipse with the ability to allow a developer to easily take over control of build, packaging, and deployment activity within the IDE. Eclipse itself manages many of these internal processes by using Ant scripts.

Available at http://jakarta.apache.org/ant, Ant is an open source application that uses XML-formatted documents to produce platform-independent build scripts. This eliminates the need to learn a script language as required by many build engines, without sacrificing any functionality. In fact, many would argue that the large variety of tasks that can be accomplished using Ant make it as powerful as any other build tool. The default name for an Ant build script is build.xml, though any file with the .xml extension could similarly be used.

build.xml

The build.xml file is the default script file used by Ant to hold its XML-based commands. When the Ant tool is invoked, it searches for the existence of this file for the definition of any specified commands. As we stated earlier, this is by no means the only file name that can be used; when other files are used, the name of the file that holds the XML-formatted commands simply has to be specified. These XML-based build scripts are known as *buildfiles* in the Ant terminology. An Ant buildfile contains a collection of tasks that are small pieces of executable code used to perform a specific action. Often a sequence of tasks are grouped together to perform a useful function for the developer, such as the compilation of files within a project. Listing 14-4 provides an abbreviated version of the build.xml file used by Eclipse to compile the J2EE web module of the Trouble Ticket application.

Listing 14-4. *An Ant Buildfile for the Trouble Ticket Web Module*

```xml
<?xml version="1.0" encoding="UTF-8"?>
<project basedir="." default="build" name="ticketWeb">

<property name="ticketWeb.location" value="C:/devl/ticketWeb"/>
<path id="project.classpath">
  <pathelement location=".deployables/ticketWeb/WEB-INF/classes"/>
  <pathelement
    location="${ticketWeb.location}/WebContent/WEB-INF/lib/junit.jar"/>
  <pathelement location=
    "${ticketWeb.location}/WebContent/WEB-INF/lib/jfreechart-1.0.0-rc1.jar"/>
  <pathelement
    location="${ticketWeb.location}/WebContent/WEB-INF/lib/commons-validator.jar"/>
  <pathelement
    location="${ticketWeb.location}/WebContent/WEB-INF/lib/standard.jar"/>
  <pathelement
    location="${ticketWeb.location}/WebContent/WEB-INF/lib/saaj.jar"/>
  <pathelement
   location="${ticketWeb.location}/WebContent/WEB-INF/lib/commons-fileupload.jar"/>
  <pathelement
    location="${ticketWeb.location}/WebContent/WEB-INF/lib/jakarta-oro.jar"/>
  <pathelement
    location="${ticketWeb.location}/WebContent/WEB-INF/lib/gnujaxp.jar"/>
  <pathelement
    location="${ticketWeb.location}/WebContent/WEB-INF/lib/jcommon-1.0.0-rc1.jar"/>
  <pathelement
    location="${ticketWeb.location}/WebContent/WEB-INF/lib/commons-beanutils.jar"/>
  <pathelement
    location="${ticketWeb.location}/WebContent/WEB-INF/lib/commons-logging.jar"/>
  <pathelement
    location="${ticketWeb.location}/WebContent/WEB-INF/lib/wsdl4j.jar"/>
  <pathelement
    location="${ticketWeb.location}/WebContent/WEB-INF/lib/struts.jar"/>
```

```
  <pathelement
   location="${ticketWeb.location}/WebContent/WEB-INF/lib/antlr.jar"/>
  <pathelement
   location="${ticketWeb.location}/WebContent/WEB-INF/lib/jstl.jar"/>
  <pathelement
   location="${ticketWeb.location}/WebContent/WEB-INF/lib/jaxrpc.jar"/>
</path>

  <target name="init">
      <mkdir dir=".deployables/ticketWeb/WEB-INF/classes"/>
  </target>
  <target name="clean">
      <delete dir=".deployables/ticketWeb/WEB-INF/classes"/>
  </target>
  <target depends="init" name="build">
      <echo message="${ant.project.name}: ${ant.file}"/>
      <javac destdir=".deployables/ticketWeb/WEB-INF/classes">
          <src path="JavaSource"/>
          <classpath refid="project.classpath"/>
      </javac>
  </target>
</project>
```

Targets

You may notice from Listing 14-4 the use of a `<target>` tag to group the `<echo>` and `<javac>` tasks. These two tags perform the compilation of sources with the `<echo>` task informing the user about the action in progress and the `<javac>` task compiling the source files. From this listing, you can also see that different tasks have different attributes that are useful to them for their specific needs. The `<echo>` tag, for instance, contains a `message` attribute that is used to specify the message to display, while the `<javac>` tag uses other attributes that are more closely related to its function.

A `<target>` element represents a functional unit of activity within the buildfile and is composed of one or more tasks that collectively complete the activity needed by the target. Each target has a unique name to aid identification and usage. Ant supports an impressive list of tasks that can be used within a target. These tasks provide such functionality as copying, deleting, and archiving files as well as executing programs, etc. Tasks are implemented as small Java classes and thus have virtually limitless capabilities. By properly manipulating the parameters passed to a task, you can use a task to perform multiple variations of a single type of activity. The `<copy>` task tag can, for example, be used to copy a file, a directory, a list of files, or a list of files that match a certain criteria. A listing of available tasks can be found in the Ant documentation at `http://ant.apache.org/manual/tasksoverview.html`.

Note In addition to the tasks provided by the Ant tool, Ant provides an extensible interface to allow developers to create their own tasks and use these tasks in their build configuration files.

Properties

Another noticeable item from the preceding listing is the use of ${ant.project.name} to represent the name of the project. In this listing, ant.project.name is a property, and its use is analogous to declaring a variable in a programming language and then using this variable. This provides the user with the ability to use a descriptive name to refer to a value within the Ant script. There are several ways of declaring properties, and here we have provided the form used in the build.xml file shown in Listing 14-4:

```
<property name="ticketWeb.location" value="C:/devl/ticketWeb" />
```

In this example, a property named ticketWeb.location is created and its value set to C:/devl/ticketWeb. This property can later be accessed using the following syntax:

```
${ticketWeb.location}
```

Ant additionally supports the reading of properties from a URL, property file, or environment variables declared within the system the Ant process is executing on. It also contains a few built-in variables such as ant.project.name and ant.file that are both used in Listing 14-4.

Types

Another important concept to creating a buildfile is the use of types. An Ant type is a data structure that is used to hold different types of data. Often this data, as is the case in Listing 14-4, is related to files, or a directory that will be included in a build, or the classpath of an application. Types provide a convenient way to pattern match and easily retrieve and store a group of related information.

Integration with Eclipse

Ant integrates easily with Eclipse to provide developers who need to manage their own build script with truly extensive capabilities. It should be noted that this is not a feature introduced into Eclipse by JST, but one that has existed previously. Nonetheless, it is a very useful feature for such exacting processes as enterprise application development. Managing an Ant buildfile within Eclipse begins with creating a configuration for the Ant build tool to make it accessible from within the workbench. Configuring this external tool is done by selecting Run ➤ External Tools ➤ External Tools from the Eclipse menu. The External Tools dialog box presented contains an option to configure the Ant build script as shown in Figure 14-4.

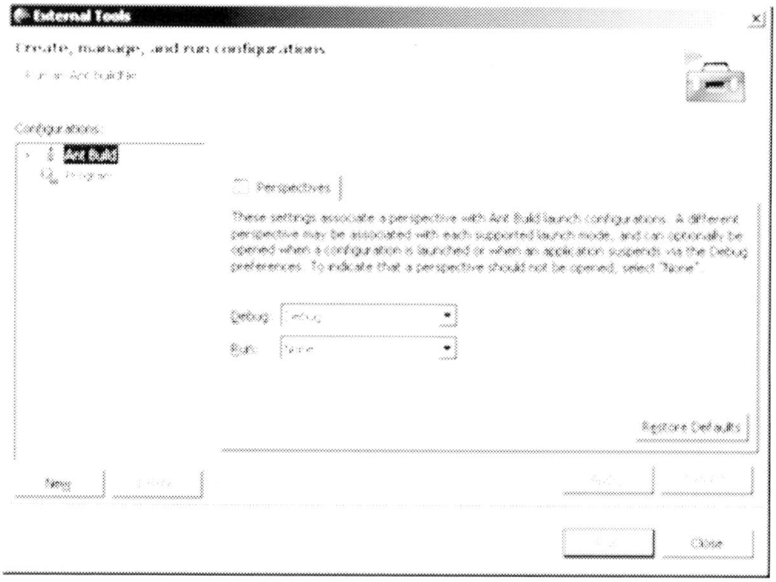

Figure 14-4. *External Tools configuration page*

With this page, a user can specify perspectives to switch to if an Ant buildfile is invoked using either the Debug or Run mode. Clicking the New button that is available on the page creates a new configuration that allows you to manage the behavior of the Ant script you will use. This configuration page also provides you with the ability to associate an Ant script with one or more projects within the workspace. Figure 14-5 shows the configuration dialog box of an Ant buildfile.

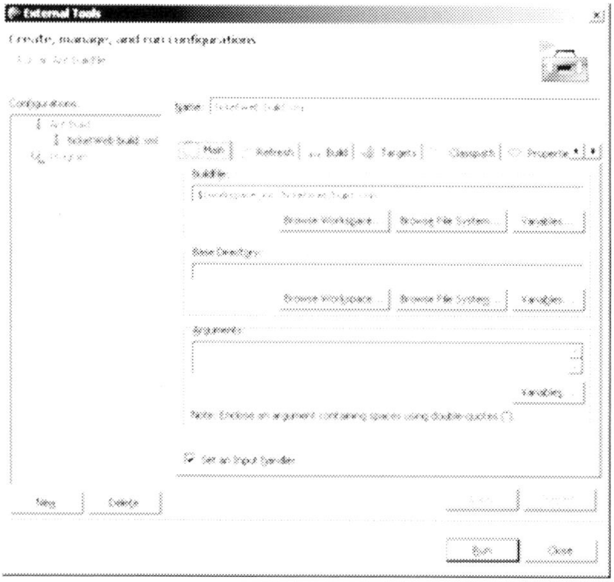

Figure 14-5. *Creating an Ant build configuration*

The tabs on the dialog box shown in Figure 14-5 are used to gather detailed information from the user about the configuration of the buildfile and how the build script will be executed within Eclipse. Most of the information prompted for by these tabs is optional. The information requested by the various tab pages includes the following:

- **Main**: Prompts for a name for the configuration, the buildfile location, variables for the buildfile, and base directory within which to execute the buildfile

- **Refresh**: Specifies whether to refresh upon completion of a build and what items to refresh

- **Build**: Specifies whether a build should be performed before the script execution and what items to build

- **Targets**: Lists a selection of targets to run and target execution order

- **Classpath**: Lists sequentially the dependent libraries to use when executing Ant

- **Properties**: Specifies additional properties and property files to use while executing the buildfile

- **JRE**: Defines the installed JRE used to execute the Ant tool and additional arguments to control its execution behavior

- **Environment**: Specifies additional environmental variables available only for the execution of the buildfile

- **Common**: Defines miscellaneous configuration information such as displaying the configuration in the Favorites menu or capturing the output in the Console View or in a file

On completion of this configuration process, the configuration information becomes integrated into the Eclipse menu and is accessible by selecting Run ➤ External Tools. The configuration is also included within the context menu and accessible from either the Run As or Debug As context menu that is shown when the buildfile is highlighted.

The Outline View that is included as a part of the J2EE Perspective provides an additional mechanism for running the Ant script within Eclipse. When the buildfile is loaded into the editor, the Outline View lists all the targets within the buildfile and allows execution of specific targets. The output from this invocation is displayed within the Console View.

ALTERNATE ANT CONFIGURATION

An alternative, and arguably simpler, method of using Ant in managing a project is to create an Ant buildfile within any open project in the workspace and then add this buildfile to the Ant View. The Ant View is accessible by selecting Window ➤ Show View ➤ Other ➤ Ant from the Eclipse menu. The Show View dialog box presented as part of this process is shown here:

Multiple buildfiles can be added to the Ant View with the view providing a mechanism to inspect all the targets available within each file and choose any target for execution. Adding buildfiles to the Ant View is accomplished by clicking the Add Buildfile icon on the view toolbar. A user is allowed to use any file type as a buildfile as long as it contains valid XML syntax and Ant targets. Eclipse immediately recognizes the file and includes it in the Ant View. This form of integration is the most flexible for users as it allows them to view all the targets in the buildfile and the tasks within each of these targets. The Ant View with a buildfile included is shown in the following illustration:

The user can then select any of the targets and execute them by using either the Run As or Debug As context menu options, or by clicking the Run toolbar button within the Ant View toolbar.

Working with Ant Buildfiles

Eclipse provides an export facility that can be used to export the internal script used by Eclipse to build your project. This exported buildfile can then be used as a starting point for modifications. You can access the export facility by selecting Export ➤ Ant Buildfiles from the project context menu and then selecting the project that you want to export the buildfile from. This process actually generates two files:

- `build.xml`: This is an autogenerated file that contains the scripts used by the IDE to build your file. You should be careful if you choose to modify this file because your updates will be overwritten the next time you run the export facility.

- `build-user.xml`: This file is referenced by the generated `build.xml` file and provides a location where you can include your targets without the file being overwritten.

We have provided in Listing 14-5 the default `build-user.xml` file that is generated by Eclipse. Listing 14-6 shows our addition of a `cleanAll` target.

Listing 14-5. *Default build-user.xml Generated for the Trouble Ticket Web Module*

```
<target name="help">
    <echo message="Please run: $ ant -v -projecthelp"/>
</target>
```

Listing 14-6. *Modified build-user.xml*

```
<property name="JBoss.serverHome"
               location="c:/devl/jboss-4.0.1sp1/server/default" />

<target name="help">
    <echo message="Please run: $ ant -v -projecthelp"/>
</target>

<target name="cleanAll">
    <antcall target="clean"/>
    <delete includeEmptyDirs="true">
      <fileset dir="${JBoss.serverHome}">
        <include name="**/log/**"/>
        <include name="**/tmp/**"/>
        <include name="**/work/**"/>
      </fileset>
    </delete>
</target>
```

The included target in Listing 14-6 makes a call to the `clean` target in the `build.xml` file and then cleans out JBoss runtime files. The location of the JBoss server configuration is specified using a `<property>` task. Figure 14-6 shows the Outline View that is displayed when the `build.xml` file is loaded into the editor.

Figure 14-6. *Outline View showing the build.xml Ant buildfile*

You may notice from Figure 14-6 that certain items have the suffix [from buildfile]; inspection of Listing 14-6 will show that these elements correspond to elements defined inside our build-user.xml file.

If you choose not to use the internal Ant buildfile generated by Eclipse, you could simply create your own file by using the XML editor (available by selecting New ➤ XML from the menu). You can also import a preexisting buildfile into the project. The Eclipse import facility accommodates this, allowing you to import the file into your workspace by selecting Import ➤ File system and choosing the file from your hard drive.

Accessing Web Applications

Once deployed, contents of a web application become available for access by users. Access to the deployed web artifacts is gained using any application capable of making HTTP requests and parsing the resulting response. This response, as we have shown in Chapter 12 and Chapter 13, is in the form of HTML documents. The most common application with which web applications are accessed is therefore web browsers because of their capability to graphically render these HTML documents. It is no surprise therefore that Eclipse provides an embedded browser with which the deployed web application can be viewed and accessed within the workbench. The built-in Eclipse web browser is accessible as part of the Internal Web Browser View and can be launched by selecting Window ➤ Show View ➤ Other ➤ Basic ➤ Internal Web Browser.

To access a deployed web application, the URL of the content desired within the web application simply needs to be requested. For most browsers, including the internal browser provided by Eclipse, this is done by entering the URL in the address bar. The URL for accessing a web application has the following generic form:

```
protocol://host:port/context/file
```

An example of a URL in this form is displayed here:

```
http://localhost:8080/ticketWeb/jsp/listtickets.jsp
```

This URL accesses the JSP created in Chapter 12. We will now break down this URL into its constituent parts and describe each of them:

- **protocol**: URLs support multiple protocols, but in the case of a web application, this must be noted as http (or https for secure access). This indicates that HTTP, which provides a transport mechanism for accessing documents over the Internet, is being used.

- **host**: The name of the server hosting the web application. During development, the same machine used for development is often used to test the application. In such a case, the special domain name localhost is used to refer back to that machine.

- **port**: The port number where the web container is listening for requests. If this is port 80, which is the default port for HTTP requests, then inclusion of the port number is optional. JBoss uses port 8080 by default to accept requests, though this port can be easily changed.

- **context**: A virtual name that represents the root of the web applications. All the contents of the packaged web application are available relative to this context name.

- **file**: The relative path structure on the server to the location of a static resource, JSP page, or servlet that is being requested from the server.

Note Certain firewall misconfigurations have been known to block reference to the localhost domain name on a machine. In such instances, you may find that using 127.0.0.1, the loopback IP address reserved for each computer, in place of the hostname "localhost" might work.

You may remember from our discussion in Chapter 13 that accessing a servlet by requesting the URL creates a request of type GET, which executes the doGet method within the servlet. Information can be passed to the servlet during a GET request using a process known as *URL mangling*. This involves appending the extra data needed by the servlet to the URL in a specific form. The URL that follows, for instance, invokes the servlet we created in Chapter 13 and passes the attributes email and status to the servlet.

```
http://localhost:8080/ticketWeb/ChartTicket?email=user@projst.com&status=open
```

Running with the Workbench

Within the workbench, a specific web artifact can be executed by selecting the item file within the Project Explorer and choosing either Run As or Debug As from the context menu. This launches the artifact in either run mode or debug mode. The difference between these two modes is that execution in debug mode provides detailed information about the execution of the application to the workbench, supplying a mechanism for testing and validating the application functionality during development.

The Run As and Debug As context menu options available for executing the application within the workbench provide the following execution options:

- **Run on Server/Debug on Server**: Deploys the web artifact to a server instance and generates an HTTP request for the selected object from the server. The server instance deployed to can be an existing server instance already available under the Servers View, or a new instance can be manually defined. The HTTP request loads the artifact into the browser configured for use within the workbench.

- **Run/Debug**: This loads the runtime configuration page that allows you to manage configuration information about the server instances already created. Creation of a new server instance can also be performed using this page. The New Server wizard we described in Chapter 11 simply provides a wizard to gather information that is recorded and stored within this page. By loading this runtime configuration editor, you are able to edit extensively the configuration details that control the execution of a defined server.

Summary

Provided in this chapter is an overview of the structure of web applications and the files and directories that could exist in a web module. We discussed the `web.xml` deployment descriptor and included a listing of some of the important configuration parameters that are often found in this file to instruct a web container on how to make services within the web application available to the public.

Archiving of web applications into WAR files is often done, and we described this as a process to each distribution of the application. We also described how WAR files could be packaged within an EAR file.

We described how a developer could take over control of the build, package, and deploy processes using an external build tool such as Ant. Ant is easily integrated within the Eclipse environment, and we provided detailed steps in setting up and using Ant within a project.

We concluded the chapter with a description of how you access web applications.

CHAPTER 15

Web Services

Web Services provide a mechanism through which distributed web-based application components existing on different platforms can interact with each other to share data-centric resources. Using Web Services technology, resources that are available to one component such as back-end applications and databases can be shared with other components and put to a variety of uses. The communication between components involved with this process is handled through the use of XML-formatted messages.

From this description, you may begin to see Web Services technology as a mechanism that provides you programmatic access to data that exists on—or is generated by—a remote system located over a distributed network landscape. This is quite correct. Web Services provide software components with the ability to expose some of the methods contained within them in a platform-independent manner. They also provide software components with the ability to invoke methods on a remote component, pass data to the method for processing during invocation, and retrieve data produced by this remote component.

These exposed methods are known as *services*, and the act of making them available is known as *publishing a service*. At the same time, Web Services make it possible for other applications' components to utilize these exposed services. This is known as *consuming a service*. At the core of Web Services lies the use of XML for communication between service providers and consumers. You will find that XML plays a big role in Web Services primarily because of the self-describing nature of XML technology and its support by many transport protocols.

The commercial benefit of this technology is immediately apparent, as it allows companies to easily provide data-centric services to customers without the overhead of maintaining a close working relationship with their clients, as is often required by many other service-based technologies. In light of its numerous benefits, many companies have embraced this technology, with notable supporters including Amazon, which has provided access to its massive database of book descriptions and reviews through the Amazon E-Commerce Service (http://www.amazon.com); and eBay, which has provided access to the many features of its online marketplace through the eBay Web Services program (http://developer.ebay.com).

In this chapter, we will discuss these Web Services and the benefits that can be derived from their use. Our primary focus will be on Java-based Web Services and the support included for them in JST. We will further describe how to provide and consume Web Services using our Trouble Ticket application to illustrate. Finally, we will discuss the Web Services Explorer tool that can be used to search for and view available Web Services, test them, and publish them to UDDI registries.

Web Services Overview

Web Services constitute a language-neutral, platform-independent technology for providing remote access to data and functionality over a distributed network. This technology achieves this by providing a mechanism to connect together the multiple services that exist in a Service-Oriented Architecture (SOA) paradigm using a platform-neutral messaging format. SOA is an architectural approach in which some components exist that support a particular business function known as a *service*. This service is then made accessible to other components that employ it for a variety of uses. Using the Amazon E-Commerce Service as an example, a developer might choose to build an application that retrieves items for sale on Amazon and displays them on the desktop. The Amazon E-Commerce Service is said to be providing a service, while the desktop application is consuming the service. SOA has been around for a while, and you might even have used it in such SOA implementations as Distributed Component Object Model (DCOM) and Common Object Request Broker Architecture (CORBA).

The advantage of Web Services over these prior implementations is the complete lack of coupling between participants involved in publishing/consuming a service. As we have established earlier, Web Services provide a platform-independent mechanism to publish and consume services across networks. They achieve this platform independence by using XML to communicate between parties involved in providing/consuming a service. XML, by virtue of being self-describing and usable by any communication protocol that supports the transmission of plain text, is extremely well suited for this activity. This immediately allows applications created in Java, for instance, to consume Web Services created in C# or Perl. Another benefit of the use of XML is the complete separation of data from presentation. Messages passed between producer and consumer can be displayed in any manner that the consumer sees fit.

You can quickly see that true platform interoperability is supported by Web Services. A J2EE web application is easily capable of consuming services hosted on a variety of different platforms. Figure 15-1 illustrates the application development possibilities that are available to you through Web Services.

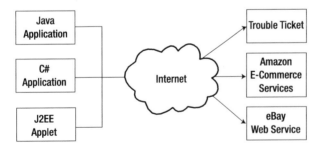

Figure 15-1. *Multiple client interaction with a Web Service*

You may notice from Figure 15-1 that the applications developed in a variety of languages can easily invoke services that run on a wide variety of platforms and are written in multiple languages. In fact, when using Web Services, there is no need to know the source language in which the service was created, or the platform it is hosted on. This is because you will interact with the service through standardized communication protocols. This is analogous to when you browse a website and do not have to be concerned about the web server type hosting the site or what language CGI scripts used by the site were created in.

One of the clients in this example is a Java application consuming multiple services from different providers. One of the service providers is a Java-based Web Service which is a part of our Trouble Ticket application. We will show you the process of creating a Web Service that will retrieve and display tickets in this chapter. The J2EE 1.4 Specification provides details on how Java-based Web Services must function in JSR-109—Implementing Enterprise Web Services. This specification provides details on how clients can connect to Web Services and how deployed components can provide Web Services in both the Web Tier and the EJB Tier. It is important to realize that JSR-109 does not describe how Web Services function, but instead how to publish and consume Web Services using Java enterprise technologies. The distinction is important because to function independently of a language or platform, Web Services must use standardized technologies and protocols.

Three important standardized technologies are utilized by Web Services:

1. **Universal Description, Discovery, and Integration (UDDI)**: This functions as the naming service for Web Services, providing them with a place to register their services for possible clients. Service providers publish their services to the registry, including the location of a WSDL file that describes how to access the service they provide. Later in this chapter, we will look at the Web Services Explorer tool that allows you to browse UDDI registries and view the various Web Services registered within them. Several such registries exist today for a variety of business, entertainment, and general-purpose Web Services. Some of these registries include the IBM UDDI Business Registry (`https://uddi.ibm.com/ubr/registry.html`) and the XMethods UDDI Registry (`http://www.xmethods.net/ve2/Interfaces.po`).

2. **Web Service Description Language (WSDL)**: This document describes the interface contract for the Web Service, including within it such items as the available operations within the Web Service, the structure of the request parameters, and response generated from the service. The types of binding supported by the service are also included in this document as well as the location of the service known as the *endpoint*. Expectedly, the WSDL file is XML-based, providing a mechanism for the service provider and consumer to easily validate that data sent to them is well formed.

3. **Simple Object Access Protocol (SOAP)**: This is a communication protocol used to share information between applications. It uses XML to specify a format for information that needs to be shared between two distributed components. This provides the ability for a service provider and service consumer to interact as long as they can both generate and parse XML documents. The SOAP document is transmitted between provider and consumer using any transport protocol such as HTTP. Besides platform neutrality, transmission over HTML has the additional benefit of allowing components to make RPC calls across network boundaries that might have firewalls.

These technologies function together to provide components with the ability to discover a Web Service, find the Web Service endpoint, and invoke operations made available by the Web Service. You may immediately notice something familiar with these three technologies: they are similar to technology services that need to exist within any technology that supports remote procedure calls. EJBs, for instance, utilize broadly similar technologies, with Java Naming and Directory Interface (JNDI) used for naming and locating EJBs, `javax.ejb.EJBObject` used to provide the interface description for the EJB, and RMI-IIOP used as the communication protocol for interacting with the EJB.

Web Services are therefore clearly comparable to any technology that supports remote invocation of procedures. The important distinction of Web Services is that since each of the three foundation technologies is based on open standards, any language or platform that supports all three foundation technologies can be used to host services. Additionally, any platform that is able to generate and parse XML documents as well as transmit documents over a network can easily consume these services. Figure 15-2 provides an illustration of how these technologies function cohesively, showing the runtime and design-time processes for a Web Service client.

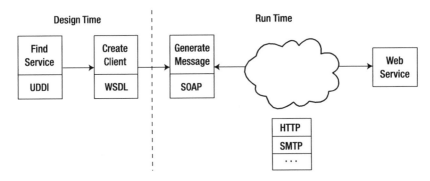

Figure 15-2. *Consuming a Web Service*

Figure 15-2 distinguishes between design-time and runtime processes when it comes to consuming a Web Service. The use of a UDDI registry to discover a Web Service and the retrieval of the WSDL file published by this service are design-time operations. The developer uses the information from the WSDL file to generate a template for SOAP messages to be sent to the Web Service as well as to support the ability to parse the response from the Web Service. At runtime, the actual message is generated and sent to the Web Service, and a request may be received.

Note Web Service operations support both synchronous and asynchronous operations, so provision of a response depends wholly on the type of operation being invoked.

Tip If you want to learn more about Web Services, we suggest you read *Beginning J2EE 1.4: From Novice to Professional* by James L. Weaver, Kevin Mukhar, and Jim Crume (Apress, 2004).

Web Services Support in JST

The ability to discover, create, and consume Web Services is a major addition to JST. This support is built upon the Apache Axis 1.2.1 toolkit (http://ws.apache.org/axis/), which provides an open source implementation of SOAP. Axis is used for easily creating and consuming Web

Services and can be employed as a stand-alone product. JST, however, seamlessly integrates this toolkit into Eclipse.

Web Services support in JST can be logically separated into the following functional groups:

- **Discovering Web Services**: JST provides the Web Services Explorer tool for the design-time discovery of Web Services by allowing you to browse UDDI registries. It further allows retrieval of WSDL files associated with these Web Services as well as invoking operations contained within them. We will discuss the Web Services Explorer Tool later in this chapter.

- **Creating Web Service**s: Support is provided for the creation of Web Services and deployment of these into defined runtime environments. Two forms of Web Service creation are supported:

  - **Bottom-up approach**: This is the creation of a Web Service from an appropriate Java class. Wizards are provided to expose methods within this class as Web Service operations, and an appropriate WSDL file is made available for clients.

  - **Top-down approach**: This process begins with an existing WSDL class. JST provides the ability to create a Java class from the operations defined within WSDL. The top-down approach would be very useful in situations where interface definitions need to be made available to clients ahead of the functionality they provide.

- **Consuming Web Services**: JST provides support for the creation of Java clients to invoke operations defined within the WSDL interface description file of available Web Services. Note that this is different from the top-down approach to creating Web Services. What is being created here is the ability to consume existing Web Services.

We will describe the process of creating and consuming Web Services in the context of our Trouble Ticket application.

Creating Web Services

Once you have decided to make services available to other applications that may need data from your application, it is time to create a Web Service. As we have stated previously, you can do this using either the bottom-up or the top-down approach. We will demonstrate the bottom-up approach to creating a Web Service client that will provide a listing of trouble tickets to any clients that require such information. You may remember that we created an EJB client in Chapter 11 to retrieve such a listing. In that implementation, clients to our system must be capable of interfacing with EJBs. This effectively limits our client base to mostly Java components, although software packages exist that allow components from different platforms to interact with EJBs.

By providing a Web Service to give clients access to the trouble ticket information, we provide a more structured access mechanism to our data and the ability for multiple clients on different platforms to easily and consistently access our information.

JST provides support for the creation of three types of Web Services using two different methods:

- **Bottom-up approach**: In this form, existing Java components are exposed as Web Services with WSDL files generated from them and packaged into a web module for access using HTTP. The type of Web Service that can be created using this method is as follows:

  - **Java Bean Web Service**: Involves the creation of a Web Service from a standard Java class, allowing you to expose public methods within the Java bean for invocation by remote clients.

- **Top-down approach**: This can be referred to as the reverse engineering of a WSDL file to create a Web Service. As opposed to the previous method, which requires the existence of a Java component, this service type requires the existence of a WSDL file and creates a skeleton Java bean file from the operations defined in the WSDL file. The type of Web Service that can be created using this method is as follows:

  - **Skeleton Java Bean Service**: Involves the creation of a skeleton Java class to support operations defined in a WSDL interface definition file.

Tip WTP provides a WSDL Creation wizard that can be used to create a WSDL file, which can then be used to create a Web Service using the top-down approach. This WSDL Creation wizard can be launched by selecting File ➤ New ➤ Other ➤ Web Services ➤ WSDL from the Eclipse menu.

Web Services can also be created from servlets and stateless session beans. Servlets already possess the power to respond to remote requests and can easily be created to accept SOAP documents as input and formulate XML-formatted responses. Stateless session beans can also be easily converted to Web Services, and are the only components from the EJB Tier that can be used as such due to their stateless nature. This is because the Web Services specification does not provide support for state management.

Currently in JST, to use either of these components as a Web Service, you must create a bean class that invokes operations that exist within the servlet or the stateless session bean. The public methods of this bean class can then be exposed as Web Service methods using the Web Services wizard.

Web Services Wizard

We will provide a Web Service for our Trouble Ticket application using the Web Services wizard provided by JST. This Web Service will support the following two operations:

- `getTicket(int)`: This allows clients to retrieve information about a specific trouble ticket based on the ticket ID.

- `getTickets(String)`: This allows clients to retrieve information about trouble tickets based on the status of the ticket.

You may remember from preceding chapters the `Ticket` JavaBean class that we have created. This class, shown in Listing 15-1, will contain information about the retrieved trouble ticket. We use this class because the information being returned by the Web Service is of a complex nature and contains multiple fields.

Listing 15-1. *Ticket.java Bean Class*

```java
package com.projst.ticket.dto;

import java.io.Serializable;
import java.util.Date;

/**
 * Trouble Ticket representing something that needs to be fixed.
 *
 * @author cjudd
 */
public class Ticket implements Serializable {
    private long oid = -1;
    private String summary;
    private String detail;
    private Date submittedDate;
    private Date lastModifedDate;
    private String email;
    private String status;

    /**
     * Unique identifier for the ticket.
     *
     * @return Returns the unique identifier.
     */
    public long getOid() {
        return oid;
    }

    /**
     * @see #getOid()
     * @param oid
     *              The unique identifier.
     */
    public void setOid(long oid) {
        this.oid = oid;
    }

    /**
     * @return Returns the summary.
     */
    public String getSummary() {
        return summary;
    }

    /**
     * @param summary
```

```java
 *              The summary to set.
 */
public void setSummary(String summary) {
    this.summary = summary;
}


/**
 * @return Returns the detail.
 */
public String getDetail() {
    return detail;
}


/**
 * @param detail
 *              The detail to set.
 */
public void setDetail(String detail) {
    this.detail = detail;
}


/**
 * @return Returns the submittedDate.
 */
public Date getSubmittedDate() {
    return submittedDate;
}


/**
 * @param submittedDate
 *              The submittedDate to set.
 */
public void setSubmittedDate(Date submittedDate) {
    this.submittedDate = submittedDate;
}


/**
 * @return Returns the lastModifedDate.
 */
public Date getLastModifedDate() {
    return lastModifedDate;
}


/**
 * @param lastModifedDate
 *              The lastModifedDate to set.
 */
public void setLastModifedDate(Date lastModifedDate) {
```

```
        this.lastModifedDate = lastModifedDate;
    }

    /**
     * @return Returns the e-mail
     */
    public void setEmail(String email) {
        this.email = email;
    }

    /**
     * @param e-mail
     *                The e-mail of the person who submitted the ticket.
     */
        public String getEmail() {
        return email;
    }

    /**
     * @return Returns the status.
     */
    public String getStatus() {
        return status;
    }

    /**
     * @param status
     *                The status of the ticket.
     */
    public void setStatus(String status) {
        this.status = status;
    }

}
```

As you can see, a single instance of the Ticket object holds information about the ticket
ID, ticket summary, ticket detail, and so on. A single instance of this class will be returned
when the getTicket(int) method is called, and an array of this type will be returned when
getTickets(String) is invoked. The Java class that provides the Web Service operations is
shown in Listing 15-2.

Listing 15-2. *Bean Class That Retrieves Trouble Tickets*

```
package com.projst.ticket.ws;

import java.util.ArrayList;
import java.sql.Connection;
import java.sql.DriverManager;
```

```java
import java.sql.PreparedStatement;
import java.sql.ResultSet;

import com.projst.ticket.dto.*;

/**
 * @author hshittu
 */
public class TicketWebService {

    /**
     * Constructor
     */
    public TicketWebService() {
        super();
    }

    /**
     * Retrieves a specific ticket based on the ticket identifier
     *
     * @param id The id of the trouble ticket
     */
    public Ticket getTicket(int id) {
        String sql = null;
        Connection conn = null;
        PreparedStatement stmt = null;
        ResultSet resultSet = null;
        Ticket ticket = new Ticket();

        try {
            sql = "SELECT * FROM TICKET WHERE ID = ?";
            conn = configureConnection();
            stmt = conn.prepareStatement(sql);
            stmt.setInt(1, id);
            resultSet = stmt.executeQuery();

            if (resultSet.next()) {
                ticket = getData(resultSet);
            }
            conn.close();
        } catch (Exception ex) {
            ex.printStackTrace();
            ticket = null;
        }
        return ticket;
    }

    /**
```

```
 * Retrieves all open tickets within the system
 *
 * @param status   The type of trouble tickets to retrieve
 */
public Ticket[] getTickets(String status) {
    String sql = null;
    Connection conn = null;
    PreparedStatement stmt = null;
    ResultSet resultSet = null;
    Ticket tickets[];
    ArrayList list = new ArrayList();

    try {
        if (status == null || status.equals("")) {
            status = "%";
        }
        sql = "SELECT * FROM TICKET WHERE STATUS LIKE ?";
        conn = configureConnection();
        stmt = conn.prepareStatement(sql);
        stmt.setString(1, status);
        resultSet = stmt.executeQuery();

        while (resultSet.next()) {
            list.add(getData(resultSet));
        }
        conn.close();

        tickets = new Ticket[list.size()];
        for (int i = 0; i < list.size(); i++) {
            tickets[i] = (Ticket) list.get(i);
        }

    } catch (Exception ex) {
        ex.printStackTrace();
        tickets = null;
    }
    return tickets;
}

private Connection configureConnection() throws Exception {
    String dbUrl = System.getProperty("ticketdb.url",
                            "jdbc:derby:net://localhost:1527/ticket");
    String dbDriver =System.getProperty("ticketdb.driver",
                            "org.apache.derby.jdbc.EmbeddedDriver");
    String dbUser = System.getProperty("ticketdb.user", "sa");
    String dbPassword = System.getProperty("ticketdb.password", "sa");
    Connection conn = null;
```

```
        try {
            Class.forName(dbDriver);
            conn = DriverManager.getConnection(dbUrl, dbUser, dbPassword);
        } catch (Exception e) {
            throw new Exception("Failed to load database driver.");
        }
        return conn;
    }

    private Ticket getData(ResultSet resultSet) {
        if (resultSet == null)
            return null;
        Ticket ticket = new Ticket();

        try {
            ticket.setOid(resultSet.getInt("ID"));
            ticket.setEmail(resultSet.getString("EMAIL"));
            ticket.setStatus(resultSet.getString("STATUS"));
            ticket.setSummary(resultSet.getString("SUMMARY"));
            ticket.setSubmittedDate(resultSet.getTimestamp("SUBMITTED"));
            ticket.setLastModifedDate(resultSet.getTimestamp("LASTMODIFIED"));
            ticket.setDetail(resultSet.getString("DETAIL"));
        } catch (Exception ex) {
            ex.printStackTrace();
            ticket = null;
        }
        return ticket;
    }
}
```

On completion of this bean class, you are ready to create the Web Service that will make access to this class available to a wide variety of platforms. We accomplish the task of creating this Web Service using the Web Services wizard. The wizard can be invoked by selecting the Ticket.java file within the Project Explorer and choosing Web Services ➤ Create Web Service from the context menu. The initial page of the Web Services wizard, shown in Figure 15-3, is then presented to you. This wizard can alternatively be invoked by selecting New ➤ Other ➤ Web Services ➤ Web Service.

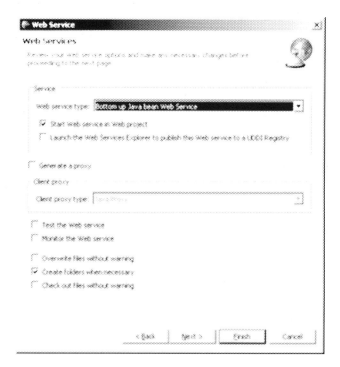

Figure 15-3. *Web Services page*

The initial page of the Web Services wizard is the Web Services page. This page prompts for the details about the creation of a service and also the optional creation of a client proxy to consume this service. For the service, details about the service type, whether to start the Web Service on completion of the wizard, and also whether to launch the Web Services Explorer to publish the Web Service is gathered.

Additionally, the page prompts for whether JSPs should be generated to test the Web Service and whether a monitor instance should be created to observe data communication between the test client and the Web Service.

The next page is the Object Selection Page, and it prompts for the object from which the Web Service will be generated. This page has two different rendered forms based on the Web Service type chosen in the Web Services page. The Object Selection Page is shown in Figure 15-4.

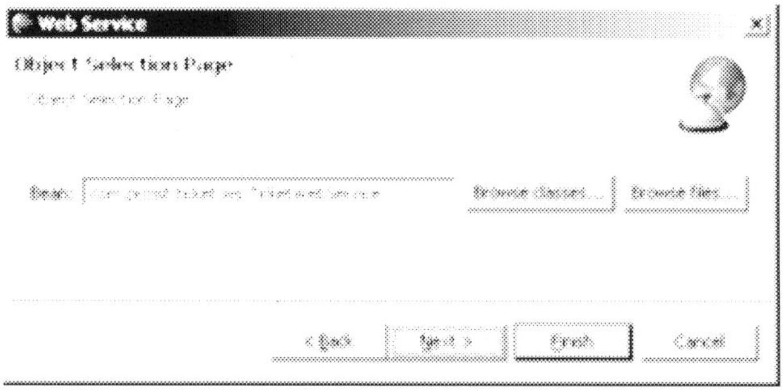

Figure 15-4. *Object Selection Page*

The form of the page shown is the version provided when a Java Bean Web Service is being generated. Table 15-1 shows the Web Service types available on the Web Services page and the type of object that is prompted for on the Object Selection Page based on each choice.

Table 15-1. *Web Service Types and Available Objects*

Web Service Type	Object Type
Java Bean Web Service	A Java bean class. The methods of this class will become operations exposed by the Web Service.
Skeleton Java Bean Web Service	The URI to a WSDL, WSIL, or HTML document to generate the Web Service Java class from.

Depending on the choice of Web Service type, some of the subsequent pages provided by the wizard might be different, as JST needs to prompt for information relevant to the type of Web Service being created. In our example, we have selected the Java Bean Web Service as the Web Service type and `TicketWebService.java` as the bean from which to expose operations. The content of this class was provided in Listing 15-2. Navigating to the next page of the wizard loads the Service Deployment Configuration page, which allows you to specify the Dynamic Web Project and web module into which you want to deploy the Web Service. Figure 15-5 shows this page, where you can specify the name of a Dynamic Web Project that exists within the currently open workspace and a web module within this project that would contain both your WSDL file and your Web Service classes.

Figure 15-5. *Service Deployment Configuration page*

Within this page, a choice of server instance to deploy the Web Service to must also be made. This choice must be either an existing Dynamic Web Project or the name of a new project that the wizard will then create. You may note from Figure 15-5 that you can alter the target server to which this project will be deployed as well as the version of the J2EE Specification that the contents of the project must conform to by clicking the Edit button. The dialog box that is presented will allow these changes to be made easily.

To complete the Web Service creation process, you will next choose from the selected bean which methods you wish to expose as operation. You can make a selection from any of the public methods defined inside the bean class. This information is entered into the Web Service Java Bean Identity page, which is loaded once you click the Next button. The page additionally provides you with the ability to specify a name for the generated WSDL file. The Web Service Java Bean Identity page is shown in Figure 15-6.

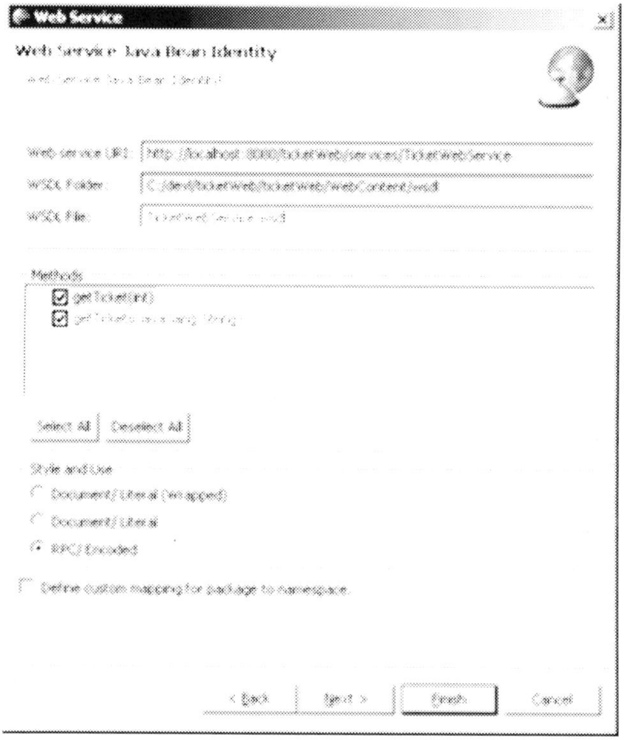

Figure 15-6. *Web Service Java Bean Identity page*

In this figure, we have chosen the two public methods that were available in our TicketWebService.java class. You may want to review the code from TicketWebService.java, which is provided in Listing 15-2. Within this class, you will find the getTicket(int) and getTickets(String) methods declared as public methods. Clicking either the Next or Finish button generates the WSDL file for exposing the Web Service. An example of this generated document is shown in Listing 15-3.

Listing 15-3. *TicketWebService.wsdl File*

```
<?xml version="1.0" encoding="UTF-8"?>
<wsdl:definitions targetNamespace="http://ticket.projst.com.ws"
    xmlns:apachesoap="http://xml.apache.org/xml-soap"
    xmlns:impl="http://ws.ticket.projst.com/wsdl/TicketWebService.wsdl"
    xmlns:soapenc="http://schemas.xmlsoap.org/soap/encoding/"
    xmlns:tns1="http://ticket.projst.com.dto"
    xmlns:wsdl="http://schemas.xmlsoap.org/wsdl/"
    xmlns:wsdlsoap="http://schemas.xmlsoap.org/wsdl/soap/"
    xmlns:xsd="http://www.w3.org/2001/XMLSchema"
    xmlns:tns="http://ticket.projst.com.ws">
    <wsdl:types>
        <schema targetNamespace="http://ticket.projst.com"
            xmlns:wsdl="http://schemas.xmlsoap.org/wsdl/"
            xmlns="http://www.w3.org/2001/XMLSchema">
            <import namespace="http://schemas.xmlsoap.org/soap/encoding/" />
            <complexType name="Ticket">
                <sequence>
                    <element name="detail" nillable="true" type="xsd:string" />
                    <element name="email" nillable="true" type="xsd:string" />
                    <element name="lastModifedDate" nillable="true"
                                 type="xsd:dateTime" />
                    <element name="oid" type="xsd:long" />
                    <element name="submittedDate" nillable="true"
                                 type="xsd:dateTime" />
                    <element name="summary" nillable="true" type="xsd:string" />
                </sequence>
            </complexType>
        </schema>
        <schema targetNamespace="http://ws.ticket.projst.com"
            xmlns:wsdl="http://schemas.xmlsoap.org/wsdl/"
            xmlns="http://www.w3.org/2001/XMLSchema">
            <import namespace="http://schemas.xmlsoap.org/soap/encoding/" />
            <complexType name="ArrayOf_tns1_Ticket">
                <complexContent>
                    <restriction base="soapenc:Array">
                        <attribute ref="soapenc:arrayType"
                                       wsdl:arrayType="tns1:Ticket[]" />
                    </restriction>
                </complexContent>
            </complexType>
        </schema>
    </wsdl:types>
    <wsdl:message name="getTicketsRequest">
        <wsdl:part name="status" type="xsd:string" />
    </wsdl:message>
    <wsdl:message name="getTicketsResponse">
```

```
        <wsdl:part name="getTicketsReturn" type="tns1:ArrayOf_tns1_Ticket" />
    </wsdl:message>
    <wsdl:message name="getTicketRequest">
        <wsdl:part name="id" type="xsd:int" />
    </wsdl:message>
    <wsdl:message name="getTicketResponse">
        <wsdl:part name="getTicketReturn" type="tns1:Ticket" />
    </wsdl:message>
    <wsdl:portType name="TicketWebService">
        <wsdl:operation name="getTickets" parameterOrder="status">
            <wsdl:input message="impl:getTicketsRequest"
                            name="getTicketsRequest" />
            <wsdl:output message="impl:getTicketsResponse"
                                name="getTicketsResponse" />
        </wsdl:operation>
        <wsdl:operation name="getTicket" parameterOrder="id">
            <wsdl:input message="impl:getTicketRequest" name="getTicketRequest" />
            <wsdl:output message="impl:getTicketResponse"
                                name="getTicketResponse" />
        </wsdl:operation>
    </wsdl:portType>
    <wsdl:binding name="TicketWebServiceSoapBinding"
        type="impl:TicketWebService">
        <wsdlsoap:binding style="rpc"
                        transport="http://schemas.xmlsoap.org/soap/http" />
        <wsdl:operation name="getTickets">
            <wsdlsoap:operation soapAction="" />
            <wsdl:input name="getTicketsRequest">
                <wsdlsoap:body
                    encodingStyle="http://schemas.xmlsoap.org/soap/encoding/"
                    namespace="http://ws.ticket.projst.com" use="encoded" />
            </wsdl:input>
            <wsdl:output name="getTicketsResponse">
                <wsdlsoap:body
                    encodingStyle="http://schemas.xmlsoap.org/soap/encoding/"
                    namespace="http://ws.ticket.projst.com" use="encoded" />
            </wsdl:output>
        </wsdl:operation>
        <wsdl:operation name="getTicket">
            <wsdlsoap:operation soapAction="" />
            <wsdl:input name="getTicketRequest">
                <wsdlsoap:body
                    encodingStyle="http://schemas.xmlsoap.org/soap/encoding/"
                    namespace="http://ws.ticket.projst.com" use="encoded" />
            </wsdl:input>
            <wsdl:output name="getTicketResponse">
                <wsdlsoap:body
                    encodingStyle="http://schemas.xmlsoap.org/soap/encoding/"
```

```
                        namespace="http://ws.ticket.projst.com" use="encoded" />
            </wsdl:output>
        </wsdl:operation>
    </wsdl:binding>
    <wsdl:service name="TicketWebServiceService">
        <wsdl:port binding="impl:TicketWebServiceSoapBinding"
                        name="TicketWebService">
            <wsdlsoap:address
            location="http://localhost:8080/ticketWeb/services/TicketWebService" />
        </wsdl:port>
    </wsdl:service>
</wsdl:definitions>
```

The tags shown in bold in Listing 15-3 represent the core parts of a WSDL document, and Table 15-2 provides a description of these core elements.

Table 15-2. *Server-specific Web Application Deployment Descriptors*

Element	Description
<binding>	Defines the communication protocols that are used by each of the operations in the Web Service
<message>	Defines the messages that are used by the Web Service by mapping simple data types or complex messages defined by the <types> element to the operation
<portType>	Defines the operations available within the Web Service and maps messages defined by <message> to operations
<service>	Defines the endpoint at which the Web Service is available

WST supports a WSDL editor that can be used to graphically edit the contents of the generated WSDL file, or any WSDL file imported into the workspace. Figure 15-7 shows the WSDL file from Listing 15-3 as presented in the WSDL editor.

Figure 15-7. *WSDL file editor*

Consuming Web Services

We have now provided a data-centric service that allows clients existing on different platforms access to information from our Trouble Ticket application. This information can easily be incorporated into a large variety of applications. To show how this information might be used, we will provide a simple web application that will invoke calls from within our Web Service, which is known as consuming the service. JST provides a wizard for the automated creation of a Web Services client in much the same way a wizard was provided to create a Web Service.

Web Service Client Wizard

Consuming a Web Service involves the creation of a Java proxy class from the WSDL file provided by the Web Service. JST uses the contract interface description from the WSDL file to generate Java code capable of making runtime invocations conforming to the contract interface. The proxy class allows any Java component type—applet, application, web, or EJB—to consume a Web Service. In our example, we have chosen to consume the Web Service in a Web Tier application.

Unlike the variable number of steps in the Web Service creation process, creation of a Web Service client is a four-step process. To start, you select File ➤ New ➤ Other ➤ Web Services ➤ Web Service Client, and you are presented with the Web Service Client dialog box as shown in Figure 15-8. This prompts for the client proxy type, whether to test the service on completion of the wizard process, and whether to monitor TCP/IP communication between the client and Web Service.

Figure 15-8. *Web Service Client page*

If you select the option of testing the Web Service, JST generates JSPs that can be used to connect to the Web Service you are consuming. The generated pages allow you to test each of the methods you wish to consume from the Web Service and view the result of this invocation. We have provided an example of this generated JSP client in Figure 15-13, which appears later in this chapter. Selecting the option of monitoring the Web Service generates a TCP/IP monitor that can be used to view contents of requests/responses between the Web Service and any clients that communicate with it. Please see Chapter 5 for our discussion on TCP/IP monitoring.

The next step is the Web Service Selection Page, which prompts for the URI to the WSDL, WSIL, or HTML file of the Web Service for which a Java proxy will be generated. We show this page in Figure 15-9 with the selection of the WSDL file from our Trouble Ticket Web Service.

Figure 15-9. *Web Service Selection Page*

You may wish to refer to Listing 15-3 for the contents of this WSDL file for which we are generating a client.

The Client Environment Configuration page is the next step, and it prompts for details about the project into which the generated files would be stored. A new or existing project can be chosen in this page to host the Web Service client. Additionally, details about the deployment server for this client project are also prompted for on this page. Figure 15-10 shows the Client Environment Configuration page.

Clicking the Edit button from the Client Environment Configuration page provides a set of pages through which you can configure your client project. These pages allow you to select a server instance for the deployment of the Web Service client, or alternatively create such a server instance if the preferred instance does not exist.

Figure 15-10. *Client Environment Configuration page*

The final step in the wizard is the Web Service Proxy Page, shown in Figure 15-11, which prompts for the location within the project selected in the preceding page where the proxy should be generated. It additionally provides the ability to define custom mappings between namespaces and package names.

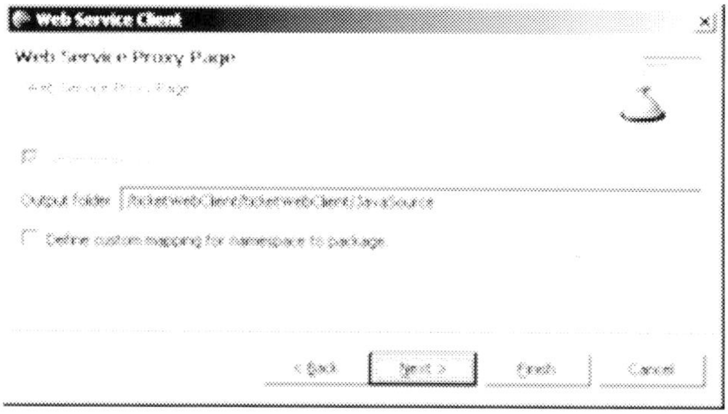

Figure 15-11. *Web Service Proxy Page*

Completion of this step generates a series of Java sources capable of invoking the Web Service whose WSDL file was used to generate the client. The generated code is built and deployed on the server instance specified in the Client Environment Configuration page of the wizard.

In the initial page of the wizard, the Web Service Client page, if you chose to test the Web Service, an additional dialog box is presented to you to specify which of the Web Service operations you intend to test. This page, the Web Service Client Test page, prompts for the type of test to generate, the project into which to place the test files, the folder structure for the files, and the methods from the generated proxy to invoke as part of the test. Figure 15-12 shows the Web Service Client Test page.

Figure 15-12. *Web Service Client Test page*

Clicking Finish on this page generates the JSPs that can be used to exercise the generated proxy classes and thus the Web Service. The code files are compiled, deployed on the selected server instance, and started within a browser. Figure 15-13 shows an example of this web-based test client generated for the Trouble Ticket application.

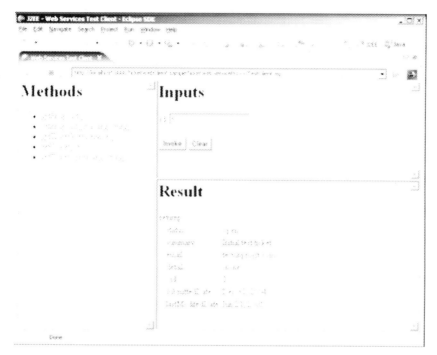

Figure 15-13. *Test client for the TroubleTicket Web Service*

Using this test harness, the process of testing a Web Service can be accomplished in three steps:

1. Select the operation to test by clicking the item in the left frame.

2. Enter appropriate values as arguments for this operation on the JSP loaded into the upper-right frame.

3. Invoke the operation and view the result in the lower-right frame.

Web Services Explorer

In the Web Services Explorer, JST provides Eclipse with a mechanism through which you can browse UDDI registries for available Web Services that can be useful to your applications. Using this tool, you can create and store queries that can be used to search any UDDI registry for Web Services. Additionally, publishing your Web Service to these registries can be performed through the Web Services Explorer. Addresses of some UDDI registries are provided within this tool including registries owned by IBM, Microsoft, SAP, XMethods (WebMethods), and Japan's NTT Docomo. The tool, however, can be used with any UDDI-compliant registry.

Launching the Web Services Explorer can be accomplished by selecting Run ➤ Launch the Web Services Explorer from the Eclipse menu, and this displays the main screen of the Web Service Explorer in the default web browser configured for use.

Tip The default browser can be changed by selecting Window ➤ Preferences ➤ General ➤ Web Browser and then choosing any browser installed on the system.

The Web Services Explorer can alternatively be launched to publish a Web Service to an available UDDI registry or to test a specific Web Service. To launch the Web Services Explorer in either of these modes, you must select your WSDL file within the workspace and, using the available context menu, choose either Web Services ➤ Publish WSDL File or Web Services ➤ Test with Web Services Explorer based on your intended action.

The test harness available within the Web Services Explorer is a very useful tool that allows you to test Web Services found within UDDI registries as well as Web Services available within your workspace without the need to generate clients. This way, you can verify the functionality of a Web Service found within a UDDI registry before deciding to consume this Web Service within your application and also test Web Services that you may be providing to others.

Figure 15-14 shows the launch window of the Web Services Explorer. In this figure, we have launched the tool within the Eclipse internal browser.

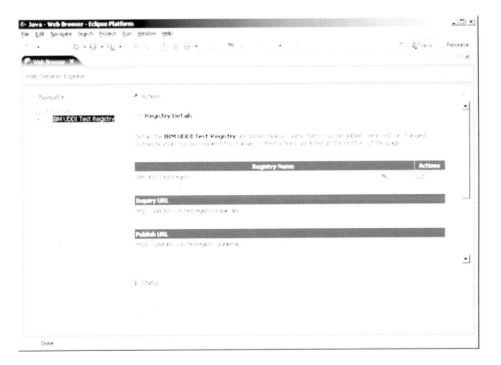

Figure 15-14. *Web Services Explorer*

You may note from Figure 15-14 the three panels provided by the Web Services Explorer. These panels supply the following functionality:

- **Navigator pane**: Similar to the Navigator View, this pane provides a tree-based hierarchical structure to view UDDI registries that are in use. As we have stated earlier, addresses of registries owned by IBM, Microsoft, SAP, XMethods, and NTT Docomo are included by default within the tool. Some of these companies support two versions of their registries including a test version for individuals to test registration of their Web Services and a main version in which valid information and services are stored. Queries created to search each of the available registries can be stored within this tool and retrieved for repeated execution. Published business, services, and service interfaces can also be browsed.

- **Actions pane**: Provides an interface with which to interact with a UDDI registry and also to test a Web Service. The following actions can be performed using this pane:

  - **Open UDDI registry**: The first step in using a UDDI registry is to open the registry. A valid UDDI registry address can be included within this pane to open a registry.

  - **Search registry**: Once a registry is opened, the contents such as businesses, services, and service interfaces can be queried using the Actions pane. The search criteria can also be saved for later execution.

  - **Publish**: Information can be published to a UDDI registry. To do this, supply a user name/password combination provided to you by the registry owner, and this information would then be supplied at the appropriate prompts within this pane.

  - **Test Web Service**: An HTML interface is autogenerated to test operations within a selected Web Service.

- **Status pane**: Displays informational messages about the state of actions performed.

We have provided in Figure 15-15 an example of the Web Services Explorer being used to test our Trouble Ticket Web Service. Using this tool as a test harness allows us to invoke operations on any available Web Service without creating a client to consume it.

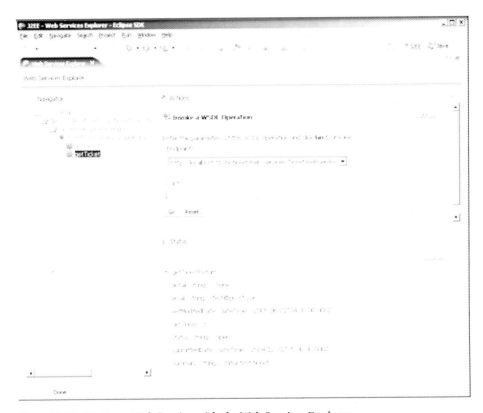

Figure 15-15. *Testing a Web Service with the Web Services Explorer*

The figure shows the invocation of the getTicket(int) operation from within the TicketWebService we created earlier in the chapter. In Figure 15-13, we provided an example of consuming this same Web Service using generated JSP files.

Summary

We have provided in this chapter an introduction to Web Services technology. We described Web Services as an implementation of Service-Oriented Architecture (SOA) that allows distributed components to publish and/or consume services made available by other components. We described the technologies pertinent to Web Services such as UDDI for discovery, WSDL for interface description, and SOAP for interaction.

JST provides several tools for the creation and use of Web Services, and in this chapter we have described such tools. Two of these that we discussed in great detail include the Web Services wizard and the Web Service Client wizard, which are used for creating Web Services and consuming Web Services, respectively.

We also took a look at the Web Services Explorer tool, including provisions of this tool to browse Web Services within UDDI registries as well as test the functionality of these Web Services. We further discussed how this tool provides users with the ability to publish information to a UDDI registry.

CHAPTER 16

Relational Databases

Most J2EE applications use a relational database to persist data. Examples of relational databases include commercial databases such as Oracle, IBM DB2, and Microsoft SQL Server. There are several noteworthy open source databases too, such as the MySQL, the PostgreSQL, and the up-and-coming Derby, the 100% Java database from the Apache group.

> **Note** If you don't have a relational database available, we recommend using Apache Derby. We will be using it throughout this chapter for our examples. See Appendix A for installation and configuration instructions.

Throughout the J2EE development process, developers must interact with relational databases in order to execute the Database Definition Language (DDL) for creating, dropping, or altering tables as well as the Data Manipulation Language (DML) for querying, updating, or inserting data. Combined, DDL and DML make up the Structured Query Language (SQL). This chapter focuses on how to use the Connection wizard, Database Explorer, SQL Scrapbook, and Data Output View found in the relational database (RDB) to perform these tasks against the `ticket` database created in Appendix A.

> **Note** While the RDB is really a component of WST, not JST, we felt it warranted its own chapter in a JST book, because interacting with a database is such a significant aspect of J2EE development.

RDB Overview

The RDB provides the tools for interacting with the database. The use of these tools includes an inherent process. The process includes creating a connection, managing the connection, executing statements, and reviewing the results. This section walks through the process to introduce the major components of the RDB.

To create a new connection, use the Connection wizard. The Connection wizard prompts for the JDBC connection configurations. See the "Managing Database Connections" section for details on using the Connection wizard.

Once the connection has been established, it will be added to the Database Explorer view. The Database Explorer is used to manage the connection. It provides the capability to reconnect and disconnect. It also enables browsing of the database components such as schemas, tables, views, and stored procedures. See "Browsing a Database" for more details on the Database Explorer.

From the Database Explorer, you can open the SQL Scrapbook. This is a SQL editor that includes SQL syntax highlighting, code assist, and content tips. The editor is automatically associated with files with extensions of *.sql and *.sqlpage (SQL Scrapbook Page). The editor also enables SQL to be executed. The SQL Scrapbook is covered in depth in the "Executing Statements" section.

The results of executing SQL statements appear in the Data Output View. The Data Output View contains a historical list of executed statements along with their results. The "Executing Statements" section of this chapter also explains how to use the Data Output View.

Creating an RDB Perspective

As discussed in the "RDB Overview" section, RDB includes the Database Explorer and Data Output Views as well as a SQL Scrapbook editor. While the Database Explorer and Data Output Views can be added to existing perspectives, they are most useful when consolidated into a single focused data perspective along with the SQL Scrapbook editor. Unfortunately, at the time of this writing, there is no Data or RDB perspective. So this section describes how to build your own custom RDB perspective consisting of the Database Explorer, Data Output, and SQL Scrapbook that looks like Figure 16-1.

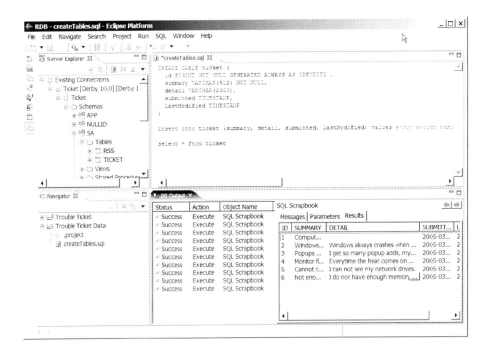

Figure 16-1. *Custom RDB perspective*

Notice in Figure 16-1 that the Custom RDB perspective includes the Database Explorer view in the top-left corner. Having the Database Explorer here makes it easy to see the open connections and tables. Expanding the tables to the columns can assist in writing the SQL statements to query the database. Below the Database Explorer is the Navigator View. This is the same Navigator View found on the Resource perspective. Including the Navigator View in the RDB perspective makes it easy to find and open *.sql and *.sqlpage files in the SQL Scrapbook. The SQL Scrapbook is in the top-right corner. When statements are executed in the SQL Scrapbook, the results appear below in the Data Output View.

To create the RDB perspective, we will begin with the original Resource perspective. We will then add the Database Explorer and Data Output Views. We will also remove the Outline and Tasks Views. In order to get the perspective to look like Figure 16-1, we will also have to rearrange some of the views. Finally, we will have to make sure we save the perspective so we can get back to the original configuration at any time by resetting it.

To create the RDB perspective, complete the following:

1. Open the Resource perspective if it is not already the active perspective by selecting Window ➤ Open Perspective ➤ Other ➤ Resource from the main menu.

2. Reset the Resource perspective to its defaults by selecting Window ➤ Reset Perspective from the main menu.

3. Save the current perspective as the new RDB perspective by selecting Window ➤ Save Perspective As, entering **RDB** in the Name field, and clicking OK.

4. Add the Database Explorer and Data Output Views by selecting Window ➤ Show View ➤ Other ➤ Database Explorer Category, selecting both Data Output and Database Explorer, and clicking OK.

5. Drag the Database Explorer view over the Navigator View.

6. Drag the Navigator View over the Outline View.

7. Close the Outline View by making it the active view and clicking its Close button.

8. Close the Tasks View by making it the active view and clicking its Close button.

9. Save the RDB perspective again by choosing Windows ➤ Save Perspective As from the main menu, selecting the perspective from the Existing Perspective listing, and clicking the OK button.

When you have completed saving the RDB perspective, it should look similar to Figure 16-1. The new RDB perspective will be used in the remainder of the chapter to interact with the ticket database.

Managing Database Connections

The Database Explorer view manages connections to one or more databases. The Database Explorer can be used to create new connections as well as disconnect and reconnect to existing connections. As you will see in the next section, the Database Explorer can also be used to browse components of a database.

In order to interact with a database, you must first configure a connection to it. Because RDB utilizes JDBC, you need to know JDBC configuration information before you begin. This information includes the database name, JDBC driver class, connection URL, user name, and password. You will also need access to the JAR file containing the JDBC drivers for your database. Figure 16-2 shows the New Connection wizard configured for the `ticket` database setup in Appendix A.

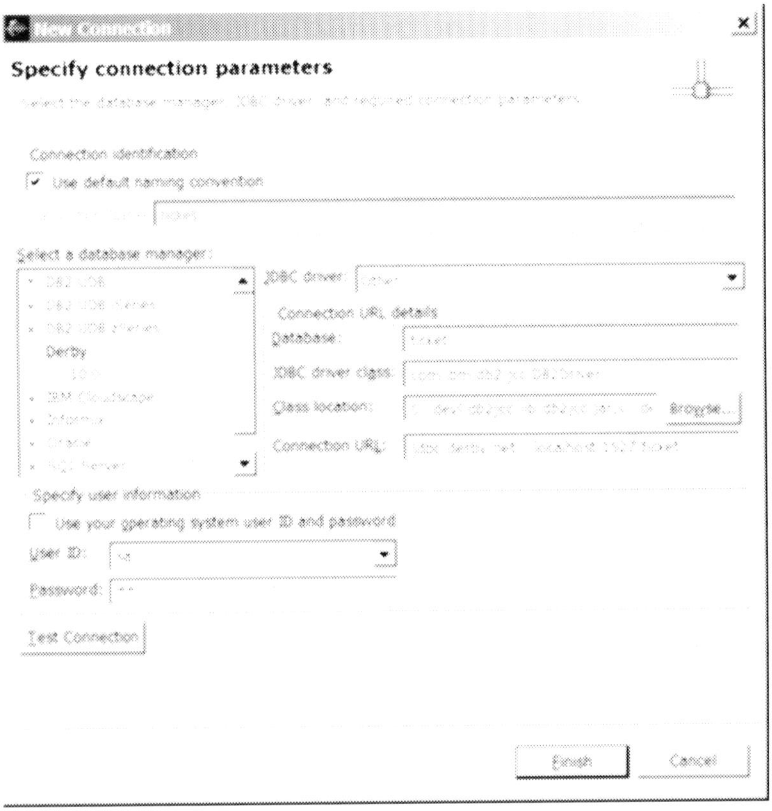

Figure 16-2. *New Connection wizard*

Notice in Figure 16-2 that the New Connection wizard is divided into three sections: connection identification, connection information, and user information. On the top is the connection identification section. This section is used to identify the connection name displayed in the Database Explorer. If the Use default naming convention option is checked, the Connection Name field will reflect the Database field in the connection information section. Unchecking the Use default naming convention option enables any descriptive name entered in the Connection Name field to be used.

The connection information section is sandwiched between the connection identification and user information sections. It consists of details of the database manager, JDBC driver, and connection URL. The Select a database manager area contains a list of popular databases. The intent is that each database in this list would contain relevant configuration information about that particular database based on the version. For example, Oracle contains the versions of 7.3, 8, and 9. Selecting a version should provide the options of Oracle's Thin or OCI drivers as well as the catchall option, Other. Selecting the desired driver from the JDBC driver drop-down list should display customized connection URL details for that driver, but unfortunately, this functionality has not been fully implemented; the only option for most databases is Other. The one example of a database with an option other than Other is Derby 10.0. In addition to Other, it includes the Derby Embedded JDBC Driver and a customized configuration (see Figure 16-3). It is, however, missing the Network Server JDBC driver configuration.

Figure 16-3. *Embedded Derby-specific connection dialog box*

Because most database definitions currently provided from WTP include Other as their only JDBC driver option, and the Apache Derby database from Appendix A is set up to run as a network server, we will explore the Other Connection URL details (refer back to Figure 16-2). The Database field typically contains the name of the database. In our example, the database we are connecting to is ticket. As mentioned earlier, the Database field drives the entry in Connection Name if the Use default naming convention option is checked. The JDBC driver class field contains a class that implements the java.sql.Driver interface. See your driver or database documentation for the proper driver class. For the network server mode of Derby, the driver class is `com.ibm.db2.jcc.DB2Driver`. The Class location field must contain the fully qualified and semicolon-separated list of all the JAR and zip files required by the database driver. If you followed the installation instructions for Derby outlined in Appendix A, you should find Derby's required `db2jcc.jar` and `db2jcc_license_c.jar` files in the `~/devl/db2jcc/lib` or `C:\devl\db2jcc\lib` directory depending on your operating system. Finally, the connection URL is a database-specific URL. See your driver or database documentation for details. The Derby `ticket` database from Appendix A uses the connection URL of `jdbc:derby:net://localhost:1527/ticket`.

Note Not all databases appear in the database manager list. Many open source databases like MySQL and PostgreSQL are not included in the list. If you are using a database that is not in the list, you can either choose Other for another database or extend WST to include it.

The New Connection wizard concludes with the user information section. In order to authenticate a user against the database, this section collects the user ID and password. You can have the wizard collect the user name and password from the operating system by checking the Use your operating system user ID and password checkbox, or you can explicitly set the user ID and password in the appropriate fields. For the Derby `ticket` database in Appendix A, we will explicitly set both the user ID and password to `sa`.

Tip The connection configuration does not currently have edit capability from Database Explorer. If you need to edit the configuration, you can either delete the connection and re-create it, or modify the file containing the configuration. The configuration is stored in the workspace `.metadata` directory with the rest of the workspace configurations. Specifically, it is in the `<workspace>/.metadata/.plugins/org.eclipse.wst.rdb.core/connection/<connection name>/connection.info` file. The `connection.info` file is in a standard property file format.

As the previous tip states, a configuration is not easily changed after it has been finished, so the wizard provides a convenient Test Connection button used to verify the database configurations. I highly recommend you use the Test Connection button. It can be very frustrating to have to delete and re-create a connection multiple times to get the configuration correct.

To create a connection to the Derby `ticket` database from Appendix A, complete the following steps:

1. Right-click Existing Connections and select New Connection or click the New Connection button on the Database Explorer toolbar.

2. In the database manager list, expand Derby and select version 10.0.

3. Select Other from the JDBC driver drop-down list.

4. In the Database field, enter **ticket**.

5. In the JDBC driver class field, enter **com.ibm.db2.jcc.DB2Driver**.

6. In the Class location field, use the Browse button to select the db2jcc.jar and db2jcc_license_c.jar files.

7. In the Connection URL field, enter **jdbc:derby:net://localhost:1527/ticket**.

8. Uncheck the Use your operating system user ID and password option.

9. In the User ID field, enter **sa**.

10. In the Password field, enter **sa**.

11. To verify the configuration, click the Test Connection button.

12. If the test is successful, click OK and Finish. Otherwise, repeat the previous steps as necessary until the test passes.

After completing these steps, you should have a ticket [Derby 10.0] [Derby 10.0] node in the Database Explorer like the one you see in Figure 16-4. In the "Browsing a Database" section, you will learn how to drill down into the connection.

Figure 16-4. *Newly added ticket database connection*

When you have completed using the database, you can disconnect from the server to free up connections and reconnect later. To disconnect, right-click the connection and select Disconnect Server or click the Disconnect button on the Database Explorer toolbar. When you want to interact with the database again, you can reconnect by right-clicking the disconnected database in Database Explorer and selecting Reconnect. When reconnecting, you will be prompted for your user ID and password.

When the connection is no longer needed at all, it can be permanently deleted. To delete a connection, right-click the connection and select Delete Server.

Browsing a Database

Once a database connection has been established, the connection can be expanded to show details of the database, including schemas, tables, stored procedures, and more. Figure 16-5 shows an example of the ticket database expanded.

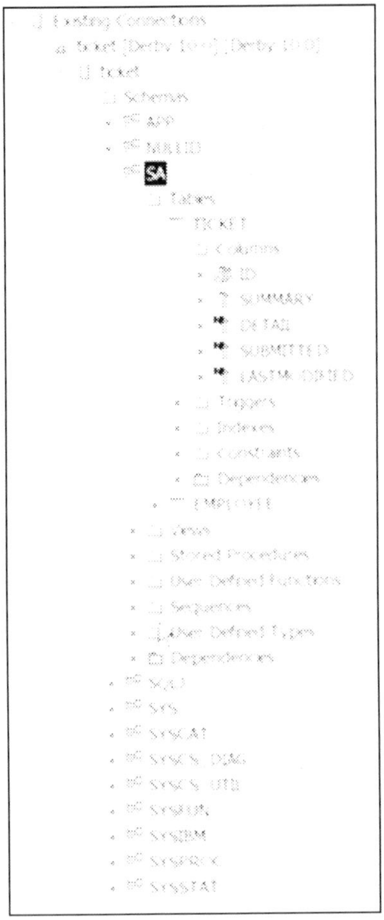

Figure 16-5. *Browsing the ticket database*

Notice in Figure 16-5 that when the ticket connection node is expanded, it reveals a ticket database (see summary of icons in Table 6-1). In the "Executing Statements" section to follow, we will use the database node to create a SQL Scrapbook for the ticket database. Underneath the database node is the Schemas folder, which contains all of the database's schemas or just the schemas the authenticated user has permission to see, depending on the implementation of the JDBC driver. Most databases create a separate schema for each user.

Each schema contains folders for tables, views, stored procedures, user-defined functions, sequences, user-defined types, and dependencies. Each folder may contain zero or more of the types denoted by the folder name. In Figure 16-5, the Tables folder contains a TICKET and an EMPLOYEE table. This database does not contain any views, stored procedures, user-defined functions, sequences or user-defined types, or dependencies, so those folders are empty.

Note Browsing capabilities may vary depending on the driver. For example, the MySQL Connector/J version 3.1.7 does not show any nodes below the Schemas node. However, the SQL Scrapbook and Data Output View were still functional.

Drilling into the `Tables` folder shown in Figure 16-5, you see each table such as the `TICKET` table contains columns, triggers, indexes, constraints, and dependencies folders. Each of these folders may contain zero or more of the types denoted by the folder name. In this example, the `TICKET` table has the following columns: `ID`, `SUMMARY`, `DETAIL`, `SUBMITTED`, and `LASTMODIFIED`. The columns have one of three icons identifying details of the column. As Table 6-1 illustrates, columns can be either nonnullable such as the `SUMMARY` column, nullable such as the `DETAIL` column, or a primary key such as the `ID` column.

Each node in Database Explorer includes a Refresh option in its context menu. Using the Refresh option causes the selected node and all of its children to be collapsed and redrawn when expanded. This is very helpful, since statements such as `create table` or other users changing the database structure can cause Database Explorer to get out of sync.

Each of the folder nodes also has an additional Filter option in its context menu. This option enables you to customize which children you want to see. For example, if you are not interested in seeing any schemas beside SA, you can apply a filter at the Schemas level as shown in Figure 16-6.

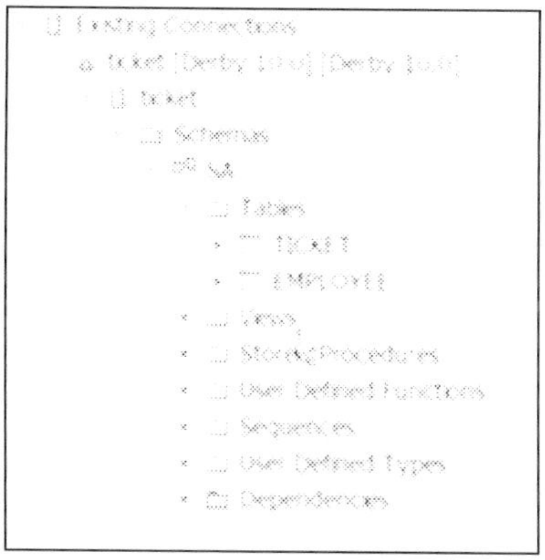

Figure 16-6. *Filtered view of the ticket database*

The filters provide the option of filtering based on an expression or specifically on selected items. Figure 16-7 shows the Filter dialog box.

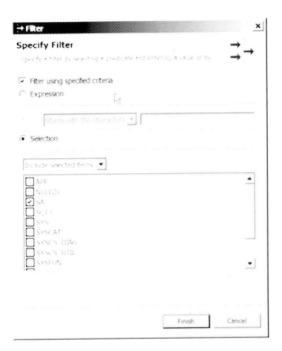

Figure 16-7. *Filter dialog box*

In Figure 16-7, the Filter using specified criteria checkbox enables and disables filtering on the selected folder. Below that are the mutually exclusive options of Expression and Selection. For expressions, you can filter based on an expression that starts with, contains, or ends with specific case-sensitive text. When using the selection, a list of all the children nodes will appear beside checkboxes. Using the drop-down menu, you can choose whether the selected children are included or excluded.

To exclude all the schemas but the SA schema, complete the following steps:

1. Right-click the Schemas folder and select Filter.

2. In the Filter dialog box, check the Filter using specified criteria checkbox.

3. Select the Selection radio button.

4. Select the SA schema from the list of schemas and click Finished.

After completing these steps, your Database Explorer should look like what you see in Figure 16-6. The only schema under the Schemas folder should be SA.

Browsing a Table

It is often helpful to see the contents of a table. So, included in the context menu of a table is an Open option. This option can be invoked by right-clicking a table and selecting Data ➤ Open. This causes a SQL select * statement to be executed against the selected table. As with the results of any SQL statement, the browse results appear in the Data Output View.

The Data Output View (shown in Figure 16-8) displays the results of SQL statements. The left side of Data Output shows a historical list of statements executed. The right side displays the results of the selected statement.

The historical list of statements contains three columns. The first column identifies the status. The Status column indicates success, failure, or in process for statements. The second column is the Action and always contains Execute. The last column is the Object Name. It will display Sample Contents when the Browse table feature is used or SQL Scrapbook when the SQL Scrapbook is used. (The "Executing Statements" section will cover the SQL Scrapbook.) Selecting a row in the list of statements will display the results and information of the statement in the right half of the Data Output View.

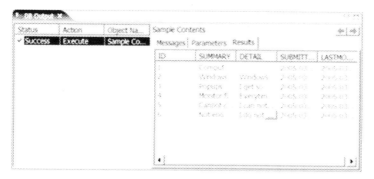

Figure 16-8. *Data Output View*

Any result set can be removed from the historical list. This can make it easier to navigate if many statements have been executed. A result set can be removed by right-clicking in the list and choosing Delete or Delete All. The Delete option will delete only the selected result set. The Delete All option will clear the entire list. In addition, the list is cleared any time Eclipse is restarted.

The results of statements are displayed in the right half of Data Output and are separated into three tabs. The Messages tab contains the statement executed, whether it was successful, and the number of affected rows. For example, the message for browsing the TICKET table (shown in Figure 16-9) includes SELECT * FROM "SA"."TICKET".

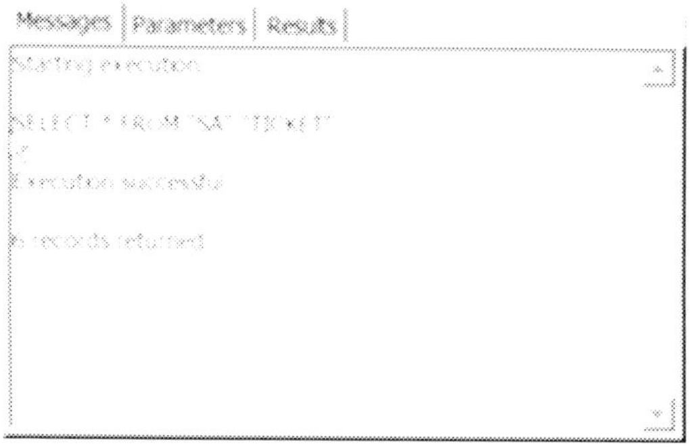

Figure 16-9. *Messages output*

The Parameters tab shown in Figure 16-10 contains a table of the parameters passed to a stored procedure if a stored procedure is invoked rather than a statement being called. The table contains the name of the parameter as well as indicating whether the parameter is an input, output, or input/output parameter.

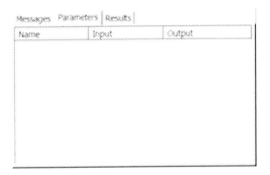

Figure 16-10. *Parameters output*

The Results tab shown in Figure 16-11 contains a table of the result set's data. The column headers match the name of the columns returned in the result set or the value of column aliases.

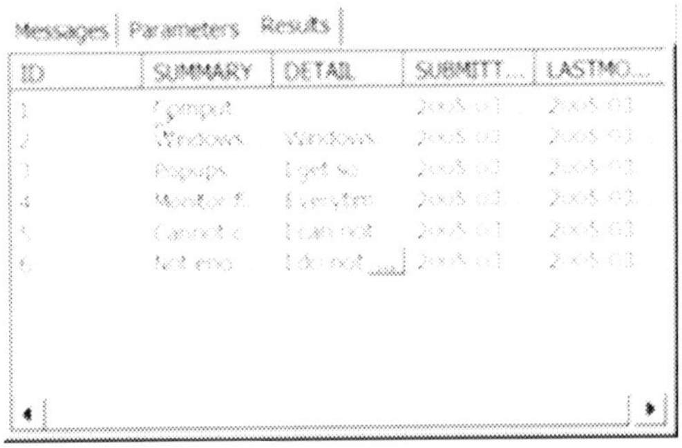

Figure 16-11. *Result set output*

Figure 16-11 shows the result of a select * operation on the TICKET table. Notice in row six that a large value in a cell may result in a button with ellipses. Clicking the button will display a dialog box containing the value of the cell.

The Results tab does have Save As and Print options on its context menu so you can save or print the results of your queries. The Save As option will save the result set data to a tab-delimited file. The Print option will print the result set data in a tab-delimited format. While the tab-delimited format works great for saving data to a file and importing it into something like Microsoft Excel, the tab-delimited format for printing is generally very difficult to read and not very helpful.

SQL File Types

RDB includes an editor that understands SQL and is automatically associated with the *.sql and *.sqlpage extensions. While these file extensions can be used interchangeably by RDB, it is recommended that you use them for different purposes to make team development clearer.

The *.sql extension should be used for files containing SQL or DDL to set up a database or commonly executed queries. These scripts will be necessary for every member of a development team in order to set up their database sandbox. Therefore, they should follow your version control conventions along with the rest of the application source code.

On the other hand, think of the SQL Scrapbook Page with the *.sqlpage extension as an interactive SQL console. The contents of the SQL Scrapbook Page may be persisted to a file. You may or may not want to apply version control to the contents of the SQL Scrapbook Page files because they could be considered developer-specific SQL.

Data Projects

Depending on how you organize your projects, you may consider creating a data project to contain your SQL and DDL scripts as well as your SQL Scrapbook Pages. Neither Eclipse nor WTP encompass the concept of a data project, so you need to use the standard Eclipse Simple Project wizard to create your project. The other alternative is to create a directory under an existing project to store the scripts and/or SQL Scrapbook Pages.

To create a data project for the Trouble Ticket application, complete the following steps:

1. Select File ➤ New ➤ Project ➤ Simple Project from the main menu and click Next.

2. Enter **Trouble Ticket Data** for the project name and click Finish.

The new Trouble Ticket Data project should be listed in the Navigator View. Now you may add SQL or DDL scripts to the project. A data project would also be a convenient place to add a SQL Scrapbook Page.

Note We will explain how to add SQL Scrapbook Pages in the "Executing Statements" section of this chapter.

Just like the data project, neither Eclipse nor WTP have a wizard for creating a SQL or DDL script. However, the New File wizard can be used to create one. The only requirement is the file contain a *.sql extension.

To create a createTables.sql script for the Trouble Ticket application, complete the following steps:

1. Select File ➤ New ➤ File from the main menu.

2. Select the Trouble Ticket Data project from the list.

3. Enter **createTables.sql** for the file name and click Finish.

In the Navigator View, you should see a `createTables.sql` file added to the Trouble Ticket Data project. The `createTables.sql` file will also open in the editor. Because of the `*.sql` extension, it will specifically open in the SQL Scrapbook editor. You may now add your application's SQL or DDL statements to the script.

Executing Statements

The SQL Scrapbook is a specialized editor that provides features for editing and executing SQL and DDL. As mentioned earlier, this editor is automatically associated with files with a `*.sql` or `*.sqlpage` extension.

In the "Data Projects" section, we explained how to create a SQL script. But how do you create a SQL Scrapbook Page? There are actually several options. The first is to use the context menu on the database node in the Database Explorer. Just right-click the database node and choose Open SQL Scrapbook. This will open a SQL Scrapbook Page in the SQL Scrapbook editor and associate it with the selected connection. The second option is to use the Open SQL Scrapbook button on the Database Explorer's toolbar. Using this method will prompt you to select a configured connection from a list of all configured connections as well as save the `*.sqlpage` file to a project in your workspace. The final option is to use the SQL Scrapbook Page wizard. This wizard can be invoked using File ➤ New ➤ Other ➤ Data ➤ SQL Scrapbook Page. The wizard will force you to choose a project in your workspace to save your `*.sqlpage` to. Then the first time you attempt to execute a SQL statement, it will prompt you to select a configured connection from the list of configured connections.

The editing features include syntax highlighting, content assist, and content tips. The syntax highlighting is not very fancy. It simply colors keywords like `CREATE` and `VARCHAR` purple. The code assist provides a context-sensitive drop-down list of keywords. For example, after the `select` keyword, invoking code assist will reveal a list of comparison operators, functions, and the `where` clause. Content assist can be invoked by using Ctrl+space, or by bringing up the context menu or the Edit menu. The content tip provides a standard tooltip with an example of the focused keyword. For example, invoking a tooltip on a `select` statement reveals `SELECT col1, col2 FROM table1, table2 WHERE table1.col1 = table2.col2;`. The content tip can be invoked by using Ctrl+Shift+space or by bringing up the context menu.

The SQL Scrapbook can also be used to execute any valid SQL or DDL for the connected database. To execute SQL, right-click in the editor and select Run SQL, and all the statements in the editor will be executed. If it is not already open, the Data Output View will open and display the results of the statements in the Results tab. If your SQL Scrapbook contains multiple statements and you only wish to run particular statements rather than all the statements, you can select the desired statements to run and execute the specified statements using Run SQL on the editor's context menu.

Summary

The WST RDB contains only the basic functionality needed to interact with the database. It enables you to connect, execute SQL statements, and browse. Future versions of the RDB may extend the functionality to include Create Table wizards, query by example, and population of test data.

APPENDIX A

Apache Derby

Apache Derby is a 100% Java standards–based relational database with a small footprint. Derby is useful for unit testing and small applications. In order to follow the examples contained within this book, you will need such a relational database. The Apache Derby database is an ideal candidate because it is open source so everybody has access to it, it is relatively easy to install, and it requires almost no administration.

This appendix provides a short history and an architectural overview of Derby, followed by instructions on how to install and configure Derby as a client/server database for the purposes of running the examples in this book.

History

Apache Derby started as the commercial database known as Cloudscape. It was one of the first available 100% Java databases. It gained popularity with early adopters of J2EE because an evaluation version was bundled with the J2EE Software Development Kit (SDK). The J2EE SDK was frequently used as a way of learning J2EE, until open source J2EE application servers became available and commercial vendors started offering free developer licenses. The J2EE SDK was a popular learning tool because it included a free reference implementation of an application server and the Cloudscape database. This combination enabled developers to quickly and easily get a development environment set up so they could focus on learning how to build J2EE applications.

Later IBM acquired the Cloudscape database in its acquisition of Informix and discontinued the practice of including Cloudscape with the J2EE SDK. IBM already had a family of databases under the name DB2, which fills the niche of high-transactional enterprise databases. IBM assimilated Cloudscape into the family by making it more compatible with the DB2 series. With the addition of Cloudscape, IBM had an offering for applications that don't need a large and expensive DB2 database. Yet using Cloudscape provides a simple migration path to DB2 as an application grows.

In the fall of 2004, IBM donated the Cloudscape code base to the Apache Software Foundation (ASF). At this time, it was renamed Derby. The ASF accepted the donation and immediately made it available in the Apache Incubator (http://incubator.apache.org), the location where all external donations begin. When the Derby project (http://incubator.apache.org/derby/) is deemed ready, it will be promoted to its host project, Apache DB (http://db.apache.org). IBM plans on continuing to sell Cloudscape and service contracts. However, Cloudscape will now be based on Derby.

Architecture

Derby can run as either an embedded database or a networked server. When run as an embedded database, only a single JVM can access the database at a time. The network server mode follows the traditional client/server model by running as a separate process that enables access from multiple JVMs and users.

Embedded Mode

The majority of enterprise applications have functional requirements requiring accessibility from multiple applications. These can include multiple end-user applications, and reporting and querying tools. So, why even expound on the embedded mode in a book about enterprise development? Well, in order to create a Derby database that is accessible from a networked Derby server, you must first create the database in an embedded mode.

Figure A-1 shows the ticket database running as an embedded database in Derby's interactive JDBC scripting tool called ij. Later in this appendix, you will see how to create the ticket database using the ij tool. While ij is connected to the ticket database as an embedded database, no other applications, processes, or JVMs can access the ticket database.

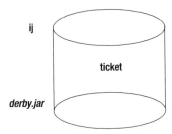

Figure A-1. *ticket database running in the ij process*

The only requirement in order to use Derby as an embedded database is for the derby.jar file that comes with Derby to be in the classpath. The embedded connection URL has a format of jdbc:derby:<databaseName>. So the ticket database connection URL would look like jdbc:derby:ticket.

Network Server Mode

Most enterprise applications require the ability to attach to a database from multiple applications, processes, or JVMs by multiple users. Figure A-2 shows the ticket database running in the network server mode and being accessed by ij, Eclipse Web Tools, and the Trouble Ticket application.

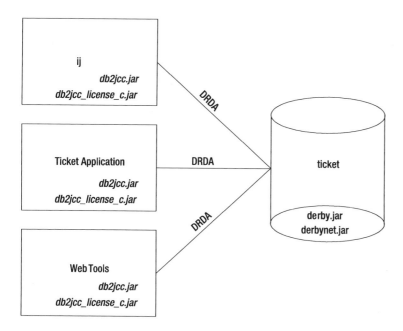

Figure A-2. *ticket database running as a network server and being accessed by multiple applications*

Using Derby in network server mode is a little more complex than using the embedded version, but is far simpler than working with most network databases. To begin, the network server must run as its own process. The easiest way to start the server is with a script or batch file. There are example startup scripts later in the appendix in the section "Running Derby Server." The server process is a Java application and must contain both the derby.jar and derbynet.jar files in the classpath.

Client applications communicate with Derby using the Open Group's (http://www. opengroup.org) open database access standard known as Distributed Relational Database Architecture (DRDA). The DRDA defines a specification for communications between applications and distributed relational databases. Both Derby and Cloudscape use the IBM DB2 JDBC Universal drivers, which are based on the DRDA specification. The drivers are contained in the db2jcc.jar and db2jcc_license_c.jar files. These files are not included in the Derby distribution and must be downloaded separately from IBM's website at http://www.ibm.com/developerworks/ db2/downloads/jcc/. The drivers are made available free of charge, but be aware the accompanying license agreement requires the original license agreement be included if the JAR files are distributed with an application. In addition, you will have to register with IBM if you have not already to download the drivers.

The Derby network server URLs differ slightly from embedded server URLs because they must include the host name of the machine running the server. The format is jdbc:derby:net:// <server>[:port]/<databaseName>. Notice the net ensures the driver manager uses the DRDA protocol and drivers rather than the embedded drivers. server is the DNS name or the IP address of the server. port is the port in which Derby is running. The default port is 1527 and can be eliminated from the connection URL if the server is using the default port. databaseName is the name of the database trying to be accessed. `jdbc:derby:net://localhost/ticket` is an example of a URL used to connect to a `ticket` database of a Derby network server running on the same machine as the client accessing it.

Using Derby

To use Derby as a network server, you must install Derby, create a new database, and run the server.

Installing Derby

To install Derby as a network server, you must download and uncompress the Derby binary distribution and IBM DB2 JDBC Universal drivers. Both are made available as zip files. For those using Unix, Linux, or OS X, Derby is also available as a `tar.gz` file.

> **Note** Use the latest official release of Derby from `http://incubator.apache.org/derby/derby_downloads.html` or `http://db.apache.org` after Derby moves from the incubator. This example uses Derby 10.0.2.1, the release version available at the time of this writing.

To install Derby, complete the following:

1. Download the `incubating-derby-10.0.2.1-bin.tar.gz` file for Unix, Linux, or OS X, or the `incubating-derby-10.0.2.1-bin.zip` file for Windows from `http://incubator.apache.org/derby/derby_downloads.html`.

2. Uncompress the `incubating-derby-10.0.2.1-bin` file to `<home>/devl/incubating-derby-10.0.2.1-bin` on Unix, Linux, or OS X, or `C:\devl\incubating-derby-10.0.2.1-bin` on Windows.

3. Rename the directory `incubating-derby-10.0.2.1-bin` to `derby-10.0.2.1` to make the directory name shorter and clearer by including only the project name and version number.

4. Download the `db2jcc_for_derby.zip` file from `http://www.ibm.com/developerworks/db2/downloads/jcc/`.

5. Unzip `db2jcc_for_derby.zip` to `<home>/devl/db2jcc` on Unix, Linux, or OS X, or `C:\devl\db2jcc` on Windows.

> **Note** This installation assumes you already have JDK1.3 or greater installed.

Creating Derby Database

As mentioned earlier, a Derby database must be created in the embedded mode. The easiest way to create the database is to use the ij command-line client included with Derby. The ij client can be executed from the command line but is more conveniently executed from a script or batch file. Unfortunately, Derby does not come with any ij scripts or batch files, so Listing A-1 provides an example of a Bash script for Unix, Linux, or OS X. Listing A-2 is a batch file for Windows.

Listing A-1. *Example of an ij Bash Script*

```
#!/bin/sh

CLASSPATH=lib/derby.jar:lib/derbynet.jar:lib/derbytools.jar:../db2jcc/lib/db2jcc
.jar:../db2jcc/lib/db2jcc_license_c.jar

java -Dij.driver=com.ibm.db2.jcc.DB2Driver -cp $CLASSPATH org.apache.derby.tools
.ij
```

Listing A-2. *Example of an ij.bat File*

```
set CLASSPATH=lib\derby.jar;lib\derbynet.jar;lib\derbytools.jar;
..\db2jcc\lib\db2jcc.jar;..\db2jcc\lib\db2jcc_license_c.jar

java -Dij.driver=com.ibm.db2.jcc.DB2Driver -cp %CLASSPATH% org.apache.derby.tools.ij
```

In Listings A-1 and A-2, the CLASSPATH variable is configured to include all the JAR files ij needs to access both embedded and networked Derby databases. The derby.jar file is included so ij can access embedded databases. The derbynet.jar, db2jcc.jar, and db2jcc_license_c.jar files are included for accessing network servers. ij and other admin tools like sysinfo and dblook are included in the derbytools.jar file.

The next line of Listings A-1 and A-2 executes the JVM, instructing it to run the main class of ij, org.apache.derby.tools.ij. Using the system property ij.driver, it instructs ij to use the com.ibm.db2.jcc.DB2Driver JDBC driver.

Once ij is running, connecting to an embedded database with the attribute create=true will create a new database. The new database will exist as a directory in the current working directory with the same name as the database. For example, connecting to jdbc:derby:ticket; create=true will create a new Derby ticket database.

To create a new ticket database, complete the following:

1. If you have not done so, create an ij script or ij.bat file like the ones in Listings A-1 and A-2 in the <home>/devl/derby-10.0.2.1 or C:\devl\derby-10.0.2.1 directory.

2. Execute the ij script or ij.bat file.

3. At the ij> prompt, enter **connect 'jdbc:derby:ticket;create=true';**.

4. To quit ij, enter **exit;**.

> **Warning** You must exit ij after creating the database; otherwise, the server will not have access to the database, since only one JVM has access to an embedded database.

After completing these tasks, you should have a <home>/devl/derby-10.0.2.1/ticket directory on Unix, Linux, or OS X, or a C:\devl\derby-10.0.2.1\ticket directory on Windows.

> **Note** ij does not have to be used interactively. ij can also execute commands in a file.

Running Derby Server

In order to start and stop a Derby server, you must execute the org.apache.derby.drda. NetworkServerControl class, passing it either a start or shutdown argument. Unfortunately, Derby does not include scripts or batch files for starting or stopping Derby servers. So Listings A-3 and A-4 are examples of startup Bash scripts for Unix, Linux, and OS X, and a batch file for Windows, respectively.

Listing A-3. *Example of Startup Bash Script*

```
#!/bin/sh
CLASSPATH=lib/derby.jar:lib/derbynet.jar
java -cp $CLASSPATH org.apache.derby.drda.NetworkServerControl start
```

Listing A-4. *Example of startup.bat File*

```
set CLASSPATH=lib\derby.jar;lib\derbynet.jar
java -cp %CLASSPATH% org.apache.derby.drda.NetworkServerControl start
```

Listings A-5 and A-6 are examples of a shutdown Bash script for Unix, Linux, and OS X, and a batch file for Windows, respectively.

Listing A-5. *Example of Shutdown Bash Script*

```
#!/bin/sh
CLASSPATH=lib/derby.jar:lib/derbynet.jar
java -cp $CLASSPATH org.apache.derby.drda.NetworkServerControl shutdown
```

Listing A-6. *Example of shutdown.bat File*

```
set CLASSPATH=lib\derby.jar;lib\derbynet.jar
java -cp %CLASSPATH% org.apache.derby.drda.NetworkServerControl shutdown
```

Notice in Listings A-3, A-4, A-5, and A-6 that the scripts and batch files begin by including the `derby.jar` and `derbynet.jar` files in the classpath. These two JAR files contain all the classes necessary to run a Derby server. Both scripts also launch the JVM with a main class of `org.apache.derby.drda.NetworkServerControl`. The only difference between the startup scripts and shutdown scripts is the passing of the `start` argument, which causes a Derby server to start up and listen on port 1527. The shutdown scripts pass an argument of `shutdown`, which stops the Derby server.

Note On Windows, the startup script cannot be named `start.bat` to match the `start` argument passed to the `NetworkServerControl` class because it conflicts with the `start.exe` program.

To start the Derby server, complete the following:

1. If you have not done so already, create a startup script in the `<home>`/`derby-10.0.2.1` directory with the contents of Listing A-3 or a `startup.bat` file in the `C:\devl\derby-10.0.2.1` directory with the contents of Listing A-4.

2. Execute the startup script or `startup.bat` file; you should see the message "Server is ready to accept connections on port 1527."

To verify the server is running, use ij to connect to the `ticket` database.

1. Execute the ij script on Unix, Linux, or OS X, or the `ij.bat` file on Windows.

2. At the `ij>` prompt, enter **connect 'jdbc:derby:net://localhost/ticket:user=sa;password=sa;';**.

If the connection is successful, you should return to the `ij>` prompt. You should also see a `Connection number: 1.` in the Derby console. If the connection is not successful, you will see a `java.net.ConnectionException`.

Note The user name and password can be anything since security is not enabled, but they must be included. Otherwise you will see a "null userid" or "null password not supported" error message.

To stop the Derby server, complete the following:

1. If you have not done so already, create a shutdown script in the `<home>`/ `derby-10.0.2.1` directory with the contents of Listing A-5 or a `shutdown.bat` file in the `C:\devl\derby-10.0.2.1` directory with the contents of Listing A-6.

2. Execute the shutdown script on Unix, Linux, or OS X, or the `shutdown.bat` file on Windows.

Summary

In this appendix, we touch the surface of the popular open source database Derby. We showed you just enough to be able to create a Derby database and run a Derby network server in order to use the examples in this book. If you want more information about Derby, visit the main Derby site, `http://incubator.apache.org/derby/`, or the Derby manuals, `http://incubator.apache.org/derby/manuals/`.

APPENDIX B

JBoss Application Server

J2EE applications like enterprise (EAR), web (WAR), and EJB JARs must run in the context of an application server. There are many commercial and open source applications servers available. The most popular commercial servers include IBM WebSphere (http://www.ibm.com/software/webservers/appserv/) and BEA WebLogic (http://www.bea.com/framework.jsp?CNT=index.htm&FP=/content/products/server/). The open source servers include ObjectWeb JOnAS (http://jonas.objectweb.org) and the focus of this appendix, JBoss Application Server (AS) (http://www.jboss.org/products/jbossas). A comprehensive list of J2EE application servers is available at TheServerSide Application Server Matrix (http://www.theserverside.com/reviews/matrix.tss).

While WTP should be compatible with any J2EE 1.4–compliant application server, we chose to use JBoss AS for the examples in this book. JBoss AS is an ideal candidate because it is open source, so everybody has access to it. The remainder of this appendix provides an overview of JBoss AS as well as installation and configuration instructions. It concludes by showing how to configure a JNDI reference to the Apache Derby `ticket` database created in Appendix A.

JBoss AS Overview

According to BZ Research, JBoss AS is the leader in the J2EE application server market. During the past couple of years, JBoss AS slowly and silently surpassed WebSphere and WebLogic in popularity and production installs. JBoss AS's popularity is due largely to the following features:

- **Open sourced under the GNU Lesser General Public License (LGPL)**: This enables organizations to deploy and embed the application server for free.

- **J2EE 1.4 certified (JBoss AS version 4.0)**: JBoss AS is the first 1.4-certified application server and the first ever certified open source application server.

- **Service-Oriented Architecture using JMX extensions**: The flexible microkernel architecture is easily extended using standard JMX extensions.

- **Relatively small footprint**: The flexible microkernel architectures enable the application server to be configured to run only necessary services.

- **High performance**: Independent benchmarks show JBoss AS performs as well as other leading application servers.

- **Clustering support**: This enables applications to scale as demand grows.

- **Aspect-Oriented Programming (AOP) model**: This enables you to transparently add service behavior to POJOs.

- **Hot deploy**: Installing or uninstalling applications is as easy as copying files to or deleting files from the `deploy` directory.

- **Community support**: The community answers questions in forums and provides free documentation.

- **Commercial support**: JBoss, Inc. provides support for a fee.

As Chapter 1 mentions, an application server contains both a web container and an EJB container. The JBoss AS is no different. Figure B-1 illustrates the JBoss AS architecture.

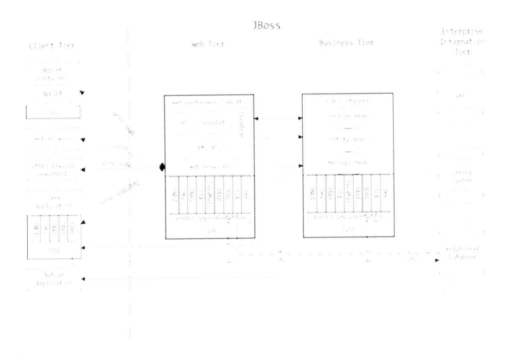

Figure B-1. *JBoss AS architecture*

When you download and install JBoss AS, you get an implementation of a web container and EJB container denoted in Figure B-1 by the vertical dashed lines. JBoss, Inc. and the JBoss community have implemented their own EJB container. However, the popular open source Apache Jakarta Tomcat (`http://jakarta.apache.org/tomcat/`) web container has been chosen to fulfill the web container requirement of the J2EE Specification.

> **Note** Earlier versions of JBoss AS alternated between the open source web containers of Tomcat and Jetty (`http://jetty.mortbay.org`). This proves the "best of breed" goal identified in the J2EE Specification is obtainable. However, since version 3.2.4, JBoss AS has standardized on Tomcat.

Using JBoss AS

In order to use JBoss AS, you must first install it. After installation, the server must be started using supplied scripts.

Installing JBoss AS

JBoss AS must be the easiest J2EE application server to install. It does not even require running an installation program or script. Just download the binary version bundled as a `tar.bz2` file for Unix, Linux, or OS X, or a zip file for Windows and uncompress it. The JBoss AS does require a JDK 1.4 or higher to be installed and accessible.

> **Note** Use the latest official release of JBoss AS from `http://www.jboss.org/downloads/index`. This example uses JBoss AS 4.0.1 sp1, the latest release version available at the time of this writing. This version includes Tomcat 5.0 as its web container.

> **Warning** Make sure the directory path JBoss AS is installed to contains no spaces.

To install JBoss AS, follow these steps:

1. Download the `jboss-4.0.1sp1.tar.bz2` file for Unix, Linux, or OS X, or the `jboss-4.0.1sp1.zip` file for Windows from `http://www.jboss.org/downloads/index` or directly from the SourceForge project at `http://sourceforge.net/projects/jboss/`.

2. Uncompress the `jboss-4.0.1sp1.tar.bz2` or `jboss-4.0.1sp1.zip` file to a local directory such as `~/devl` on Unix, Linux, or OS X, or `C:\devl\` on Windows.

> **Note** For more information on installing and configuring JBoss AS, see "Getting Started with JBoss 4.0" at `http://docs.jboss.org/jbossas/getting_started/startguide40/` or the JBoss 4 Application Server Guide at `http://docs.jboss.org/jbossas/jboss4guide/r2/html/`.

After the installation, you should have a directory structure similar to the one shown in Figure B-2.

Figure B-2. *JBoss AS directory structure*

In Figure B-2, you can see the root directory is jboss-4.0.1sp1. Just beneath that are the bin, client, docs, lib, and server directories, which contain various items as described here:

- The bin directory contains scripts for starting and stopping the JBoss AS as well as other scripts.

- The client directory contains the JAR files client applications such as a Swing application that might need to interact with the JBoss AS. The client directory also contains a jbossall-client.jar file, which encompasses all the other JARs in the client directory to make deployment easier and the client application classpath smaller.

- The docs directory contains DTDs and schemas used by the JBoss AS configuration files. The DTDs and schemas are also a great source of documentation regarding configuration options. License of other open source projects used by JBoss AS are also included in the doc directory. The docs/examples directory contains examples of different resource and service configurations. For instance, there is an Apache Derby configuration example we will discuss in the section "Configuring Derby Datasource" later in this appendix.

- The lib directory contains JAR files that belong on the server's classpath. It is intended to only include the JAR files that come with JBoss AS, so you should not add JAR files to this directory. The "Server Configurations" sidebar explains the proper place to put your JAR files and third-party JARs such as datasource drivers.

- The server directory contains different server configurations. See the "Server Configurations" sidebar for more information on JBoss AS configurations.

Running JBoss AS

In JBoss AS's bin directory, you will find scripts for starting and stopping the JBoss AS process. On Unix, Linux, or OS X, the run.sh script will start the default server configuration that corresponds to the configurations found in the server/default directory. On Windows, the run.bat script does the same thing. Other server configurations can be started by passing the server configuration name as a parameter to the run script. See the "Server Configurations" sidebar for more information about running alternative server configurations.

The shutdown.sh script on Unix, Linux, or OS X, or the shutdown.bat script on Windows can be used to stop the server. Alternatively, if JBoss AS was manually started in a console window, you can use Ctrl+C to stop the server.

SERVER CONFIGURATIONS

One of JBoss AS's most impressive features is the ability to scale down as well as up. If you need a lean server with a small memory footprint, JBoss AS can be configured to run only the bare minimum services you require. This is accomplished through *server configurations*. Server configurations are stored in directories under JBoss AS's server directory (see Figure B-2). JBoss AS comes with three preconfigured configurations: minimal, default, and all.

The minimal configuration starts no services except logging. Default, as indicated by the name, is the default configuration and starts all the commonly used services including the Tomcat service, administrative applications, and an embedded Hypersonic database. The all configuration starts every service that comes bundled with JBoss AS; it includes the default configuration services as well as clustering, IIOP, SNMP, and remoting.

Figure B-2 shows the common configuration directories under the default configuration: conf, data, deploy, lib. Additional directories of data, log, tmp, and work are created when the server is started up for the first time. The data directory contains the contents of the embedded Hypersonic database configured in the deploy/hsqldb-ds.xml configuration. The log directory contains logs for its particular server configuration. The tmp directory is a temporary directory the server uses for staging deployments. The work directory contains the uncompressed web applications and servlet code generated from JSP pages.

The remaining conf, lib, and deploy directories can be used to configure JBoss AS before and in some cases while the JBoss AS process is running. The conf directory contains XML- and property-based configuration files. These files can be used to configure things like logging, the HTTP port, and services started at startup. The lib directory contains JARs needed by the specific server configuration. This is the location for third-party JARs such as database drivers. If you have your own JARs that are shared across applications, this would be the place to put them, assuming they are not already included in a WAR, EAR, or EJB JAR.

Warning Classes in the server configuration lib directory are shared across all applications in this configuration. If you need to update the JAR, you will have to restart the entire server. In addition, static values will be shared across all applications.

The deploy directory is unique because changes here happen real time while the JBoss AS process is running. To install an application, simply copy the EAR, WAR, or EJB JAR file into this directory and it will be immediately loaded and configured. Remove the EAR, WAR, or EJB JAR file, and the application will be unloaded. Replace the EAR, WAR, or EJB JAR file, and the application will be hot-swapped by unloading the running application and all of its classes and automatically load the new application. It can also be used to start new services and/or new configurations like pooled datasources.

To create a new custom configuration, simply copy one of the existing server configurations. Then add or remove the appropriate services. One approach for the example Trouble Ticket application would be to make a copy of the default server configuration and name it `ticket`. This is similar to the concept of domains that some other application servers like WebLogic have. The goal would be to have a named configuration with all the application or related application's configurations organized together. This also preserves the original default configuration if you need to get back to it.

To execute a server configuration other than the default configuration, execute the run script, passing the name of the server configuration to run. For example, to run the all configuration on Unix, Linux, or OS X, enter **./run.sh all**, or on Windows enter **run all**.

To start the default server configuration, follow these steps:

1. Open a command prompt and change directories to JBoss AS's `bin` directory. For example, on Unix, Linux, or OS X, use `cd ~/devl/jboss-4.0.1sp1/bin`; on Windows, use `cd C:\devl\jboss-4.0.1sp1\bin`.

2. Execute the run script by entering **./run.sh** on Unix, Linux, or OS X, or entering **run** on Windows or double-clicking the `run.bat` file in Windows Explorer.

3. When the server has finished the startup process, you should see a startup message similar to `[Server] JBoss (MX MicroKernel) [4.0.1sp1 (build: CVSTag=JBoss_ 4_0_1_SP1 date=200502160314)] Started in 20s:489ms` in the console window.

JBoss AS contains some web-based administrative applications including a Tomcat status page, a JMX console, and a JBoss web console. These applications are automatically started when JBoss AS's default server configuration is run. You can visit these applications to ensure the server has started properly.

To verify JBoss AS started correctly, follow these steps:

1. Open a web browser.

2. Navigate to `http://localhost:8080/` if the server is running on the same machine as your browser. Otherwise, substitute your server name or IP address for `localhost`.

3. Verify that the resulting web page looks like the one in Figure B-3.

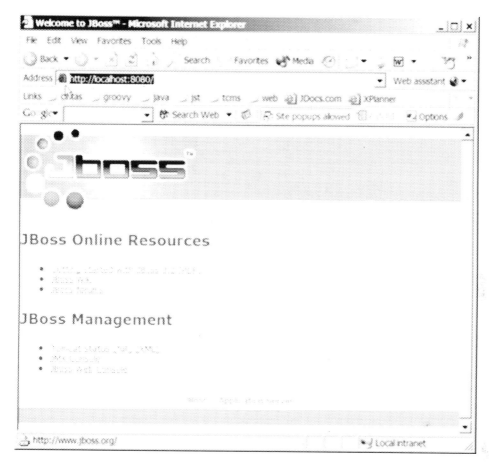

Figure B-3. *JBoss AS administrative applications*

Configuring Derby Datasource

A key function of J2EE applications servers is to manage resources. Datasource connections are one of the primary resources you should let the application server manage. The application server will automatically handle difficult issues like *connection pooling*. Connection pooling enables multiple applications to share datasource connections in order to reduce the expense of establishing new connections for each request. In addition, application servers usually provide tools for administrators to monitor the number of connections being used and provide the ability to add new connections to the pool at runtime if necessary.

In order to use a datasource, you must first configure it. The process of configuring a datasource is application server–specific. Many have a web-based administrative console for configuring the datasource. JBoss AS, however, uses an XML-based configuration file that can be dropped into the server configuration deploy directory. This can even be done while the application server is running. JBoss AS will recognize the new configuration file and automatically configure the datasource. You can find examples of configuration files for most common

databases in JBoss AS's `docs/examples/jca` directory on Unix, Linux, or OS X, and `docs\examples\`
`jca` on Windows. The file names include the database name followed by the required `-ds.xml`
extension.

Note JBoss AS does include a `derby-ds.xml` file to demonstrate an Apache Derby configuration. Unfortunately, the example is tailored to configuring an embedded Derby database and not a network server like the one set up in Appendix A.

A JBoss AS datasource configuration file contains the standard JDBC configuration information to connect to a database such as the connection URL, driver class, user name, and password. It also contains a JNDI name that can be used by an application to look up the datasource. The JNDI name may be referenced in deployment descriptors for container-managed entity beans or directly in the source code itself. The configuration file can also contain instructions for the application server such as pool sizes and time outs. Listing B-1 shows an example of a configuration file for the Apache Derby database configured in Appendix A.

Note We recommend naming the datasource configuration file the name of your database followed by a `-ds.xml`. For example, the `ticket` database would be `ticket-ds.xml`.

Listing B-1. *Appendix A's Apache Derby Datasource Configuration*

```xml
<?xml version="1.0" encoding="UTF-8"?>
<!-- Pro Eclipse JST Plug-in Ticket DB data source -->
<datasources>
  <local-tx-datasource>
    <jndi-name>jdbc/ticket</jndi-name>
    <connection-url>jdbc:derby:net://localhost:1527/ticket</connection-url>
    <driver-class>com.ibm.db2.jcc.DB2Driver</driver-class>
    <user-name>sa</user-name>
    <password>sa</password>

    <min-pool-size>5</min-pool-size>
    <max-pool-size>20</max-pool-size>
    <idle-timeout-minutes>5</idle-timeout-minutes>
    <track-statements>true</track-statements>
  </local-tx-datasource>
</datasources>
```

The example in Listing B-1 shows the root element of a datasource configuration file is a `datasources` element. Contained within the `datasources` element is a block that describes the specifics of the connection, with the parent element determining the connection type. Connection types can determine whether the datasource supports distributed transactions

(XADataSource), nondistributed transactions (non-XADatasource), or no transactions. In this case, it identifies this connection is a non-XADatasource with local transactions. Next is the JNDI name. This example uses a JNDI name of jdbc/ticket. The datasource name java:/jdbc/ticket can be used to look up a pooled datasource connection in either source code or deployment descriptors. The connection-url, driver-class, user-name, and password values are all discussed in Appendix A.

The min-pool-size of 5 instructs JBoss AS to immediately create 5 connections to the datasource. This happens during the initial configuration and/or restart of the server. The configuration limits the number of connections that can be created to 20. As an application scales or during heavy traffic, the application server may create additional connections if the existing connections are already being utilized. max-pool-size limits this number. max-pool-size can also be useful when databases have connection limits due to licensing. So connections are not left open indefinitely, idle-timeout-minute can be configured to close the connections. Of course, it will only close connections until it reaches the minimum pool size.

The last element is track-statements. track-statements is a debugging technique designed to warn when JDBC code does not close statements or result sets. Not closing statements and result sets leads to connection leaks and ultimately running out of connections in the pool when the max size is reached. It is recommended that track-statements be turned off for production.

> **Note** For more information on the definitions and possible datasource configurations, see
> http://docs.jboss.org/jbossas/jboss4guide/r2/html/ch7.chapt.html#ch7.jdbc.sect or the
> jboss-ds_1_5.dtd file in JBoss AS's docs\dtd directory.

JBoss AS will also need access to the datasource drivers. The drivers should be placed in the server configuration's lib directory. Adding the drivers to the lib directory will require the server process to be restarted in order for JBoss AS to find the appropriate classes.

To configure a datasource for the Apache Derby database set up in Appendix A, follow these steps:

1. Copy the db2jcc.jar and db2jcc_license_c.jar files to the ~/devl/jboss-4.0.1sp1/server/default/lib directory on Unix, Linux, or OS X, or the C:\devl\jboss-4.0.1sp1\server\default\lib directory on Windows.

2. If JBoss AS is currently running, restart it.

3. Create a JBoss AS datasource configuration file in a temporary location with the contents of Listing B-1 and a name of ticket-ds.xml.

4. Copy or move ticket-ds.xml to the ~devl/jboss-4.0.1sp1/server/default/deploy directory on Unix, Linux, or OS X, or the C:\devl\jboss-4.0.1sp1\server\default\deploy directory on Windows.

5. In the JBoss AS console, you should see an information message indicating the datasource was bound to the configured JNDI name. For example: INFO [WrapperDataSourceService] Bound connection factory for resource adapter for ConnectionManager 'jboss.jca:name=jdbc/ticket,service=DataSource Binding to JNDI name 'java:jdbc/ticket'.

To validate the datasource was also added, you can use JBoss AS's JMX Management Console. Through this console, you can interrogate any JMX bean running in JBoss AS. To see whether the datasource is available, you need to use the JNDIView service. This service has a list method that returns a tree of JNDI names. Included in the list should be the new jdbc/ticket name. Figure B-4 shows the jdbc/ticket name in the JNDI View.

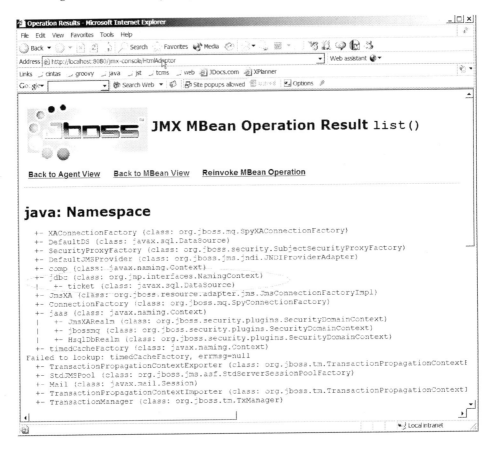

Figure B-4. *Apache Derby datasource listed in the JNDI View*

To verify the JNDI name is bound, follow these steps:

1. Open a web browser.

2. Navigate to http://localhost:8080/jmx-console/. This is the same JMX console application available from the administration page you loaded earlier to ensure JBoss AS was running.

3. Select service=JNDIView under the section jboss.

4. Click the Invoke button under java.lang.String list() (see Figure B-5).

5. Locate the ticket datasource name in the java: Namespace section. It should look similar to what we showed previously in Figure B-4.

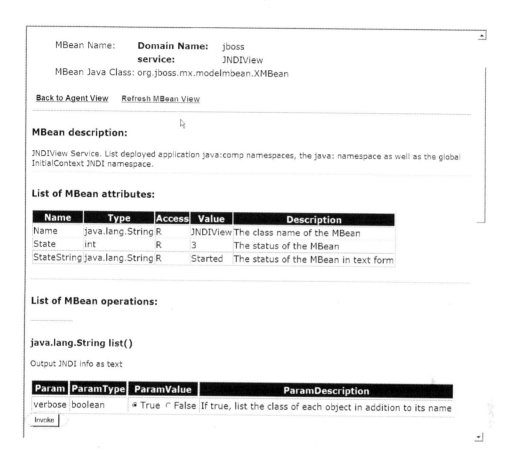

Figure B-5. *JNDI info Invoke button*

Summary

This appendix concludes the process of setting up a development environment that includes an Apache Derby database and a JBoss AS. It explains how to install and configure the JBoss AS. It also included instructions on how to configure a datasource for the database installed in Appendix A.

Index